Davis, California 95611

EL MUNDO ZURDO 2

SELECTED WORKS FROM THE MEETINGS OF THE SOCIETY FOR THE STUDY OF GLORIA ANZALDÚA
2010

EDITED BY
SONIA SALDÍVAR-HULL,
NORMA ALARCÓN
AND RITA E. URQUIJO-RUIZ

aunt lute books
San Francisco

Aunt Lute Books
P.O. Box 410687
San Francisco, CA 94141
www.auntlute.com

Cover design: Amy Woloszyn, amymade.com
Text design: Amy Woloszyn, amymade.com
Cover Art: Alma R. Gomez

Senior Editor: Joan Pinkvoss
Managing Editor: Shay Brawn
Production: Soma Baral, Chenxing Han, Aileen F. Joy, Alexa Kelly, Jada Marsden, Kara Owens, Erin Peterson, and Shaun Salas

Funding for the production of *El Mundo Zurdo* was provided in part by support from the Vessel Foundation, Three Dog Foundation, and the San Francisco Arts Commission.

Library of Congress Cataloging-in-Publication Data

El mundo zurdo 2 : selected works from the 2010 meeting of the society for the study of Gloria Anzaldúa / edited by Sonia Saldívar-Hull, Norma Alarcón, Rita Urquijo-Ruiz. -- 1st ed.
    p. cm.
    ISBN 978-1-879960-86-2 (acid-free paper) 1. Anzaldúa, Gloria--Criticism and interpretation. 2. Mexican Americans in literature. I. Saldívar-Hull, Sonia, 1951- II. Alarcón, Norma. III. Urquijo-Ruiz, Rita.
    PS3551.N95Z793 2012
    818'.5409--dc23
                            2012015962

Printed in the U.S.A.

10 9 8 7 6 5 4 3 2 1

CONTENTS

ANZALDÚAN LITERARY/ POLITICAL THEORIES

INTRODUCTION

BEFORE *BORDERLANDS* AND BEYOND: "MAKING THE WORD LUMINOUS AND ACTIVE"[1]

SONIA SALDÍVAR-HULL

As this volume of *El Mundo Zurdo 2* goes to press, we mark the 25th anniversary of the monumentally influential *Borderlands/La Frontera*. Anzaldúa's legacy, however, began years before this publication. In 1981, with the initial printing of *This Bridge Called My Back: Radical US Women of Color*, we first read about "el Mundo Zurdo." Typical of Anzaldúa's quiet way of enunciating path-breaking ideas, in just the few paragraphs that served as the introduction to the last section of the anthology, she presented a visionary theory that she would develop throughout her lifetime as a writer and philosopher. From the start she confounded us with her spiritual, mystical visions, sounding echoes of a long-forgotten or destroyed cultural memory that included hints of an indigeneity that had already been colonized out of our racial recall; "india" had been reduced to an epithet used by dark skinned elders in the South Texas of her youth in the 1950s.

Even today, when Chicana/os engage in the attempt to decolonize history[2] and claim that mestizaje, they are considered appropriative, nostalgic in the worst way. Surely, this negation is the mark of the beast, in this case, of hegemonic incorporation. As George Hartley argues below, these critiques tend to miss the subtleties of Anzaldúa's formulations and "in the end contribute[s] to the further fragmentation of North American decolonization movements by erasing up front the radical potential of refigurations of mestizaje such as Anzaldúa's new mestiza." Indeed, the borderland of South Texas is not Mexico and Anzaldúa's writings demand to be read in their historical context. Read through the lens of historical materialism, Anzaldúa's claim of indigeneity in Texas, with its legacy of a genocidal Texas Ranger militia, is much more complex than the romanticized Aztec warriors of the Chicano movement imagination; hers was a dangerous, radical move.

In the 1977 poem, "The coming of el mundo surdo," (*Reader* 36-37), Anzaldúa offers a vision of this left-handed world, which we now elaborate as the site of the interstitial subject. When she writes the poem, however, she is clear sighted about the "sad things in [her] head," and her dream is to "break out of bondage" and construct what she develops in *Borderlands* as a utopian world that a new mestiza consciousness can produce. She imagines that there will be a decolonized future when "Together we will walk / through walls" (36), walls that we can certainly understand in our own historical moment as the border walls erected by the Department of Homeland Security, further militarizing the US/Mexico border. Melina Martinez testifies how living with the wall in her own back yard stirs up a burgeoning political consciousness in her and in people in her South Texas Valley community.

Perhaps having the Anzaldúan metaphoric barbed wire fence made concrete with the Wall allows the seeds of decolonization to mature in the twenty-first century. After all, in "The coming of el mundo surdo," Anzaldúa foresees a time when "a collective of wo/men/ and androgynes will proclaim" their subjectivity in order to "prepare the way/Love is the doctrine" and live in a world transformed by the hermeneutics of love, with all its revolutionary potential (*Reader*, 37). Other feminist theorists who move in the constellation of U.S. third world feminisms would agree. Chela Sandoval, in language more prosaic than Anzaldúa's, sees that "it is love that can access and guide our theoretical and political '*movidas*'— revolutionary maneuvers toward decolonized being" (*Methodology*, 140.1).

In "La Prieta," which Anzaldúa began formulating in 1979 (Keating 23), we find a further elaboration of that left-handed world, declaring that "those people who feel at home," are "the colored, the queer, the poor, the female, the physically challenged" who can form "an international feminism" that is the design for a new type of revolution (*Bridge*, 196). This essay is where she lays out the preliminary articulations she will develop the rest of her life and particularly in *Borderlands*. But in 1979 she had already begun conceptualizing the new political, feminist philosophy, writing of the struggles of "a colonized peoples throughout the world, including Third World Women in the U.S." (197). Even then Anzaldúa challenged dualistic thinking, arguing for "autonomy" but not "separation," often calling for a "revolution" incited by love and spiritual work (*Bridge*, 196).

The Mundo Zurdo she inscribes in the final section of "La Prieta" is her "own universe" (*Bridge* 209). It is home for "the queer groups, the people that don't belong anywhere, not in the dominant world nor completely within our own respective cultures" (209). Here she speculates about a process of politicization, the conocimiento that she will fully develop years later in "now let us shift...the path of conocimiento...inner work, public acts." El Mundo Zurdo, even in its first inception, is a site where difference is acceptable, where diverse people with their differences "can live together and transform the planet" (209).

In Sandoval's oppositional theories, el Mundo Zurdo figures as a possible site for developing a "differential mode of social movement (that which transforms and allies all other modes of social movement)" (*Methodology*, 139). It would rely "on ...a 'cyber' consciousness, a 'differential' consciousness, that operates as process and shifting location" (139). In Anzaldúa of the 1970s, we find in her vision of el mundo surdo the genesis of an emancipatory, decolonizing theory of Chicana lesbian, U.S. women of color feminism.

This volume, *El Mundo Zurdo 2*, shows the range of Anzaldúan theoretical influence. From Laura Pérez's erudite elaboration of Anzaldúa's spiritual teachings that link politics with soul-work and spiritual activism to Sunshine Maria Anderson's discovery of alternative discourses in the community art venues in East Los Angeles, we see through Anzaldúan serpent eyes a discourse that motivates conocimiento in its spiritual and political manifestations. In her perceptive reading, María del Socorro Gutierrez Magallanes comprehends the historical context of La Prieta's Texas, where the operating ideology is a virulent racism "that in its display simultaneously justifies conquest, colonization and occupation." Theresa Delgadillo deploys Anzaldúan thought through an innovative route, as a crucial element in "critical migration studies." With Marion Rohrleitner's equally original insights, we can see how Anzaldúan theories travel from the borders of the Mexico-U.S. third world to the island of Hispaniola in the works of contemporary U.S. third world feminist writers, the Haitian American Edwidge Danticat and Dominican American Eloida Pérez. Anzaldúan epistemology also travels and permeates Laurel Boshoff's reading of a Maori girl's personal and political awakening.

In a tri-authored epistolary narrative, Aurora Levins Morales writes to Gloria and in true Anzaldúan spirit, decries the devastation of subaltern women's bodies, poisoned by the toxins of capital. Levins Morales makes community with the woman whose "glucose [was] making tidal waves in [her] blood," certain that Anzaldúa would join in a political protest against the devastation of the "ecological web." Also in this piece, Qwo-Li Driskill notes how Anzaldúa's writing now makes sense to her as "radical" disability theory and as part of disability studies.

The theories we glean from the body of Gloria Anzaldúa's work, from mundos surdos to transformative bridges, from borderlands to third spaces, from facultad to conocimiento and spiritual activism, all engender a radical, politicized, spiritual, decolonized subject in process. The essays that follow interpret Anzaldúan thought with its multiple implications and draw on Anzaldúan theory to illuminate other texts, other sites that dwell in Nepantla.

In the mid 1970s Anzaldúa wrote the poem "The New Speakers" (*Reader*, 24-25) about poets who would make a difference, serve as "our age's mouthpiece," and would not be "hung/ -up on the art for art trip." Always ahead of her time, she seemed to foresee a time when the once silenced subaltern could speak and be heard:

We don't want to be

Stars but parts

of constellations.

As we witness in the following essays, her "luminous and active" poetic and philosophical words are both.

ENDNOTES

1 See the Gloria Anzaldúa "Foreword to the Second Edition" to *This Bridge Called My Back,* 1983, n.p. I would like to thank Christina Gutierrez and Megan Wallace for their expert assistance in getting the manuscript of this volume prepared for publication.

2 See Emma Pérez's *The Decolonial Imaginary* for the classic articulation of what we call Third Space Chicana feminist theory.

THE PERFORMANCE OF SPIRITUALITY AND VISIONARY POLITICS IN THE WORK OF GLORIA ANZALDÚA[1]

KEYNOTE ADDRESS

LAURA E. PÉREZ

I have come a long way with Gloria since first reading *This Bridge Called My Back* in the mid-eighties, as a sister Chicana and radical woman of color, and then giving my copy of *Borderlands* away like a disease, after erasing my mad pencil markings correcting or challenging the author throughout the book's margins. I was a graduate student, half of me about order and footnotes and foolproof arguments, the other half about radical politics and, at least theoretically, about experimental poetics. And here was this flaw of a book about a different kind of knowing, a knowing we could only access by seeing how fallen apart we actually were, how colonized our wholeness. A book too much a solo flight into the unknown, the instinctual, and the scary-as-hell "*facultad*."

To embrace *Borderlands* at that time would have been to pay to be jumped: an unadvised *revolcada* from head to toe that promised worse than nothing, to the taunting tune of "I know more than Freud." In 1987, Anzaldúa's book was an invitation into the deeper recesses of margins I already inhabited, not the exodus promised by a graduate school where I only ever came across two other Chicana/os in the entire humanities and social sciences, one of whom did not want to come out and play.

But by 1990, not only had I bought a new copy, I was teaching it, as I have continued to do, sometimes two to three times a year. It has been a steady, twenty-year intravenous drip of the Anzaldúan way. The transfusion was complete in the early 1990s, in one of the first papers I ever presented, in high *macha* mode, at a philosophy conference. There I argued that Anzaldúa's *Borderlands* presented us with a new philosophical framework outside of western binary thought, a different way to think and conceive the making of meaning, a way beyond the hegemonic: a multiply queer way of knowing.[2]

In the spring of 1998, I published an essay discussing the centrality of the spiritual and the psychic or *la facultad* as other ways of knowing in *Borderlands*. That essay, "Spirit Glyphs: Reimagining Art and Artist in the Work of Chicana *Tlamatinime*," argued that a decolonizing politics of spirituality was at work, alongside gender, race, class, and/or sexual critiques in the work of Anzaldúa, Moraga, Castillo, and Cisneros; in visual artists Yolanda Lopez, Yreina Cervantez, and Ester Hernandez, and in film maker Frances Salome Espana, alongside many others. That essay became the cornerstone of a book that grew up around it, a book I conceived as an altar, and that focused on the spiritual and aesthetic hybridities of over forty artists in various media, published in 2007 as *Chicana Art: The Politics of Spiritual and Aesthetic Altarities*.

In the opening paragraphs of *Altarities*, I recounted that my journey to spirituality in the work of Chicana art began reluctantly, in the early 1990s, after reading a white feminist theorist who exhorted feminists to take up science and defy their gendered lot in the touchy feely, unscientific. What was disturbing to me was that in a chapter recounting the history and development of the concept of gender in the United States, when summarizing the contributions of Anzaldúa, she silenced the centrality of spirituality in her work and failed to engage her critically for it, as we would have expected given the rest of the book. I felt that this was, at best, a condescending act of solidarity with a woman of color feminist. And I said so to a friend, who said that I should write about it.

But there was no way that I was going to commit intellectual suicide in the basic black, piranha world of fashionably atheist, leftoid academics for whom religion and spirituality on the personal level were good for snide appetizers.

At that time, spirituality and religiosity were not generally conceived of as a terrain of, let's face it, "first" world political struggle, let alone as a site of consciously decolonizing ideology, alongside, gender, sexuality, class, and racialization, as Anzaldúa, and so many U.S. women of color in her generation, and those following, did in their literary essays, poetry, stories, novels, and visual art.

Nonetheless, with Anzaldúa as the psycho pomp, I was dragged, then led, through an underworld, into a different politics of lived being, one seeking anchor in a more real, complex, and most importantly, integral conception of subjectivity as multiple and changing, and of coexistence as interdependent, simultaneous, and in which difference is valuable and necessary to the whole. This was a perennial philosophy found across the globe's ancient peoples of individual and social being as a path of continual growth and transformation, and of human and social health through integration and empowerment, rather than social marginalization, psychic fragmentation, and disempowerment.

Anzaldúa's way spoke powerfully to me as a person to whom the visual was very important. In *Altarities*, as I had argued in an earlier essay called *"El desorden,"* I wanted to make a feminist and an interdisciplinary argument: that Chicana feminism was the product of many languages, including those of visual and performance art, and of literary art, and not only of feminist journalism or scholarly articles. I wanted to argue that the arts, through their own languages, were a way of making meaning, of thinking, indeed of cutting edge insights and theories. It was life-blood to me that the arts spoke other than linguistically or that when they were word-based, that they spoke through poetic suggestion and fiction, rather than through a belief in definition and denotation.

And so it was that in spite of my "No way" to writing about spirituality in *Borderlands*, I found myself, both in my personal life and in my research and teaching, continually accompanied by Gloria and the psychological and spiritual mythological roadmap of multiple and simultaneous planes of existence that she created to navigate these times: bridges and borderlands; the Coatlicue State; *nepantla*; the practice of making face, making soul, and later, *conocimientos y desconocimientos*.

Therefore, I want to honor Gloria Anzaldúa, as a tremendous thinker, artist, activist, a tremendous spirit who wrote of the necessity and rewards of transformation, of creating other ways beyond the binary logic of the various dominations we have been shaped within, beyond the dominating logic which is the foundation of colonialism and the patriarchy, heternormativity, religious intolerance, and unjust social orders which preceded the invasion of the Americas and the subsequent five hundred years of inhumanity against a majority of this continent and the planet.

From *This Bridge Called Our Back,* to *Borderlands/La Frontera*, and up through *Making Face, Making Soul*, into *this bridge we call home*, in her deeply compassionate essay within it, "now let us shift...the path of conocimiento... inner work, public acts," and now, still, through her posthumously published writings, Gloria broke ground for the rest of us. She showed us pathways beyond the internalization of hatreds that render us various shades of living death. Because this was not about writing, about metaphors, but about real survivals, real transformations, towards real better presents and futures, she was careful to not hide the dangers and fearsomeness that lay ahead.

I don't know that I have ever read a writer, not even Anais Nin, so committed to exposing herself, to patrolling her own duplicity and fear, as Gloria Anzaldúa. Writing was a spiritual path for her, a spiritual practice among other spiritual practices. Through it, she engaged in meditation, reflection, and self-scrutiny and, this, in turn, allowed her to gaze at the social world made by humans more clearly and to scry a vision of a different, better way of being.

Gloria's writing was her embodied thinking, and I dare say, her prayer or incantation, her words of power, delivered with intentionality, as performative act. As she pointed out in *Borderlands*, she understood writing as image-making, a calling forth from the imagination that, at its core, was performative, and powerfully so.

My "stories" are acts encapsulated in time, "enacted" every time they are spoken aloud or read silently. I like to think of them as performances and not as inert and "dead" objects (as the aesthetic of Western culture think of art works). Instead, the work has an identity; it is a "who" or a "what" and contains the presences of persons, that is, incarnations of gods or ancestors or natural and cosmic powers. The work manifests the same needs as a person, it needs to be "fed," *la tengo que bañar y vestir.* (*Borderlands* 67)

She wrote of her book as alive, as needing to be bathed and dressed, even as a kind of "precocious girl-child" (*Borderlands,* 66). She distinguished her aesthetics from the formal virtuosity of modern decades, increasingly emptied of any kind of social or visionary power, and gradually reduced to mute decoration. Instead, she sought to resuscitate the *tlacuilo's* and the *tlamatinime's* performative path of the red and the black inks, one among many ancient and cross-cultural, intentional and sacred ways of object making, not necessarily called "art." "Picture language precedes thinking in words; the metaphorical mind precedes analytical consciousness," she wrote (*Borderlands* 69). Thus, she strove to return to art making as an image-producing activity, an awareness of its actual, literal power in this time when even the thought of art as powerful is laughable, or at best, seen as a moment of insight that might move us emotionally or intellectually.

Her project was more ambitious than formal virtuosity, in fact, not possible through it, really. She sought to restore to consciousness the awareness of psychic power itself as the seedbed of image-making and therefore of thought itself and its omnipresent embeddedness in material reality, beginning with our own bodies: our guts, our genitals, the flickering thoughts escaped from our unconscious recesses. For her, the flesh was also the dwelling place of the unfleshed; the body itself, a borderlands and a *nepantla.*

The *Interviews,* and last year's publication of *The Gloria Anzaldúa Reader,* a selection of decades of her writings, both edited by AnaLouise Keating, show how hard and continuously Gloria worked on harnessing the performative power of the imaginal. It is no coincidence that *Borderlands* is a multi-generic or hybrid text. The multiple, and simultaneous registers on which it performs together enact a way of being and consciousness that sees much, at once. Its language is the language of simultaneity, and of *conocimiento,* drawing its strength on the fuller truths of what we actually are as humans, that is, spiritual and psychic, and what is happening on these levels, as indicated by heart, gut, and desire as sites of spiritual or psychic speech, as it were, and not only by what has been programmed into our brains by culture and through *familia* as truth or permissible.

Anzaldúa wrote that she hated institutionalized religiosity (*Interviews*). Instead, she spent her life as an artist-intellectual-spiritual guide, a *tlacuila tlamatinime,* uncovering spiritual power and disempowerment that go by other names. She sought to decolonize, that is, to extricate spirituality from its institutionalized control at the hands of dogmatic churches and its debasement by dominant intelligentsia. She sought to de-ghettoize a more complex notion of spirituality and a more empowering one, one that is anchored in the mind and body, as embodied, and therefore necessarily enacted in the flesh and in thought. She studied world spirituality, psychology, philosophy, and the arts searching for knowledge beyond that which reproduces the present orders.

Like the philosophers of old and their continuum in the cross-cultural spiritual teachers of the present, she sought wisdom. And like them, she sought not only for herself. She was therefore a seeker and an activist, and somewhat like Gandhi and Martin Luther King, Jr., she sought in the universals of ancient spiritual truths from all quarters of the globe a way for humans to live better, to live more fully, more justly, more honorably. Like so many spiritual teachers, she was a gender bender, seeing no solace in the socially corrupt strictures of gender and in *metiche* (busybody) prohibitions labeling how love and desire must or must not flow in disregard of how in nature, love and desire actually exist.

Anzaldúa wished to perform the path of integrity, the struggle for wholeness, the acceptance of all the Glorias, as she put it, of all the selves that in moments like sexual and spiritual ecstasy in particular co-existed consciously, harmoniously, no longer fragmented off as a habit of social rejection and self-loathing. She conceived of being and existence as spiritual and thus of everything natural as interrelated. She wrote of feeling great connection with plants, animals, the ocean, the sky, even inanimate objects like corral posts and windmills. In her short stories, she sought to fictionalize the experience of characters stretching beyond their conceptual and physical borders to pass through or unify with other beings and objects.

She was able to write of the spiritual as a borderlands, alongside the geopolitical U.S.-Mexico border, and cultural, psychological, and sexual borderlands because she had lived her interest in the paranormal and in non-institutionalized world spiritualities as taboo. She is remarkable for having set out to weave together the many innovative and visionary strands of the sixties and seventies as a form of political activist social action theory. Born in 1942, she lived these decades with open eyes: for in 1960 she was 18, and by the still-happening mid-1970s, in her mid-thirties.

The sixties and seventies were not only a cultural and political renaissance in this country, they were also a spiritual revival and break with a past of institutionalized religiosity. If Black and Chicana/o Power were freshly minted as such and spread like wildfire among massive numbers, along with the Gay and Lesbian and feminist liberation movements, so did Eastern spiritualities, the resurgence of Native American and African diasporic spiritualities, and the mushrooming of new religious movements, neo-pagan magic, and goddess-rituals. Indeed, Gloria trod the risky path of immersing herself into New Age spirituality, into UFO literature, astrology, and other forms of the occult. I wonder if this fearlessness of hers was because she nearly died four or five times and because of this, as with other psychics, this human capacity became pronounced in her, a door, as it were, left thereafter ajar?

With the publication of the *Interviews/Entrevistas* in 2000, I believe that the women will be separated from the girls, or more precisely, the daring from the timid. The gauntlet that Anzaldúa threw down there, refusing us a dull moment in our companionship with her, was to more fully elaborate on often glossed snapshots in *Borderlands*: possession, merging, and outright sexual trysts with spirit beings and aliens. What can be done with that? There's really no way to make nice with that against her many critics, among those Chicanas and Native American women who view her as little more than a Latina New Ager. What will philosophers and theorists now wanting to write from *nepantla* as a freshly discovered so-called decolonial space do with this if they don't politely ignore it or drop her like a hot potato?[3]

And I have to smile because I realize that Anzaldúa's body of work as a whole has made it difficult to vampirize its power, ripped off and unacknowledged as her complex concepts of borderlands and queerness continue to be, worldwide. Anzaldúa was really talking about gnosis, literally, not metaphorically. She didn't only mean that the oppressed experience cultural and social reality differently and therefore have a different point of view from which to tell reality, in the style of Akira Kurosawa's *Rashoman*. What would political science look like if it located power within the psyche, as Anzaldúa did, and not only in its external management via the state or social blocs?

Anzaldúa is not the first to suggest that revolution as social transformation cannot happen in any lasting way without inner transformation. Marxists and Socialists argued the point a hundred years ago, face to face with Marx and his correligionaries. The bearers of a directly transmitted spirituality and philosophy thousands of years old, the Hindu social activist yogi, Gandhi, whom I mentioned earlier, the late Tibetan Buddhist, Chogyam Trungpa, and the Vietnamese monk, Thich Nhat Hanh, have also explained that inner transformation affects our bodies and society simultaneously, causally, and thus that social revolution cannot be just or lasting without inner revolution, first.

Spiritual masters of traditions across the globe and across time make clear that spirituality and religiosity are about power. But greater power, beyond parlor tricks, is earned and developed through self-discipline and unwavering commitment to the right use of power in service of the greater good, over self-aggrandizement and enrichment, they have told us. Chogyam Trungpa said the spiritual path is a warrior's way, for it takes a warrior to not close one's heart in the face of so much suffering and to remain in love with the world and to be a beacon of healing love within it. Gandhi, a yogi whose path was through social action, who developed a powerful form of non-violent spiritual activism, said it was not for the faint of heart, but rather a path of courageous self-sacrifice for a world we might not live to see. Martin Luther King, Jr., learned this way from Black religious social activist elders who had sought Gandhi out in India, and like Gandhi, did not live to see the way he peacefully led through a spiritual politics of love.[4]

At her core, Gloria Anzaldúa was also a spiritual activist. And I want to frame her study and practice of many different spiritualities not as a meaningless, shallow New Ageism, but rather as an excavation and a *rescate*, a rescuing of universal and enduring truths in this time of what I consider a neocolonizing secularism that privatizes spirituality to cage it and denies spirituality or the scope of its nature to disempower us individually and collectively, both against materialist money lords and "religious" fundamentalist power-mongers. This is an investigation that she undertook in the face of the irony of post-structuralist atheism and the arrogance and myopia of western scientific atheism, both, in my view, herd-like postures that attempt to pacify us with the fiction of intellectual superiority over our ancestors and almost the entire population of the country and the planet.

For Gandhi, truth, God, and love were one. For Anzaldúa, the truth of being was our oneness and interdependence, founded in a common nature that is spiritual.[5] Anzaldúa sought to translate the meaning and function of the spiritual through comparative study of the religions and spiritual practices of many peoples. A kind of decolonizing Joseph(a) Campbell, she looked for coincidences and commonalities beyond imperialist and Eurocentric Darwinian catalogs of primitive religiosities. And from this perspective, she was not afraid of speaking of essences in the face of the rise of extreme social constructivism in academia, an extreme of the argument that how we think and are is due to how the societies we are born into shape us.

Anzaldúa was in fact a spiritual teacher, though she did not call herself that. I think that instead she understood her responsibility as a public figure in the "making face and soul" of those who heard and read her. She navigated the New Age, astrology, Don Juan, Seth, magic ritual, meditation, paranormal exercises, contact with UFOs, and prophetic vision not to conduct weekend vision quests for $500 or to gather groupies to vampirize psychically and do her *mandados* (bidding). Throughout her work, I see the surviving words of the Nahua and Maya ancients guiding her ethics of self-knowledge and service to others, guiding her journey through the bric-a-brac of the spiritual market place of the last four decades. "Not this, not that," I imagine her saying to herself, as she separated treasure from junk.

Anzaldúa's rediscovery in the areas of spirituality and politics was that spirituality was political activism. It could be passive, or called by another name, such as political ideology, or will power, and reproduce reality as the status quo, or spirituality could be active, consciously deployed as a performance, an action creating effects that matter politically. Thus Anzaldúa dedicated herself to thinking about consciousness as a very real, spiritual, and productive site, which, if invisible, is visible in its effects.[6] If Frantz Fanon has been invaluable in helping us to think about the internalization of colonial thought in, for example, discussing the self-loathing colonized peoples have been force-fed by racist regimes of power, and if Foucault has helped us to think better about the way in which we internalize power in general and at large in policing ourselves for the state by wanting to be good citizens, party to hegemony in whatever measure possible, Anzaldúa goes even further. For discourse and ideology are not just powerful intellectual phenomena with effects that are materialized on the social, cultural, economic, and political planes. Discourse and ideology are themselves the effects of spiritual awareness or ignorance, of *conocimiento* and *desconocimiento*. We are not merely subjected to and produced by the politically, socially, economically, and culturally empowered of our times. We are not merely a walking net of interpellations, soft clay misshapen by the constant *manoseadas* or manhandling of mass media, law, and education.

At our core, within Anzaldúan thought, we are all by nature powerful beings, and "being-becoming" is the reclamation of the right use of that power. Unlike the invitation to the cloisters, the monastery, the yogi's cave, or to discipleship, Anzaldúa's message and methodology is radically simple, and cross-culturally classic: know thyself, as the lintern read above the oracle at Delphi, and to thine own self be true, as Shakespeare's Polonius advised.[7] We are the compass on the road that she told us was made as we journeyed it. *"Caminante, el camino se hace al caminar."* If a mystic, as she identified herself several times, it was to come back and tell us about it, like a big sister, in order to get us to move and do something to empower ourselves in the world.

However, in direct opposition to the path of ascetics, for Anzaldúa, the path of spiritual awareness for herself and others in some way like her, born into negatively racialized, gendered, and sexed bodies, must first embrace and heal, *desembrujar*, as it were, unbewitch the despised, gendered body of color, traumatized further as a *mita y mita*, a gender half and half. Chogyam Trungpa, I believe, once noted that exercises immolating the ego were not appropriate for U.S. beginners because their egos were not healthy. How much more true is this for people of color, women, and queers, generally from poor social backgrounds to boot? The sad statistics of suicide, disproportionate physical and mental illnesses, and dropping out among our ranks top to bottom, say it all.

In Anzaldúa's worldview, the body is a wretched cage against which the spirit flails only to the extent to which we have been taught to desacralize our bodies, our authentic feelings, thoughts, and desires as suspect, unworthy, or evil. Instead, she wrote that:

> We have to recognize the total self…. And we have to work with the body. To not say 'Oh, the body is dirty and vile and we should escape it because it's a prison. The flesh is a prison, and the spirit is all-important; we should discard the body and let it rot.' No. It's the other way around. Matter is divine also." (*Interviews* 103)

Borderlands has not turned out to be a vehicle of demonic possession as a young undergraduate warned me the very first semester I taught it twenty-plus ago: it was the beginning of an exorcism, an exorcism that continues to be guided by a litany of readings of the work of this very brave and generous woman, a woman not afraid to be called crazy or New Age or light weight, because what was at stake was more important than her reputation among the intelligentsia of the day. In this sense, Gloria Anzaldúa knew that she was sacrificing herself as she wrote, in her very beautiful poem of 1977, and to which she returned in a later essay:[8]

The coming of el mundo surdo
(For Joya Santanlla)

"This is not Pharoah's Egypt and we are not his slaves."
—*The Passover Plot*

I walk among you
I see sad things in my head
not being free is being dead

This is the year
the people of peace
break out of bondage

Together we will walk
through walls by the lunar
light see our
left-handedness
with our third eye

I am the temple

I am the unmoving center
Within my skin all races
sexes all trees grasses
cows and snails implode

spirals lining thought
to feeling

The day of I am is now
I discard the wings
and claws I wear to
disguise my humanness
A collective of wo/men
and androgynes will proclaim me
One will prepare their way
Love is the doctrine

I am becoming-being
the questor the questing the quest
You and I have already met
We are meeting we will meet

The real unknown is feeling
The real unknown is love
do not be afraid
to touch each other
We go naked here.

This is not the year of revenge
Give it up give up that hatred
of yourself rise up reach
Come to me my sister-brother
We will share the moment
We are the awakening feminine presence
We are the earth
        We are the second coming

(*The Gloria Anzaldúa Reader*, 2009: 36-37)

I want to end by writing that I am very grateful to Gloria Anzaldúa for naming the place which by necessity we must occupy, *nepantla*, as the place of visionary politics for unrequited social justice lovers. In that place, the social world is thankfully disturbed, its logic upended. Here we together begin to imagine and thus call into being a visionary, political eros that is simultaneously individual and social, spiritual and political. Here, it is true that we are different and same, we the many, the unknown, the welcome, where self is also somehow other, *donde tu eres mi otro yo, segun los maestros maya*, where you are my other me: *In' Lakesh*.

ENDNOTES

1 This essay was originally presented as the keynote lecture of the third Society for the Study of Gloria Anzaldúa conference at University of Texas, San Antonio, November 4, 2010. I would like to thank the two Normas, Dr. Norma Cantú, this newbie organization's founder, and Dr. Norma Alarcón, for thinking of me when considering the special themes of the conference, performance and art.

2 "Negotiating New American Philosophies: Anzaldúa's *Borderlands / La Frontera,*" Philosophy, Interpretation, Culture, Mind Annual Conference, Binghamton University, NY, April 1993.

3 For Anzaldúa's own analysis of "dependent" academic critics of this aspect of her work, see *Interviews*, pp. 18-19.

4 On the role of Mohandas K. ("Mahatma" i.e., Great Soul) Gandhi's role in SNCC, the Student Non-Violent Coordinating Committee and its effect on the Black Civil Rights Movements, including that led by Martin Luther King, Jr., see Wesley C. Hogan, *Many Minds. One Heart. SNCC's Dream for a New America* (University of Carolina Press, 2007).

5 "...everything is spiritual....nothing is alien, nothing is strange. Spirit exists in everything; therefore God, the divine, is in everything....Everything is my relative, I'm related to everything." (Interview with Weigland, *Interviews,* p. 100).

6 On consciousness, see *Interviews*, p. 20, her 1982 interview with L. Smucker and the preface interview with AnaLouise Keating to Smucker's.

7 Anzaldúa put it this way in her 1983 interview with Weiland: "We have to recognize the total self, rather than just one part and start to be true to that total self, that presence, that soul" *Interviews:* 103.

8 On what she imagined the future understanding of her work, see *Interviews,* pp. 18-19.

WORKS CITED

Anzaldúa, Gloria and Cherríe Moraga, ed. *This Bridge Called My Back: Writings by Radical Women of Color.* New York: Kitchen Table: Women of Color Press, 1983. Print.

Anzaldúa, Gloria. "Turning Points." *Interviews/Entrevistas.* Ed. AnaLouise Keating. New York: Routledge, 2000. 17-70. Print.

---."Within the Crossroads: Lesbian/Feminist/Spiritual Development." *Interviews/Entrevistas.* Ed. AnaLouise Keating. New York: Routledge, 2000. 71-127. Print.

Pérez, Laura E. "Negotiating New American Philosophies: Anzaldúa's *Borderlands/La Frontera.*" Philosophy, Interpretation, Culture, Mind Annual Conference. Binghamton University, New York. April 1993.

IMMIGRATION, THE IMMIGRANT, AND THE RACIALIZED BODY

LA PRIETA: AN ACROBAT, EXPERT IN THE ACT OF EQUILIBRIUM

MARÍA DEL SOCORRO GUTIÉRREZ MAGALLANES

"Yo ando por la cuerda floja con facilidad y gracia. Me extiendo sobre los abismos. A ciegas en el aire azul. La espada entre los muslos, una espada calentada por mi carne… Ando la cuerda—una acróbata en contrapaso, experta en el acto de equilibrio" [1]

In this essay, I maintain that in the autobiographical text *"La Prieta"* by Gloria Anzaldúa, as an expression of what I name, "Chicana political autobiography,"[2] the body of the author is unfolded as matter and also as a body marked to become unveiled as a metaphor: a *bridge*. As matter, the body is shown as a territory marked by violence, discrimination, exclusion and racism. As a metaphor, the body is embodied as a bridge that through imagination, writing, language, tongue, skin and voice allows crossing from one way to another, taking on all the complications of a body situated in multiple crossroads. In other words, in the refererenced text, the body of Gloria Anzaldúa is racialized by multiple social experiences, and at the same time it is metaphorically transformed by the author into a bridge towards social recognition and towards a belonging to multiple communities, towards resistance and freedom in her horizon and utopia, i.e., *El Mundo Zurdo,* via self-affirmation, self-recognition, self-figuration, self-representation and imagination.

Some questions I approach the text with are the following: Who speaks in the figuration of a life? What body does the narrative come from? Who narrates and is constructed as an *I?* What equilibrium is achieved between autonomy and commitment, between the I and the We/-? What is narrated and from where? How? Why? What experience is visibilized? How is that step taken from the personal to the political, from the individual to the collective? I will try to respond to these questions tracing the path that took Anzaldúa from being a ciphered body articulated with the wounds inflicted by others that made it a racialized body to being a metaphor: a body transformed into a bridge.

Before I continue, I will present a set of important biographical elements of Gloria Anzaldúa. She was born in Texas in 1942, and she passed in California in 2004. Throughout her life she was a teacher, an activist, a poet, a writer, a literature professor and a theoretician of cultural and ethnic studies in the United States. Her work in different cultural arenas is precursor and constituent of what was considered a long process, questioning dominant epistemological paradigms in the U.S. academy during the 1980s. Her work translated into the construction and consolidation of critical and leftist thought which did have some influence in the academy, especially in what we now know as feminist women-of-color theory in the U.S., in Ethnic Studies in general and in Chicano/a Studies in particular. A lot of her literary and theoretical work is founded on the narrativization and theorization of her experience as a poor, working-class, Chicana lesbian, especially in the form of autobiographical texts. One of which is precisely the text "*La Prieta*" (Anzaldúa, 1987).

THE TAINTED AND RACIALIZED BODY: *MORENA, MUY PRIETA, INDIA, MEXICANA*

In the text "*La Prieta,*" Anzaldúa begins her narrative speaking of her birth and some of her "excessive" physical and racial characteristics. These are observed and spoken of by her grandmother "Mamá grande Locha," a woman we suppose is an important person in the identity and perception of Anzaldúa's self. This we assume because Gloria speaks of her in the very first line of her autobiographical text and because she mentions her as the first person in the world that observed her as she was born. She refers to her grandmother as the person that "inspected" her and legitimized and de-legitimized her at the same time.

Anzaldúa narrates how her grandmother refers to her physical characteristics, racializing her when she observes her at birth. In this way, Anzaldúa integrates into the memory of her body a sign of worthlessness. It is important to note this because Anzaldúa, in her first enunciation as a narrator in this text, presents herself in the narrated world as a body in the voice of her grandmother while clearly in opposition to her. She introduces herself with her grandmother's voice as different, as "other," as *"india, de mancha oscura, con señal del indio, de sangre mulata…morena, prieta, y distinta a…los hijos güeros"* (157). She presents herself to the narrated world through the eyes of her grandmother, a woman Anzaldúa describes as *"española, un poco alemana, el rastro aristocrático debajo de su piel pálida, de ojos azules y cabellos enroscados, en un tiempo rubios"* (157). Anzaldúa is birthed *"india"* in a world narrated by the voice of her *"española"* grandmother.

In this way, from her birth Anzaldúa's body was racialized by her grandmother's and her mother's discourse. Both women belonging to a Texan society, the territory where her narrative is articulated, a territory that was first conquered and colonized by the Spaniards and secondly occupied by the Anglos. In this Texan society, racism is an operating ideology that in its display simultaneously justifies conquest, colonization and occupation: an ideological operation that informs the identity configurations of racialization and exclusion.

Throughout her life, in her family (particularly with her mother and grandmother), Gloria Anzaldúa was singled out because of her dark skin, which was consistently referred to as an undesired and despised skin color. In her mother, Gloria narrates, if the girl would go out *"a tomar el sol o jugar o si se ensuciaba la ropa al jugar, haría pensar a otros que era una india o que era una mexicana sucia"* (157). By putting the voices of her mother and grandmother in her narrative, Gloria weaves the internalization of her family's lived racism in South Texas, even if they are sixth-generation Texans. This reveals the structural racism internalized by folks who have lived there for many generations.

The voice of the racialized body of Gloria Anzaldúa speaks of shame and fear, about the pain and wounds caused by her mother's words. Nevertheless, she also understands and expresses that her mother, as is the case with many people of color, has been a subject of racism and multiple forms of oppression: for being dark-skinned, for being a woman, for being poor and working class. Anzaldúa does not intend or want to portray her mother as the villain of her life, but she does want to show how the very same people who are subjected to racism reproduce ways of internalized racism. Gloria says: "*a mucha mierda nuestra, como nuestro propio racismo, nuestro miedo a las mujeres y a la sexualidad*" (158). What Anzaldúa intends in this text, in part, is to narrate her experience as she lived it and internalized it without betraying herself, not to "*traicionar(se) a sí misma*" (158). That is to say, she wants to speak with the truth of her wounds in her body and her identity, as inflicted even by her own family and community, as painful as they might be. Anzaldúa displays a paradoxical textual and discursive strategy here. She begins to give place, space and voice to her wounds in her writing as she throws herself and her body into an abyss in search of equilibrium.

IN SEARCH OF EQUILIBRIUM: AN ACROBAT *EN CONTRAPASO A CONTRATIEMPO*

In her narrative, Anzaldúa is in search of equilibrium between narrating the truth from a place of enunciation of the self and narrating with clarity how the women in her life configure her from their internalized racism. This is a crossing place where the *I* is a configuration of the dialogue between her and the women in her life and her world. In this way Anzaldúa narrates the experience of her pain and the women that are so important in her life without making them the villains of her story. In search of equilibrium, narrating the truth from the pain caused by her grandmother's disgust and her mother's shame, Anzaldúa looks for ways to let go of the guilt she has carried in her body and on her back for years, a pain and guilt that do not belong to her. Likewise, Gloria is sure that shame and guilt do not belong to the women that are so important to her. To narrate from the multiple wounds helps her comprehend her mother and grandmother. To narrate with the truth is a commitment to equilibrium she assumes with integrity and imagination, for she knows how to "*andar por la cuerda floja con facilidad y gracia*" (168). This is her search.

In her text, what is unfolded in Anzaldúa's words is a narrative creation of the self that balances out between the I and the Us/We. As Jerome Brunner sustains with respect to writings of the self, the creation of the I/Self is a narrative art, to invent and re-invent the self, which resides in an interior and exterior side, and in a balancing act between autonomy and commitment. This act is constituted by memory, feelings, ideas, beliefs and subjectivity, as well as the appreciation of others and the numberless expectations that we derive very quickly, even unconsciously, from the culture we are embedded in.

The narrative acts directed to the creation of the *Self* are typically guided by tacit and implicit cultural rules of what the self should and should not be. This is precisely what is unveiled in the autobiographical text "*La Prieta*"; the narrative creation of Anzaldúa´s self that tries the balancing act of narrating her experience without betraying herself or making villains of others who made her who she is. That is to say, on the one hand, to narrate the self from an experience of the internalized racism of the central figures in her life that was projected towards her and, on the other, to narrate and create another self or another I from a collective. In doing so, she is also getting rid of the guilt, the hatred and the bitterness that do not belong to her, neither to her nor to the collective.

THE MATTER: THE GENDERED BODY

In her narrative Anzaldúa continues to tell her life from the crossings of pain, betrayal, wounds and images "*que la espantan*" (158). One of those images is that of her body as a body marked as different from other girls'. In addition to having been racialized at birth, Anzaldúa's body was also gendered in what a doctor told her mother about her: Gloria is a girl with the mark of an "*esquimal.*" Anzaldúa red spotted her diapers as a baby girl. She started her period as a child, and this led her to have a much accelerated growth, as if she was an adult woman even at an early age. This physical condition led her mother to pin a towel in her underwear and to tie her upper body with cotton bandages so she would not differ from other girls her age. Her mother would tell Gloria: "*mantén las piernas cerradas Prieta,*" as if between her legs she carried shame and the malignant sex. The image that her mother had of her was of a girl "*marcada, anormal, rara*" which affected her in such a way that Gloria felt that her mother was ashamed of her and that her mother felt guilty for making Gloria "*víctima de su pecado… de fornicar antes de la ceremonia de boda*" (158-159).

COMMITMENT: TO HER MOTHER AND HER COMMUNITY

In the acts and words of her mother, Anzaldúa not only localized the conflict as a tension of the religious Catholic dogma and the role the church plays in subjugating women to such beliefs, but Gloria also signals to a type of power battle between her and her mother that has more to do with the contradiction created by the need to have autonomy from and commitment to her family. This tension informs and confirms her own construction of her self. According to what Gloria narrates, this battle has to do with her mother's need to require obedience from Gloria because of all the care she required as a girl and because she was a child different from the others and from her own siblings. The image that her mother had of Gloria made her feel as "*un ser ajeno de otro planeta*" (159). To distance herself from her mother and other people in her family and community, she turned to books and to solitude in search of her autonomy.

AUTONOMY: THE WORLD OF LETTERS AND HER FATHER'S DEATH

The image and figure of the father that Gloria traces with her words is that of a person who "*dejó caer en (su) regazo una novelita de vaqueros del oeste de 25c, el único libro que se podía conseguir en la botica*" (159); her father is the person who led her to the act that changed her forever: the act of reading. The act of reading was the act that defined her autonomy. In this part of her narrative, Gloria situates very clearly the meaning of her entrance to the world of letters and literacy. In this, she underlines her reading in the racist code provided by *the novelitas de vaqueros*, where Mexicans were represented as maids, villains, drunkards, Indians and beasts. It is this same racist ideology she later found and identified in her Anglo teachers. The other image of Gloria´s father is of him *"muriéndose, la aorta se le reventó mientras que manejaba, la camioneta se volteó, arrojó su cuerpo y la camioneta se volcó sobre su cara.* Blood in the pavement" (159). Anzaldúa refers to the death of her father as an event that also changed her life forever; his death destroyed the myth that there would be a male figure in her life that would care for her. Without explicitly saying it, from that accident on, Gloria lost the possible subjection of the protector father figure, and she was obliged by circumstance to search and struggle for her autonomy. She searched for her autonomy in a new world, a world of letters, in a narrative of the self, invented, re-invented and imagined by her own self.

THE WOUNDED BODY: *LA ESPADA ENTRE LOS MUSLOS, UNA ESPADA CALENTADA POR MI CARNE*

Another image in her autobiographical text *"que la espanta"* and one that also configures her, as a woman-subject is her menstrual period and the doctor visits, "men in white," every 24 days. She had to put up with doctors' comments that what she had was *"pura imaginación,"* the mark in her gendered body as an abnormal woman. She narrates that her body suffered unbearable pain every 24 days and that she was cut by the knife of a man dressed in white to remove some tumors. She narrates that she was *"chingada abierta y violada por la vara de un hombre blanco"* (163).

She sustains that this experience led her to a border situation: *"descortezarse hasta el hueso y hacer(se) abosolutamente vulnerable"* (163). This experience leads her to make herself vulnerable. Another passage in her text narrates how her body is persecuted, torn, strangled, violated and thrown from a bridge by a burglar. The burglar terrorizes her in her dreams. She throws rocks at him, runs behind him, reaches him with the help of others, and they put him in jail. Nevertheless, her body lives permanently in fear with the ghost of the aggression, since the burglar threatened to come back for her. With these images Anzaldúa narrates the experiences of a body denied, hurt, wounded and violated. She also narrates experiences of a body willing to value itself, to heal itself and to defend itself with stones, dreams and even with its very life.

NARRATIVE AND THE CREATION OF THE SELF/I: SELF-REPRESENTATION AND SELF-CONFIGURATION

As Brunner proposes about the creation of the Self/I, for Anzaldúa the expression of her human condition in certain historic circumstances provides the point of departure for a process of creating the self via the autobiographical text of "*La Prieta*." This creation is an instrument to unveil and denounce via the narrated word, the cultural hegemony of the elite as well as the possibility to struggle against it. To struggle against the oppressions lived by the community she belongs to, Anzaldúa refers (in her autobiographical text) to her memories, feelings, wounds, denials, rejections, ideas of rebellion, beliefs and the appreciation others have of her or not, also, the expectations, deceptions, affiliations that come from the culture to which she belongs.

Anzaldúa narrates and creates herself on a tacit *autobiographical pact*[3] or referential pact which confirms the most appropriate public narrative of the Self. According to Philippe Lejeunne, to say or to tell others about the self turns out not in the private form, as was thought of in the past, but rather as a dialogic form where the other is always implicated in the self and the self is always implicated in the other. In this sense, no autobiographical text is ever complete, for she or he who writes such a text asks which subjective process is presented in the narrative: she or he who is, she or he who wants to be, or she or he who others want her or him to become.

Regardless of this unfinished process in the text "*La Prieta*," Anzaldúa begins her journey of self-representation and self-figuration pointing to what she does not do, to what she is not, and how she truly is, even if it becomes uncomfortable for her own family, her community and the society she is part of. Gloria speaks about how she was referred to as "*machona, india ladina*" because she did not behave like "*una buena chicanita*" should. She also talks about her refusal to take on the traditional role of the woman and how she was "*marimacho y andaba con botas, no le tenía miedo a las víboras ni a las navajas, demostraba el desdén hacia los roles de las mujeres, partió a la universidad, no hacía hogar ni se casaba, era política y estaba al lado de los campesinos*" (161).

This led her to trace the degrees of autonomy as an individual when she narrates, *"El rol tradicional de la mujer era una silla de montar que yo no me quería poner"* (162). In an act of equilibrium, Gloria distances herself from what was painful and damaging in her own family and in her social and cultural education and formation. At the same time, she forged commitments to the communities to which she belonged and became an ally in the struggle for justice for farmworkers, poor folk, lesbians, the gay movement, women of color, progressive whites, all of whom for her were part of or could be part of her *Mundo Zurdo*.

It is what she calls *"El estirón entre lo que es y lo que debe ser"* (165). In her self-figuration and in getting rid of obedience and passiveness, Gloria narrates that she started to *"[u]sar botas y pantalón de mezclilla de hombre y andar con la cabeza llena de visiones, con hambre de palabras y más palabras…dejar de andar cabizbaja, rechazar la herencia y desafiar las circunstancias"* (162). With this, she started to unlearn the belief that to be *"blanco es mejor que ser moreno"* (162). While she laments that there will be people of color who will never unlearn this, Gloria turns the self-hate she grew up with into self-love. It is with this that Gloria begins her journey of self and collective figuration: by letting go of and unlearning the self-hate and reaching out to the self-love. *"Y apenas ahora, que el odio de mi misma, el que pasé cultivando durante la mayor parte de mi adolescencia, se convierte en amor"* (163).

EXPERIENCE: GAINED SELF-REPRESENTATION

Anzaldúa turns to her personal and collective experience by first giving it historicity; she identifies collective historical processes where she situates herself as an individual. She makes visible historical subjects when she considers herself one of them and configures herself as one of them. She unwinds and unlearns the modes and mechanisms that operate or function to reproduce systems of exclusion, racism, sexism, homophobia and dehumanization. Anzaldúa does precisely what Joan Scott[4] suggests; she struggles for and achieves the process of visibility for the denied, excluded and hidden subjects in History.

In the personal and intimate levels, Gloria narrates, without hesitation, some of her loved ones' behavior, such as her mom's and siblings'. She criticizes the gender-based differential treatment not only exercised by her mother but also by her own siblings. She also talks about the personal decisions of leaving for college, of not getting married, of not having children and of having love and political relationships with whomever she desired. Anzaldúa continues to relate her political adherence to the struggle of the *campesinos* in the Chicano Movement to build the Farmworker's Union headed by Dolores Huerta and César Chávez (161).

In the collective, Anzaldúa tells her experience and conditions of poverty and hunger that she and her family lived and of the other Mexican families around hers, all of who worked in the field and whose bodies were sprayed with pesticides. Here Anzaldúa narrates the collective experience of Mexican families and how the agro business exploits the labor force of the workers and taints the bodies of the workers with insecticides in the fields.

FROM MATTER TO METAPHOR: GLORIA´S BODY AS A BRIDGE

According to Elsa Muñiz y Mauricio List:

> *Las sociedades contemporáneas han experimentado ciertos cambios en la concepción de los procesos de construcción de las subjetividades. Es entonces cuando el cuerpo de los sujetos cobra una significación particular, ya que deja de pensarse como materia y se percibe como metáfora, situándose en el ámbito de lo que nos gustaría ser y de la posibilidad de alcanzar casi cualquier forma que desde la imaginación podamos desear, gracias a la "agencia" que supuestamente tenemos sobre nuestro cuerpo y a las posibilidades que en los contextos contemporáneos existen para hacerlo.*[5]

In this sense, the denied, tainted, racialized, wounded and violated body of Anzaldúa stops thinking of itself as matter to reconfigure itself into a metaphor when she embarks herself into a journey, a struggle for selfrepresentation as a *body-bridge* that is "*columpiada por el viento, un crucero habitado (y atravesado) por torbellinos, Gloria la facilitadora, montada a horcajadas en el abismo*" (165). She also transforms herself when she makes explicit her membership in multiple communities, such as those of women, the Third World, the gay movement, the feminist movement, the socialist revolution, the New Era, magic, the literary movement, the art movement. That bridge to multiple belongings makes her who she is: "*Una lesbiana feminista tercermundista inclinada el marxismo y al misticismo. Me fragmentarán y a cada pequeño pedazo le pondrán una etiqueta*" (165).

ANZALDÚA'S BODY INHABITED BY THE SPIRIT OF AN ACROBAT, EXPERT IN THE ACT OF EQUILIBRIUM

Finally, I close this essay with Gloria Anzaldúa's own words which to me are the heart of her transformation in her process and journey of self-representation, from body-matter to body-metaphor, from a racialized body to a *bridged* body:

> *La mezcla de sangre y afinidades, en vez de confundirme o desbalancearme, me ha forzado a lograr un cierto equilibrio. Las dos culturas me niegan un lugar en su universo. Entre ellas y entre otras, yo construyo mi propio universo. El Mundo Zurdo: Yo me pertenezco a mi misma y no a cierto grupo... Yo ando por la cuerda floja con facilidad y gracia. Me extiendo sobre los abismos. A ciegas en el aire azul. La espada entre los muslos, una espada calentada por mi carne... Ando la cuerda- una acróbata en contrapaso, experta en el Acto de Equilibrio.* (Anzaldúa, 1998: 168)

That bridge is Anzaldúa's body, that body which is "*La Prieta,*" the one who lives as an acrobat in search of equilibrium.

NOTES

[1] Anzaldúa, Gloria. "*La Prieta.*" En: *Esta puente mi espalda. Voces de mujeres tercermundistas en los EEUU.* Moraga, Cherríe & Castillo, Ana. Eds. Translated by Ana Castillo & Norma Alarcón. Ism Press, 1998. 168.

[2] This proposal is part of a larger dissertation project where I propose the reading of these types of texts from the lens of what I call "Chicana political autobiography." Under this framework the expressions of the Chicana political autobiography, paraphrasing Roland Barthes on the crossings between History, Society, Politics and Literature, are literary works that present signs of history at the same time that they present a resistance to it. (Barthes, 1960: 19)

[3] Lejeune, Philippe. *On Autobiography*. Minneapolis, University of Minnesota Press. 1989. & *Le pacte autobiograhique*. Paris, Seuil, 1975. Lejeune, with his concept of "autobiographical pact" defines the contract between the author or subject of enunciation and the reader where the first one is committed mainly to understanding the life of the speaking subject in relationship to others with some inexact historical marks yet dealing with them. It should be clear that to read or to interpret any autobiographical text, writing or enunciation, there are fictional components to them and that not everything that is fiction or imaginative is necessarily false. Before anything, the autobiographical pact presents a plane where it is understood and agreed that the telling of the narrative is based on an ethical terrain and not in a factual result *per se*. Lejeune, among others, recognizes that any act of re-constructing the past is necessarily supported by the naturally selective and subjective memory of the person who writes or narrates or speaks.

[4] Scott, Joan. "Experiencia." Traducción al español de Moisés Silva en *revista de estudios de género*: La Ventana." Guadalajara, Jalisco, 2001. (Translation from this text into English is mine.) In this article Scott calls for conferring historicity to experience to identify the dominant patterns of a specific human activity and the ideology that sustains it; to pay attention to the historical processes that through discourse position subjects and produces their experiences. According to Scott, "It is not the individuals that have the experience, but the subjects that are constituted via the experience." This definition of experience turns not into the origin of our explanation, nor in the definitive evidence because it has been seen and felt what sustains what we know, but rather into something that we want to explain, that from which knowledge is produced. To think of experience in this way, to explain experience and locate it in a historical process that constitutes it, is to give it historicity, the same way in which historicity is given to the identities that it produces, argues Scott.

[5] Muñiz, Elsa & List, Mauricio. IV International Congress on Science, Arts and Humanities. *El cuerpo descifrado*. 27 - 30 of October, 2009. Ciudad de Puebla, Puebla, México. UAM-A, BUAP, ENAH,UAB, GESyS, FES-Iztacala-UNAM, Revista Kiné.

REFERENCES

Anzaldúa, Gloria. *"La Prieta"* En: *Esta Puente Mi Espalda. Voces de mujeres tercermundistas en los EEUU*. Moraga, Cherríe & Castillo, Ana. Eds. Translated by Ana Castillo and Norma Alarcón. Ism Press, 1998.

Barthes, Roland. *"Histoire ou litterature?"* En: *Sur Racine*, 1960.

Bruner, Jerome. *La Fabrica de Historias. Derecho, literatura, vida*. FCE, Argentina, 2002.

Lejeune, Philippe. *On Autobiography*. Minneapolis, University of Minnesota Press. 1989.

--- *Le pacte autobiograhique*. Paris, Seuil, 1975.

Pratt, Mary Louise: *Towards a Speech Act Theory of Literary Discourse*, Bloomington: Indiana University Press, 1977.

Scott, Joan. *"Experiencia" traducción de Moisés Silva. En: Revista de estudios de género La Ventana,"* Guadalajara, Jalisco, 2001.

THE BORDER WALL: HOW, WHY AND WHAT'S NEXT?

MELINA M. MARTÍNEZ

Borders are set up to define the places that are safe and unsafe, to distinguish us from them. A border is a dividing line, a narrow strip along a steep edge. A borderland is a vague and undetermined place created by the emotional residue of an unnatural boundary. It is a constant state of transition. (Anzaldúa , *1987/2007, 25*)

SOUTH TEXAS

In her work, the words of Gloria Anzaldúa (1987), a South Texas native, carefully describe what it means to live in a borderland. Her words acknowledge the space of constant transition embedded in daily life on the border. Her idea of "borders" is often vividly carried into discussions of conceptual borders. A greater understanding of physical borders such as the U.S. Mexico border provides insight about the nature of borders, helping her to more readily address conceptual borders.

Many of you know Gloria's work in a more formal manner. I am relatively new to the work of Anzaldúa. I am happy to have the privilege to be welcomed so graciously. I am responding from Gloria's homeland, the borderlands of South Texas.

THE BORDER WALL

In South Texas the border wall takes on various forms. In some areas there is nothing but steel pylons. In others there is a combination of cement with steel. The wall reaches eighteen feet into the air. It extends for miles at a time. Then, abrupt gaps in the fence erupt.

Initially perplexing, the gaps become an area of interest. When the fence was proposed, The Working Group on Human Rights and the Border Wall at the University of Texas at Austin conducted a study that examined the areas where gaps would appear and where they would not.

The Department of Homeland Security (DHS) released a map indicating where the proposed fence would be erected. On the map the fence was indicated by a solid line; there were, however, areas that had a dotted line. The dotted lines represents where gaps in the fence would exist. The Working Group took a map of preexisting census data and compared the two maps to see if any disparities could be identified. Some of the factors that the study compared are education and income; race, ethnicity, and language; and citizenship and origins. The study illuminated a concept known as the 'Gaps of Privilege' meaning they found there were various disparities (Wilson et al, 2008). Places marked for "gaps" had populations with higher incomes and a lower number of Hispanics.

GAPS OF PRIVILEGE IN ACTION

In the panel discussion *Seeds of Hope: The Border Wall One Year Later* at El Gran Salon, the term "gaps of privilege" described the economic disparities found in the proposed construction of the "Border Fence" present where the fence would and would not be constructed.

Eloisa Tamez, who is the first landowner (El Caloboz Ranchería, Texas-Mexico Border) to refuse to sign away her land rights to the U.S. Government, was sued by the Department of Homeland Security (DHS). In a personal interview, Dr. Tamez explained that she had been contacted by the DHS at her place of work where she refused to speak about the issue. She later denied permission to access her land for surveying. Despite her refusal, the DHS responded by surveying her land.

When she learned that the DHS would be suing her, she fought back. A federal judge ruled that the two parties must meet to resolve the issue within a given time frame. While Dr. Tamez was out of town at a conference, private contractors moved the materials onto her land. Before a restraining order could be issued, the wall was already under construction, (Tamez, Personal communication, 2010). Within two weeks it was completely built. Two miles down the road from Eloisa's home the wall stops. There is a slight pause in the structure where River Bend Resort, a popular winter Texas haven, is located. On the other side of the resort the wall resumes its course.

CONFLATING TWO THREATS

One question continues to emerge: how could it be possible for the fence to be built when local opposition seemed so great? Dr. Terence Garrett, an associate professor at the University of Texas at Brownsville and Texas Southmost College, comes to the border issue having already studied the creation of the Department of Homeland Security. In a personal interview, Dr. Garrett argues that 9/11 made the wall possible, meaning congress took issues of immigration and issues of terrorism and conflated the two threats (Personal Communication, Garrett, April 27, 2010).

In the Immigration Policy Center (IPC) [2009] report "Breaking Down the Problems: What's Wrong with Our Current Immigration System," a discussion of the United States immigration issue at hand is highlighted; for twenty years the U.S. government has been hung up on completely eliminating "unauthorized immigration through enforcement efforts at the border and in the interior of the country, but without success—and without fundamentally reforming the broken immigration system that spurs unauthorized immigration in the first place." The findings released by IPC present logical steps for directly dealing with the current problems in immigration law. The IPC's Special Report provides accurate information for policymakers, the media, and the general public to use. The report addresses how the current immigration system works, where its failures are as well as inadequate responses to the flood of immigrants. Comprehensive immigration reform is necessary. Building up "enforcement only" solutions has not worked.

There has always been a faction in government that is anti-immigration. The strategy of conflating the Real ID Act (2005) and the Secure Fence Act (2006) functions as the means through which the construction of the wall is justified: "the Secretary of Homeland Security shall have the authority to waive, and shall waive, all laws such Secretary, in such Secretary's sole discretion, determines necessary to ensure expeditious construction of the barriers and roads under this section," (Hise, 2008). The Real ID Act handed over power while the Secure Fence Act dictated control.

WHY THE BORDER WALL?

I began focusing on the U.S. Mexican Border Fence/ Border Wall primarily due to proximity. Initially, my drive to school was uneventful. I would drive by Hope Park in downtown Brownsville on my way to classes each day. I never thought much of the drive until the construction of the Border Wall began. At the time of the wall's construction I lived in a house a few miles away. Something began to stir inside of me as the land was cleared for the "fence."

I remember the first night I saw the wall. I was driving with a friend down 281, known locally as Old Military Highway. We stopped on the side of the road, walked through a farmer's field, and stood staring up at the structure. The sight was beautiful and grotesque, beautiful like a work of land art; mammoth geometric repetition planted in natural landscape. Grotesque when I think about the meaning of the structure. Grotesque when I consider how some humans use their abilities to create symbols of hate (mis-used power). The creative process became a way of knowing and understanding the subject. In a journal entry I try to articulate what I see and feel:

> *I have not completely made sense of my feelings towards the fence that was recently constructed in my hometown, which is an object I now see on a daily basis on my way to class. What becomes clear to me as I drive around the city running errands and 'taking care of business,' is that I rarely feel a sense of affection or attachment or even awareness of local landmarks. The lack of sensation quickly dissipates when my eyes catch a glimpse of the U.S. Border Fence. Immediately, a rise of emotion swells in my chest and all at once I feel. I feel disgust, hate, anguish; I also feel joy, a sense of awe, and presences of beauty. Perhaps, it is the juxtaposition of feelings I encounter within myself when I see the fence that provokes my curiosity to learn more about the structure. My own conceptual bias is one of distaste for the wall as it is locally known. A part of me is disappointed in humanity. I cannot help but think, with all of our sophistication, we could have done a better job at alleviating illegal immigration, combating terrorism and stopping drug trafficking. My visual bias towards the wall, however, is a sharp contrast to my conceptual distaste. Visually I am mesmerized, flabbergasted by the beauty of the structure. It is monumental to a single individual standing before it. Line and repetition are gracefully incorporated into the landscape. A conflict rises within me and I strive to find meaning in what I feel.*

In 2008, I organized an exhibition held at Galeria 409 called ¿Qué Piensas? What Do You Think: The U.S.-Mexican Border Wall, For or Against? Throughout the experience I felt the pulse of communal opposition. Although the exhibition was open to entries of any stance, no works in favor of the wall were submitted. From what my eyes and ears were telling me, the community stood against the construction. A year later the wall was plowing its course along the South Texas border. A community spoke; although we did not want the wall, it still came to us.

My routine drive to school became juxtaposed with a historically monumental construction led by the United States Government. National policy had come into my community, quite literally. I tried to suppress my feelings of anger (toward the hidden agenda the fence represents). Yet, each day I was confronted with the reality of being on my way to a place that nourishes my mind, a school where our slogan is "knowledge knows no boundaries," and here the federal government was building a physical and colossal "No Trespassing" sign for our neighbors. The experience forced me to recognize how arbitrary a borderline is, "Borders are set up to define the places that are safe and unsafe, to distinguish us from them," (Anzaldúa, 1987/2007, p. 25). The imaginary and real lines assign who will and will not have certain opportunities. I would have preferred to continue living in a kind of sublime ignorance, but proximity wouldn't allow it.

THE COST

The non-fiction book *Confessions of an Economic Hit Man* (2006) written by John Perkins offers insight into the possible reasoning for building the wall. The wall is not meant to stop illegal immigrants but to slow it down, (Hise, 2008). Why funnel the great cost of construction into a barrier? An Economic Hit Man is a highly paid individual whose job is to justify huge international loans that funnel money back to U.S. companies through massive engineering projects.

The estimated cost of the wall is about seven and half million dollars per mile. Under the Secure Border Initiative, an office under Customs and Border Protection, Boeing was able to secure a private contract in 2006, and it's called SBInet (Stana, 2008). They won an indefinite contract, which has no maximum value on how much they can spend. It's a three-year contract with three-year optional advance. And their task is to do *whatever it takes* to secure the northern and the southern borders (Del Bosque, 2009).

WHAT NEXT?

After writing, reading, talking, listening, interviewing, questioning, photographing, drawing and painting, I finally came to the realization that I alone could not come up with a solution. Initially, I felt extremely dissatisfied because I could not generate some sort of solution to alleviate this inhumanity. Now, I realize it's okay not to know what to do yet. Identifying a problem is the first step to finding resolution.

My job has been, and will continue to be, identifying the depth of this issue and sharing those findings with others. I work with the purpose of creating a space where dialogue about border issues has room to emerge.

I've outlined what I perceive the issue to be, including people's lived-experiences of the actual methods DHS used to complete the wall as well as how, at a policy level, the wall became possible. I have also briefly addressed a possible rationale about why the wall was built as opposed to comprehensive immigration reform. In terms of what's next I'll leave you with a quote.

Don't give in Chicanita... Your lineage is ancient... strong women reared you... and yes they've taken our lands. Not even the cemetery is ours now... But they will never take that pride... Perhaps we'll be dying of hunger as usual but we'll be members of a new species... Like old skin will fall the slave ways of obedience, acceptance, silence. (Anzaldúa, 1987/2007, p. 225)

WORKS CITED

Anzaldúa, G. *Borderlands/La Frontera*. San Francisco: Aunt Lute Books, 1987. Print.

Del Bosque, M. "Homeland Security Doesn't Know if the Border Wall Works." *Texas Observer* 2009. Print.

Garret, T. Personal Interview. 27 April 2010.

Goodman, A. "Holes in the Wall: Texas Border Wall Bypassing Wealthy Residents with Bush Admin Ties." *Proceedings of the Democracy Now: The War and Peace Report*, 2008. Web. http://www.democracynow.org/2008/2/27/holes_in_the_wall_texas_border

Hise, S. "Wild Versus Wall." *Sierra Club*, 2008. Web. http://arizona.sierraclub.org/conservation/border/borderfilm.asp

"Breaking Down the Problems: What's Wrong with our Immigration System?" *Immigration Policy Center: American Immigration Council*, Oct. 2009. Web.

Perkins, J. *Confessions of an Economic Hit Man*. New York: Plume, 2006. Print.

Stana, R. "Secure Border Initiative: Observations on Selected Aspects of SBInet Program Implementation." Vol. 08-31T. United States Government Accountability Office, Oct. 2007. Web.

Tamez, E. Personal Interview. April 2010.

Wilson, J. Gaines, et al. "An Analysis of Demographic Disparities Associated with the Proposed U.S.-Mexico Border Fence in Cameron County, Texas." The Rapport Center for Human Rights and Justice, 2008.

NATION, MIGRATION AND BORDERLANDS: HUMAN MOBILITY VS. IMMIGRATION IN ANZALDÚA

THERESA DELGADILLO

This essay broadens the scope of our consideration of Gloria Anzaldúa's thought to consider her intervention into the discourse of immigration and citizenship. Long considered critical to the development of theory and scholarship in gender, sexuality, ethnic and cultural studies—and, as I argue in my recent work, to religious studies, Anzaldúa's work has been studied from a number of perspectives. In this essay, I suggest that Anzaldúa also makes an important contribution to critical migration studies, one that merits greater attention in an era of intense immigration debate in multiple countries for the alternative visions of citizenship and belonging that she explores.

Anzaldúa's strong assertion of belonging and her claim to the space of South Texas and the U.S.-Mexico border have long been read in support of present-day efforts by Chicano/as to assert their belonging as natives of lands that are now a part of the U.S., and to emphasize strong and ongoing historical and cultural ties to Mexico. Making these strategic claims manifest in narrative, method and theory form a central part of Anzaldúa's project, though not its entirety. I argue also that Anzaldúa theorizes mobility in ways that simultaneously undercut nationalist claims and authorize Chicano/as and Latino/as in the U.S. as she offers a different model of belonging.

As she observes in "Now Let Us Shift ... The Path of Conocimiento ... Inner Work, Public Acts," the dangerous and unsettling violence that marks all facets of contemporary human life falls upon people of all nationalities. She hints here at the possibility that new forms of individual and collective affiliation may be necessary:

> At the crack of change between millennia, you and the rest of humanity are undergoing profound transformations and shifts in perception. All, including the planet and every species, are caught between cultures and bleed-throughs among different worlds—each with its own version of reality. (541)

These new interpenetrations have been wrought by a global system, she continues, that:

> condones the mind theft, spirit murder, exploitation, and genocide de los otros. We are collectively conditioned not to know that every comfort of our lives is acquired with the blood of conquered, subjugated, enslaved, or exterminated people, an exploitation that continues today. We are completely dependent on consumerism, the culture of the dollar, and the colossal powers that sustain our lifestyles (541).

Addressing an audience residing in the relative comfort of the U.S., Anzaldúa connects shifting perceptions and the juxtaposition of differing worldviews with glimpses into the material conditions that underwrite both that comfort and advance migrations at multiple levels; she sees the possibility of new collective formations in these very conditions. Her text calls readers to action, to "find a path through the dark woods/ ... claim these puentes "home"... si se puede .... Now let us shift" (576), in ways that prompt us to consider the current debates around immigration and globalization from an Anzaldúan perspective.[1]

HUMAN MIGRATION AND THE PHYSICS OF MOVEMENT

Mobility and migration appear repeatedly in Gloria Anzaldúa's work as motors of cultural and social change. Just as importantly, she cites migration as a natural human phenomenon which creates the conditions for cultural and social change, although the latter cannot occur, and certainly not in ways transformative of oppressive social orders, without consciousness, action, and intent.[2] To privilege the physical action of mobility and migration in this way is not only to recognize the physics of movement, but to embrace physics over a strictly logocentric or intellectualist perspective. Mobility matters. It changes us. It changes who we are individually and socially. A daughter of the Americas, and of societies created by the migrations of peoples, Anzaldúa, in emphasizing migration as both essentially human and generative of social change, makes an important intervention into the nationalist politics of citizenship, a contested subjectivity in her experience, for if mobility is intrinsically human and generative then social and legal determinations of belonging need to be reconciled with this understanding.

Key passages in *Borderlands,* considered in tandem with later interviews and essays, shed light on an Anzaldúan intervention into the politics of immigration. In the decade prior to the publication of *Borderlands,* the question of immigration policy again entered the public sphere as migration from Latin America increased, not least because of the violent conflicts in Central America, in which the U.S. was involved, which prompted people to flee to safer ground, but also as greater numbers of Mexicans facing economic difficulties journeyed to the U.S. Indeed, as a recent article in *Mother Jones* magazine notes, shortly after the 1980s showdown between major meatpacking companies such as IBP and Hormel and the United Food and Commercial Workers Union in which workers lost, these companies began actively recruiting Mexican migrant labor. Several media sources, and scholars, have documented the overwhelming reliance of this industry on undocumented migrants, mostly from Mexico, and both the harrowing conditions of their border-crossing and the deeply exploitative, and even brutal, working conditions under which they labor.[3] These events, coupled with the long-standing discrimination that Chicano/as have faced in the U.S. since their nineteenth-century incorporation into the U.S., the many ways that they are continually perceived as "foreigners," and which Anzaldúa addresses in her autohistoria, may have been very much in her consciousness as she composed *Borderlands*.

We do know that the strong concern for social justice that shines throughout Anzaldúa's ouvre would likely have prompted an ongoing interest in U.S. immigration policy and debates. Since then, draconian legislation passed in Arizona, Georgia and South Carolina, has upped the ante in efforts to demonize and scapegoat migrants and to prevent them from enjoying both civil and human rights.[4] In light of these recent events, returning to consider Anzaldúa's borderlands perspective, and how it addresses migration, is particularly important. If we take into account how she melds together key passages where she considers migration with remembrances and discussions of her own experiences of belonging, citizenship, mobility and displacement, we can identify alternative models of belonging, or revised notions of citizenship prompted by the borderlands experience, but perhaps useful to global migration issues.

MUST MIGRATION = DISPLACEMENT?

Why is Anzaldúa's intervention important? As sociologist of ethnicity Tomás R. Jiménez notes, "the intellectual foundations of the study of immigration and ethnic change were built without considering the Mexican-origin experience" (8). Chicano/as constitute a unique population with a unique relationship to the U.S., as he observes, recognizing that Mexican-Americans are both "a colonized group *and* an immigrant group; an old immigrant population *and* a new one; part of the established native-born population *and* the foreign-born population" due to the fairly stable and steady migrations of Mexicans into the U.S. over the past one hundred years (8, 22, 24). Jiménez's focus on the uniqueness of Chicano/a ethnic identity and assimilation offers a social scientific parallel to the content of Anzaldúa's poetry and narratives that address this same phenomenon, in her case as life story, and theory generated from that life story, rather than data. In the first chapter of *Borderlands* alone, there are *six pages* devoted to a consideration of homeland and *eight pages* on destierro and migration, suggesting their importance to both story and theory, to autohistoria. Interrelated in her text, the question of belonging, of homeland, remains intimately linked to issues of displacement and migration. Her narrative also welds together the fates of Chicano/as without land and migrants from Mexico, both displaced peoples now sharing the same space.

The oft-quoted opening description of the border that Anzaldúa offers in *Borderlands/La Frontera,* that of a scab over a wound, brings the historical, and perhaps haunting, dispossession of Chicano/as in the U.S. Southwest sharply into focus, but it also casts this loss as an ongoing rather than a past phenomenon by employing the metaphor of the scab rather than the scar. The scar marks an event in the past while the scab is the more recent wound still healing. Her visualization of the significance of the border resonates throughout her recall of this historic displacement:

> In the 1800s, Anglos migrated illegally into Texas, which was then part of Mexico, in greater and greater numbers and gradually drove the *tejanos* (native Texans of Mexican descent) from their lands, committing all manner of atrocities against them. Their illegal invasion forced Mexico to fight a war to keep its Texas territory....*Tejanos* lost their land and, overnight, became the foreigners. (28)

Given my argument, this passage may, at first, appear to undercut my suggestion that Anzaldúa's intervention into critical migration studies naturalizes migration as a route toward imagining new forms of belonging. After all, if migration is a human phenomenon then how could one characterize any migration as "illegal"? Wouldn't this be an example of movement altering the social in irrevocable ways? However, this remembering of the history of displacement operates within the framework of that displacement; it cannot, after the fact, recall as entirely natural a migration planned and executed for territorial enrichment that relied on the calculated inhumanity of forcing others out or subjugating them. That kind of migration takes place on another plane, the plane of property, legality, and citizenship through which it justifies itself as an exclusionary movement. To become a "foreigner" in one's own land is to suffer an exclusion from the new order that migration organized to bring into being. The appearance of "illegal" here is a rhetorical ploy to undercut contemporary xenophobia by reminding the xenophobes of their own status and history as migrants, but it also situates belonging and not-belonging within the frameworks of colonialism and nationalism, revealing the exclusionary mechanisms by which these function.

THE VIOLENCE OF POLICING BELONGING

In another passage, *Borderlands* details the military and juridical measures by which the nation-state authorizes some migrations but delimits others:

> Many, under the threat of Anglo terrorism, abandoned homes and ranches and went to Mexico. Some stayed and protested. But as the courts, law enforcement officials, and government officials not only ignored their pleas but penalized them for their efforts, *tejanos* had no other recourse but armed retaliation. (30)

This reference to the 1916 San Diego uprising underscores the desperation of those juridically and socially excluded from the new social order.

Raised in a Tejano/a agricultural community, Anzaldúa writes from the perspective of this displaced people, incorporating into *Borderlands* the accounts of Mexican-Americans losing their land, becoming sharecroppers, working as migrant agricultural laborers side-by-side with Mexican bracero workers. These events inform a familial and collective history, but also the economy and society of South Texas. In one interview Anzaldúa weaves together her understanding of how her immediate "family lost their land to whites because of taxes and dirty manipulation" (87) with what befell her extended family when "grandmothers, uncles, and aunts sold their mineral rights for a few dollars" (88) with the broader historical picture of "land grants from the time when Texas was Mexico" (88), recalling how her "grandmother was born in one of the first settlements in South Texas" (89).[5] In her account, the palimpsest of the landscape of South Texas reveals multiple forms of migration that shaped this space from colonial outpost to settlement at the far reaches of the nation to new colonies and nations. There is a claim here to native birthright and long-standing habitation in the many generations cited but more importantly, there is a protest against exploitation and manipulation, a protest against systems of belonging that require the dispossession of some.

This critique becomes even more pronounced in her description of the simultaneity of policing borders and policing humans—indeed, these unfold synonymously—in the actions of the Border Patrol, wherein ideologies of belonging become manifest in the present-day:

> The Border Patrol hides behind the local McDonalds on the outskirts of Brownsville, Texas or some border town. They set traps around the riverbeds beneath the bridge. Hunters in army-green uniforms stalk and track these economic refugees by the powerful night vision of electronic sensing devices planted in the ground or mounted on Border Patrol vans. (33-34)

This biopolitics of "immigration control," has become only more pointed in the wake of extreme measures implemented post 9/11 and as regimes of exploitation come to rely ever more on these measures in times of economic contraction. As *Borderlands* reminds us: "…the illegal refugees are some of the poorest and the most exploited of any people in the U.S." (34).

The vision and compassion evident in this critique of regimes of exclusion emerges, as Anzaldúa tells it in a number of texts, from her own process of wrestling with the exclusions encountered as a Chicana, a lesbian, and a woman. Her multiple negotiations suggest a route that she describes metaphorically as "crossing over" or "kicking a hole" in the old fences, language that emphasizes the significance of the U.S.-Mexico border, the exclusions it enacts and the exclusions enacted to preserve it in particular ways for certain peoples, in her formation but also in her view of new forms of belonging: "Every time she makes 'sense' of something, she has to 'cross over,' kicking a hole out of the old boundaries of the self and slipping under or over, dragging the old skin along, stumbling over it" (71). I want to suggest that the "hole" Anzaldúa sees as necessary here also represents a rupture to the exclusions of "citizenship" that prop up the literal boundary at the heart of her work. Making a hole in the border fence, in the physical manifestation of that exclusionary notion constitutes a first step in re-making ideologies of belonging. The brutality of maintaining current ideological investments becomes evident not only in *Borderlands'* discussion of the Border Patrol, but also in the predatory behavior it spawns on the other side of the border: "Smugglers, *coyotes, pasadores, enganchadores* approach these people or are sought out by them" (33).

MIGRATION AS HUMAN MOVEMENT

I have often pondered why Anzaldúa mentions the theory that North America was populated long ago by peoples migrating from one continent to another via the bridge of the Bering Strait. She adds to that story an account of the indigenous migration from north to south America embodied in Nahuatl culture, linking these two movements in a narrative of the Americas as the site of multiple, historic migrations, before concluding: "We have a tradition of migration, a tradition of long walks. Today we are witnessing *la migración de los pueblos mexicanos*, the return odyssey to the historical/mythological Aztlán. This time, the traffic is from south to north" (33). But why go that far back? What is important about that human history for a borderlands perspective? In linking these events, she marks the "native" belonging of Chicano/as to the Americas, and the southwestern U.S. in particular. Yet, it seems also to reflect an understanding of migration as a deeply natural, a human act—in our DNA so to speak. So, when she references contemporary migration from Mexico to the U.S., she isn't only claiming a historical basis for this "reverse migration," she is also underscoring the significance of human movement historically. Very critical of sexism and homophobia within Chicano/a ethnic community, as well as reigning paradigms of mestizaje and religiosity, *Borderlands* is not engaged in an ethnocentric or nationalist project. In both her work before and after *Borderlands*, Anzaldúa's trajectory is toward coalition with the like-minded and similarly-driven regardless of ethnicity or race, which would also suggest that her discussion of migration, though grounded in the U.S.-Mexico borderlands experience, is not only about defending U.S.-Mexico migration.

In *Borderlands* "illegal" border crossing—making a hole in the fence—becomes a metaphor for the change she envisions; this becomes a necessary act in the creation of a different kind of belonging, one not limited to ethnocentric national paradigms that limit belonging, be they U.S., Mexican or Chicano/a. Her language ties the move toward mestiza consciousness with dismantling the most prominent manifestation of national exclusion, the border:

> It is her reluctance to cross over, to make a hole in the fence and walk across, to cross the river, to take that flying leap into the dark, that drives her to escape, that forces her into the fecund cave of her imagination where she is cradled in the arms of *Coatlicue*, who will never let her go. If she doesn't change her ways, she will remain a stone forever. *No hay más que cambiar.* (71)

We might usefully consider any number of daily movements for survival or activist interventions into immigration policy as moments wherein just such an opening into re-defining belonging is under construction. Places such as municipally sponsored day labor halls may be a step toward the recognition of the dignity of work and workers and respect for surrounding communities, a bridge. Activist work to eliminate HIV discrimination in immigration policy or undocumented pro-DREAM students visibly advocating policy change each represent new openings in the fence of exclusion that Anzaldúa calls us to make wider.[6]

Though inherently exclusionary, citizenship becomes even more suspect in the borderlands, where migrant and Chicano are alike, both agricultural field workers and both subject to deportation without the proper documents. Her recollection of just an event emphasizes how legality is not a guarantor of rights—even more so today in the U.S. with the recent passage of so-called anti-immigrant legislation. Where migrant and Chicano/a are alike, following Anzaldúa, is that neither enjoys full acceptance or the rights that routinely accompany citizenship. This lesser status for some and the way it embodies particular expectations about the ethnicity, race and phenotype of U.S. citizens, has been methodically constructed via U.S. immigration policy over the past one hundred years at least.[7] Historian Philip Gleason notes that the U.S. maintains "a latent disposition toward an ethnically defined concept of nationality" (62).[8] The literature on this subject reveals a strong investment in Anglo-American ethnicity, identity and culture as the ideal citizen, a quality of citizenship that undergoes a change, a further abstraction into whiteness as quality for full citizenship with the defeat of Reconstruction and the grudging acceptance of other white ethnics, primarily those from Western Europe, into the fold of ideal citizenship. In the case of the latter, ideal immigrants become ideal citizens.

However, in addition to the legal distinctions between the rights and responsibilities accorded to a citizen in contrast to those accorded an undocumented migrant—or, to use Victor Romero's phrase "non-terrorist others," to underscore the differentiation necessary to more properly see persons who are undocumented, overstays, foreign born adoptees, and even permanent residents who have committed crimes as persons—in the space of little more than a decade, the U.S. has advanced policies that create a permanent wedge between citizens and non-citizens, regardless of residency status. The U.S. has significantly expanded its ability to act arbitrarily in defining belonging in recent years. For example, a child might be granted permanent residency upon migration with his or her family, however, now later criminal convictions can be retroactively applied to deny permanent residency. New immigration policy also re-defines certain misdemeanor violations as felony violations, increasing arbitrariness in policing permanent residency (Romero 161, Coutin 193-95). These measures effectively subject resident non-citizens to a state of permanent surveillance, permanent non-belonging, permanent possible deportation dependent on the whims of the nation state's immigration policy.[9]

As citizens who were and are subjected to discrimination, dispossession and state-sponsored violence, Chicano/as do not easily reaffirm the enduring belief in the U.S. as a utopian site of economic advancement that the experience of white ethnic migrants continues to underwrite.[10] In the very different trajectories of these ethnically and racially diverse populations, the contours of citizenship as exclusion emerge. Rather than buy into the narrow notion of belonging that citizenship in the U.S. embodies, which would reproduce conservative preferences such as normative heterosexuality, traditional gender norms, amnesia about social movements and the denial of labor rights, Anzaldúa opens the road to another model for belonging, one more expansive, based not on nationalism but on human rights. This seems even more important to her writing in the aftermath of 9/11 and the essentialist racial profiling and ethnic and racial discrimination it provokes, events which prompt her to recognize the pulse of the times as one dominated by "feelings of bewilderment, sorrow, and fear—the U.S. borders of 'safety' had been violated and many people could no longer see our country the same way. Rather than reflect on this arrebato (breach), some of us screamed for revenge" (*Home* 4). She does not retreat in the face of this, or shy away from calling attention to how the U.S. has never been "safe" for all, but instead asks us to re-make ourselves, to become a bridge.

Seeing migration as an enduring human phenomenon does not become an apologia for the exploitations and injustices migrants face, or for acts of conquest, in Anzaldúa. Instead, it appears to reinstate, and revise, a discourse and category of governmentality elaborated in the 1945 UN Charter and repeated thereafter in various forms in the bodies and declarations of this and other international organizations.[11] As Inderpal Grewal notes in her discussion of the adoption of this discourse in the struggle for women's freedom and equality, human rights discourse produces subjects where previously there were only objects, as well as particular kinds of relations, movements and knowledge (and in the case of women's rights, not all positive or progressive).[12] Whereas human rights discourse has been typically employed in relation to the "developing" countries, in this case the move invokes it as an instrument for achieving greater social justice for migrants everywhere.

WHAT IS BRIDGEWORK AT THE NATIONAL LEVEL?

After the protracted silencing of debate on questions of immigration and its relation to national security and on state power and executive authority to spy on, detain, imprison, deport, torture or assassinate—interrupted only by the 2006 nationwide protests against the scapegoating of immigrants and for a path to legalization—we have, once again, entered into a renewed period of public discussion and activism on these questions in the U.S. The implementation of the U.S. Secure Communities program most likely dampened the emergence of an activist response, but now as the country finds itself with a new administration, in the midst of a serious economic downturn, the end of a particular anti-terrorist effort and preparations to end wars abroad, there exists mounting pressure for federal passage of the DREAM Act and federal intervention against anti-immigrant legislation approved in several states as well as heightened calls for federal legislation providing a path to legalization.

Anzaldúa tells us that bridges are "passageways, conduits, and connectors that connote transitioning, crossing borders, and changing perspectives" (*Home* 1), and that they are necessary: "there are no safe spaces... Staying 'home' and not venturing out from our own group comes from woundedness, and stagnates our growth... Bridging is the work of opening the gate to the stranger, within and without" (*Home* 3). What then is bridgework in relation to immigration policy? What coalitions must be built? What more expansive notions of belonging, or of citizenship need we focus on developing? What are the rights of the undocumented?

Legal scholar Victor Romero, premising his view on the twin tenets of anti-essentialism and anti-subordination in Critical Race Theory, suggests an equality of treatment for all residents of the U.S.[13] Legal movement with such an aim, rather than the continued propping up of exclusions, would seem to fit with Anzaldúa's vision of belonging. In this view, anti-essentialism rejects notions that similarity can be attributed on the basis of phenotype, that individuals can all be treated the same based on their presumed participation in a group/category/race, such as citizen, immigrant or undocumented. The anti-subordination principle focuses on whether legal change diminishes or augments oppressions (Romero 5). He asks: "So here is the dilemma: to what extent should the Constitution protect noncitizens—immigrants, undocumented persons, tourists, foreign students—in the United States?" (Romero 1). And his answer is as follows: "In my view, the best reading of the Constitution is one that provides as much parity as possible between citizen and noncitizen, regardless of formal immigration status" (Romero 5). Only this kind of parity can contribute to dismantling the divisiveness of the new social order that Anzaldúa so cogently describes:

> We are experiencing a personal, global identity crisis in a disintegrating
> social order that possesses little heart and functions to oppress people by
> organizing them in hierarchies of commerce and power—a collusion of
> government, transnational industry, business, and the military all linked
> by a pragmatic technology and science voracious for money and control.

This system and its hierarchies impact people's lives in concrete and devastating ways and justify a sliding scale of human worth used to keep humankind divided. (*Home* 541)

Past exclusionary policies, such as the Chinese Exclusion Laws of the 1880s, were driven, as Romero observes, by limited choice between two options: assimilation or exclusion (163-4). As we know, language, culture, race and ethnicity were considered in policy determinations of who could assimilate, who could eventually become a citizen. Now we live in an era where the notion of dual citizenship is no longer an exotic idea, but a concrete reality for growing numbers of people. Is it possible to hope for a form of national belonging that is not culturally, linguistically, racially, ethnically limited? Is it possible to recognize that, indeed, such sub-groups exist in all nations? In immigration jurisprudence two models of action exist—separation and convergence, yet, according to Romero, both might be models for arbitrary inaction. In the separation model, power over immigration is separate from power over an immigrant's personal rights, while in the convergence model, government has the power over both, and, therefore, may restrict immigrants' right to vote. In the former, immigration policy might regulate the conditions and requirements of entry and stay, but personal rights are not dependent on immigration status. The danger of reading this as lack of responsibility to protect immigrants' personal rights runs high without a shift toward a stronger and more comprehensive legal standing for all residents or a more effective and comprehensive route toward legal citizenship. What new steps might we take to break down the divisive and brutal barriers separating undocumented from citizen today? In *Borderlands*, Anzaldúa speaks not from the position of citizen, but from the in-between and outside, to imagine new ways of belonging. In *Borderlands/La Frontera* she calls us to effect those new ways of belonging by stepping outside of frameworks we already know, and she reminds us: "Nothing happens in the 'real' world unless it first happens in the images in our heads" (109).

NOTES

1 "Now Let Us Shift…The Path of Conocimiento…Inner Work, Public Acts." *This Bridge We Call Home*. New York: Routledge, 2002. 540-578.

2   These latter three she envisions as elements that might manifest in any aspect of being, whether it be intellectual, physical, emotional or psychic, but they remain fairly equal in her perspective, no one elevated above the other, which is telling. In this perspective, physical movement informs a way of being as much as an intellectual worldview.

3   See "The Spam Factory's Dirty Secret," by Ted Genoways. *Mother Jones.* Mon. June 27, 2011.; "270 Illegal immigrants Sent to Prison in Federal Push," by Julia Preston. *New York Times.* May 24, 2008.; and Paul Apostilidis's *Breaks in the Chain: What Immigrant Workers Can Teach America about Democracy.*

4   SB1070 became law in Arizona in 2010 and according to Randal C. Archibold, writing in *The New York Times,* "proponents and critics alike said was the broadest and strictest immigration measure in generations, would make the failure to carry immigration documents a crime and give the police broad power to detain anyone suspected of being in the country illegally. Opponents have called it an open invitation for harassment and discrimination against Hispanics regardless of their citizenship status." See "Arizona Enacts Stringent Law on Immigration." *New York Times*, U.S. Politics Section, April 23, 2010.

Georgia House Bill 87 took effect on July 1, 2011, with some provisions of the bill blocked by ruling of the federal district court. Georgia's bill allows authorities to check the immigration status of anyone without a valid ID, and penalizes individuals and businesses that transport, rent to, or employ undocumented immigrants. See "Georgia Immigration Law Taken to Court" by Stephen Ceasar. *Los Angeles Times.* June 2, 2011.

South Carolina's Illegal Immigration and Reform Act takes force on January 1, 2012, and requires employers to enroll in and use the U.S. Department of Homeland Security's E-Verify system to establish employee eligibility to work. See South Carolina Department of Labor, Licensing and Regulation website, accessed on 8/13/11 at http://www.llr.state.sc.us/immigration/ South Carolina's law, according to John Eby, would allow "local law enforcement officers the authority to detain a person while determining whether the person is in the country legally, but only after the person has been stopped on suspicion of another crime. It states that an investigation into the person's immigration status could only begin if the person failed to present a valid I.D." The bill also establishes a statewide Illegal Immigration Enforcement Unit and imposes new fees on wire transfers of money out of the U.S. of at least $5.00 or 1 percent on amounts over $500.00, but exempts businesses from this fee. See "SC Immigration Bill Passes Senate" by John Eby, March 10, 201, on WYFF News 4 Web Site, accessed on 8/13/11 at http://www.wyff4.com/news/27155560/detail.html#ixzz1Ux2Wwule

5   "Within the Crossroads: Lesbian/Feminist/Spiritual Development. An Interview with Christine Weiland (1983)." In *Interviews/Entrevistas/Gloria E. Anzaldúa.* Ed. AnaLouise Keating. 71-127.

6 The DREAM Act (Development, Relief, and Education for Alien Minors Act) was first brought to Congress in 2001 and most recently re-introduced into the U.S. Congress on May 11, 2011. The DREAM Act would allow many immigrant youth who have been raised in the U.S. since childhood to apply for temporary legal status and to eventually obtain permanent legal status and eligibility for citizenship if the students complete either two years of college or military service. The Dream Act would also "eliminate a federal provision that penalizes states that provide in-state tuition without regard to immigration status." Source: Website of National Immigration Law Center, accessed on 8/13/11 at www.nilc.org/immlawpolicy/dream/dream-bills-summary-2011-05.pdf and www.nilc.org/immlawpolicy/dream/DREAM-changes-summary-2010-12-03.pdf

7 As Victor Romero notes, 1924 Immigration legislation limited "non-white" immigrants from southern and eastern Europe, upholding an Anglocentric view of citizenship (4). For further on exclusions enacted via immigration policy, see *Alienated: Immigrant Rights, the Constitution, and Equality in America*. See also Desmond King's *Making Americans: Immigration, Race, and the Origins of the Diverse Democracy*; David G. Gutiérrez's *Walls and Mirrors: Mexican Americans, Mexican Immigrants, and the Politics of Ethnicity*; Susan Bibler Coutin's *Nations of Emigrants: Shifting Boundaries of Citizenship in El Salvador and the United States*; Ali Behdad's *A Forgetful Nation: On Immigration and Cultural Identity in the United States*.

8 Philip Gleason, "American Identity and Americanization," in *Concepts of Ethnicity*, ed. William Petersen, Michael Novak, and Philip Gleason.

9 See also Bill Ong Hing's *Deporting Our Souls: Values, Morality, and Immigration Policy*.

10 See Bonnie Honig on how the myth of immigration undergirding U.S. exceptionalism validates the nation in a capitalist way by promoting the belief in the universal possibility of economic advancement, in a communitarian way by re-creating family and community units, in a traditional way by bringing patriarchal models of family back to the nation, and in a liberal democratic way by choosing citizenship and validating the nation (74-5). In *Democracy and The Foreigner*.

11 This form of governmentality, and the kind of minimal commitments to act in concert with other nations that could, at times, provide an arena for social justice movements otherwise severely constrained from any voice at international level, has been severely challenged, and diminished, by U.S. government policies of the 21st century.

12 See Chapter Three, "'Women's Rights as Human Rights': The Transnational Production of Global Feminist Subjects" in Inderpal Grewal's *Transnational America*.

13 See Romero's *Alienated: Immigrant Rights, the Constitution, and Equality in America*.

WORKS CITED

Anzaldúa, Gloria. *Borderlands/La Frontera*. [1987] San Francisco: Aunt Lute, 1999.

——. ed. *This Bridge We Call Home*. New York: Routledge, 2002. Print.

——. *Interviews/Entrevistas/ Gloria E. Anzaldúa*. Ed. AnaLouise Keating. New York: Routledge, 2000. Print.

Apostilidis, Paul. *Breaks in the Chain: What Immigrant Workers Can Teach America about Democracy*. Minneapolis: U of Minnesota P, 2010. Print.

Behdad, Ali. *A Forgetful Nation: On Immigration and Cultural Identity in the United States*. Durham, N.C.: Duke UP, 2005. Print.

Coutin, Susan Bibler. *Nations of Emigrants: Shifting Boundaries of Citizenship in El Salvador and the United States*. Ithaca: Cornell UP, 2007. Print.

Grewal, Inderpal. *Transnational America: Feminisms, Diasporas, Neoliberalisms*. Durham, N.C.: Duke UP, 2005. Print.

Gutiérrez, David G. *Walls and Mirrors: Mexican Americans, Mexican Immigrants, and the Politics of Ethnicity*. Berkeley: U of California P, 1995. Print.

Hing, Bill Ong. *Deporting Our Souls: Values, Morality, and Immigration Policy*. Cambridge: Cambridge UP, 2006. Print.

Honig, Bonnie. *Democracy and The Foreigner*. Princeton, N.J.: Princeton UP, 2001. Print.

King, Desmond. *Making Americans: Immigration, Race, and the Origins of the Diverse Democracy*. Cambridge: Harvard UP, 2000. Print.

Petersen, William, Michael Novak and Philip Gleason, ed. *Concepts of Ethnicity*. Cambridge, MA: Harvard UP, 1982. Print.

Romero, Victor. *Alienated: Immigrant Rights, the Constitution, and Equality in America*. New York: NYU Press, 2004. Print.

EMIGRANTES AMBIENTALES I: AFTER FALLOUT

KAMALA PLATT

Fallout comes in the color of warblers here.
The birds blew in following April chill-storms.
Swallows piling high to stay warm—
some suffocate, as others die
for lack of food—no insects moving
as temperatures glide down.
We will live from crisis to crisis now…
In January, temperatures bottom out, turn
comforter-covered community garden plots
to compost fodder, spoiling new year feasts.
Hypothermic sea turtles, progeny
of a hundred million years
are warehoused, bathed in plastic kiddy pools
by early responders hoping to reverse genocide.
We will live from crisis to crisis now…
Drought follows deluge follows drought
The hundred-year drought, an annual deal, now.
Time speeds as we age, scientists say—
Is Earth revolving faster? Can she get away this time?
Eco-empires issue mandates

to catch what the sun has to say,

and at the same time pull poison out upon

the most sacred of pueblos

in order to make corp-profit by lighting the planet

all the while knowing only nuclear time does not speed up

nuclear does not waste away, age or reduce to half price.

We live from crisis to crisis now...

What of the next generation? What of the seventh?

EMIGRANTES AMBIENTALES II: VALLES Y SALUD

KAMALA PLATT

From el valle maravilloso, mágico,
delta of the grand river
to Valles San Joaquín and Silicon,
where computer sales sail, kindles soar above fruit
that freezes or never forms for lack of pollinating bees
or lies unpicked—where have all the workers gone?
No matter, nothing is edible anyhow, grapes gone "Sun Mad"
as poisons morph proteins in tiny bodies
from Mission to Bhopal; from campos en Viet Nam
to calles en Chicago y ciudades from coast to coast.
No juice here, orange, a calavera color, now
its agents reap disease on holy grounds stirring ancient déjà vu
as the continent, herself, recalls the European plagues.
environmental migrants, illegalized on the corpus
of our madre; felonized in the embrace of our padres
país sin tierra, nations without planet
turtle with no island.
We live from crisis to crisis now…

EMIGRANTES AMBIENTALES III: PADDLING TOGETHER

KAMALA PLATT

I knew paddling a line down the Río Grande El Río Bravo
would not be easy though the river carries the canoe and
droplets on wood-grain dry cloudy on the paddle in my lap:
I wince as strangers' border banter pierces my mestiza tongue.
Sun and breeze beckon our spirits.
Kingfishers mascot the boats downstream.
Kiskadees and kingbirds call from high branches
against chachalaca chisme, the gossip issuing from the
mesquite and huisache beyond thickening river cane.
"Two years ago there was no hyacinth,"
my partner remarks as we steer away from thick tangles
of the succulent green mass, metastasized—
feeding on the health of its watery host…
We live from crisis to crisis now…
Around a bend in time, steel and concrete
pop up like running bamboo sprouts.
They are leftovers of a far away war,
warmed over, soldered with the heat of fear—
a border wall to still someone else's demons.
Ours bounce over and back like in an ancient ball game.
We all create crisis, live crises now, unabated
because they stimulate economies and win elections.
Earth and her people, our collateral,
our damaged goods, our sacrificial flesh.
I reach out of the canoe to place a memorial wreathe

on the waters where those who reached el otro lado
entered heaven, while their comrades paced onward
not yet knowing the Estados Unidos might be hell,
knowing only they needed work to pay bills, feed families.
None of us knowing, all earth is in crises together.
None of us knowing, seven generations are in crises together.

PRACTICING CONOCIMIENTO

SWEET DARK PLACES: LETTERS TO GLORIA ANZALDÚA ON DISABILITY, CREATIVITY, AND THE COATLICUE STATE

AURORA LEVINS MORALES, QWO-LI DRISKILL, AND LEAH LAKSHMI PIEPZNA-SAMARASINHA

I. LETTER FROM AURORA LEVINS MORALES

Dear Gloria,

Well, here it is el Día de las Muertas again and I've come to sit with you awhile. The living are busy trying to excavate your soul, writing all kinds of papers about the meaning of your life, spinning analyses from your words, arguing about the true significance of when you said this or that, digging up quotes to prove that you do or don't posthumously support hundreds of positions on thousands of issues. It's the usual mix of thoughtful insight and the absolute nonsense people invent when they're forced to churn out theory in order to keep their jobs in the middle of a depression. Some of them, I'm sorry to say, have even canonized you! I know. It's a hell of a thing to do to a flawed human being just because she had some great ideas and a strong writing hand and told her own truths. People are desperate for guides, so they remake us into oracles, and miss half the lessons our lives could offer them.

The questions on this particular table are about why you refused to identify as a disabled woman, and what illness and pain have to do with what you called the Coatlicue state, that well-mapped region of chaotic breakdown leading to revelation.

That question about how people identify, which battles we take on and how and when and with whom, gets so loaded with judgment, with accusations of having let down the team, with diagnoses of self-betrayal by those who made different choices. We choose which ground to fight on for such a mix of reasons: what feels urgent, what feels hopeful, whether we have a good band of fighters to stand with, how much of ourselves we can bring to each struggle. I spent years reading the lives of early 20th century Jewish feminists, trying to decipher what led them to fight on the terrains of gender, class and Jewishness in varying combinations. So much depends on solidarity.

In the late seventies and early eighties there was no place for me to stand as a bisexual woman. The fluidity of "queer" did not yet exist, and the lines of sexual identity were rigidly drawn. The oppression was bitterly painful, between the toxicity of heterosexism on one side and the often brutal rejection by lesbians on the other, cutting me out of the places I most longed to be. But there was not yet a critical mass of people I could fight beside to claim my place.

Most of the rooms I entered in those years were impossible to bring my whole self to, for many different reasons. But some of those silencings, those barriers, were being thought about and struggled over by many, many people, and we took it on together. So I fought about racism and then about anti-Semitism, and the battles were difficult and complex (as a Jew of color, they still are), but there was often critical mass. I had enough people who shared enough ground that I could fight for myself and others, win some battles, and not be demolished.

For you to shout out to the world, "Hey, not only am I a dark-skinned working class Tejana lesbian, but I'm disabled, too!" to draw attention to yet another way you were oppressed, and for this to do you good, you would have needed a strong, vocal, politically sophisticated, disability justice movement led by queer working class women and transpeople of color who understood your life, and it wasn't there yet. You would have needed people who saw that all the ways our bodies are made wrong, held responsible for our own mistreatment, blamed for showing the impact of oppression, all the ways our nature is called defective, are connected, rooted in the same terrible notions about what is of value. Who would have understood to the core your reasons for brewing all those herbal teas, knowing it's dangerous to enter the doors of the medical-industrial complex, and that there are things we need in there.

If you were here now, maybe what we've been constructing these last few years would be enough, would look to you like a place to rest, to be known. Oye, comadre, sometimes history leaves us stranded, waiting for a train that's still being built, five or ten years up the tracks. Have some pan dulce. Can't touch it myself, what with the diabetes and the gluten allergy, but the dead can eat whatever they want.

What I'm really interested in is that state you named after your ancestral goddess, the Coatlicue state, in which a shattering lets in light. Of course being Boricua not Mexica I call it the Guabancex and Oyá state, after the storm goddesses, the deities of creative destruction, of my Taíno and West African ancestors. The landscape of my homeland is regularly uprooted by hurricanes, those wild, whirling, spirals of wind and water spreading out vast arms out to pluck trees and houses and lives from solid land, drive bits of metal right through tree trunks and take giant bites out of cement.

In the structure of a hurricane, the strongest, deadliest winds are closest to the core, but the core itself is clear, calm, full of light. Illness has been one long hurricane season for me, chunks of cement and metal roofing flying through the air, big trees made into heaps of splinters and shredded roots. What takes me to the core, to the place of new insight is listening with all my being to the voice of my own flesh, which is often an unbearable task. What lets me bear it is political, is a deep ecological sense of the web in which my flesh is caught, where the profound isolation of chronic illness forces me to extend my awareness beyond individual suffering, beyond the chronic pain of my muscles and joints, the endless exhaustion, the mind-bending build up of toxins where nausea and nightmare meet, dragging me from my bed at 3 A.M. to lift cups of bitter tinctures to my lips with cramping hands, and leach the poison from my own liver.

In the steepest pitch, the darkest hour, in the ring of deadly wind, the only salvation is to expand, to embrace every revelation of my struggling cells, to resist the impulse to flee, and hold in my awareness both things: the planetary web of life force of which I am part, and the cruel machinery that assaults us: how greed strips and poisons landscapes and immune systems with equal disregard, how contempt for women, and the vastly profitable medical-industrial complex conspire to write off as hysterical hundreds of thousands of us bearing witness through decades in bed, while we're told all we need is a change of attitude.

To think, for example, not just about the side effects of anti-seizure drugs, or the need for stable sleep, but also society's hatred of unruly bodies, the frequent killing of epileptics by cops, and those 20th-century eugenicists who built "colonies" to protect society from our bad seed, yes, the same people who sterilized 37 % of all Puerto Rican women of child-bearing age, the same people who traveled to Nazi Germany to lecture about building a master race.

When my body feels as if it's tearing itself apart, when I'm in the nightmare condition, shaking and nauseated, my vision full of flashing lights, my legs too weak to stand, the only path out is deeper. Did you hear that Mami has cancer in the marrows of her bones? For her the key to peace is acceptance and a mind fixed on the present, but for me the material roots of my illness and hers are essential, medicinal, and rage clarifies things for me. I need to map it, and not just for myself. Our bodies, the bodies of two Caribbean women who were born and grew up in the 20th century, amidst war and industry and political repression, hold political truths about the world we live in, about damage and resistance, about truth telling and healing, and so did yours, with its infant bleeding and rocketing glucose.

There are days when I pretend I have no body, not to enter the windstorm of physical, spiritual, emotional and political pain that waits there. Sometimes clarity is intolerable. If I write about our bodies I will be writing about the "chemical revolution" that began by retooling leftover weapons into peacetime product, and has saturated our environment with 100,000 new molecules, which, in a reckless euphoria of avarice, we were all blithely assured would bring better living to all. If I write about our bodies I am writing about the land and what has been done to it. I am writing about unbreathable cities and abandoned coffee farms and tainted water, about starvation and death by thirst deliberately built into business plans. I am writing about the agricultural choices forced on people whose economic lives are ruled from afar, of shade trees clear cut for slightly higher production, leaving a wake of cancer and erosion, of massive advertising campaigns to persuade Puerto Rican women that canned vegetables and Tang are more "civilized" than fresh calabaza and orange juice, about what crossing the border does to the Mexicana pancreas.

And going in, going deeper, allowing the pain, there is the moment when I come clear: this isn't just a tale of damage. It's also a chart of where we need to go. The transformation of the planet into a sustaining and sustainable eco-social system moves along pathways we can't entirely see, but with their hungers and injuries and amazing capacity for renewal, our bodies have both a great store of critical information, and something like night vision. These three bodies I am writing about, my mother's, my own and yours, are not "statistically significant" but we have other significance. We are not representative, but we are extremely relevant.

The mountain moving day is coming. DDT on my father's work clothing entered the fatty tissue of my toddler body and is still there. Parathion sprayed in our home against disease-carrying mosquitoes ignites the nerve pathways in my brain. Sexual violence has impaired my digestion and increased the excitability of my neurons. *I say so yet others doubt it.* Formaldehyde leaking from new carpets and particleboard in the place we moved to when I was pregnant has left tracks of hysteria throughout my immune system. *Only a while the mountain sleeps. In the past all mountains moved in fire.* All over the world women sick in bed are thinking about these things. Those of us with electricity and computers and literacy write to each other. Susan in Santa Fe and Maria in Cayey and Beverly on Vashon Island and Julie in Arizona and Lisa in Washington, DC and Naomi in New York City. All over the world people whose bodies tremble and mutate, whose lungs labor, who sweat and cramp and can't remember what they were saying, are making connections. *Yet you may not believe it.*

Gloria, if you were here now, among us, with your endlessly bleeding womb and glucose making tidal waves in your blood, you would not be silent about this because you would not be alone. I think if we called on you to bring the story of your body to this circle, you would come.

There is no neutral body from which our bodies deviate. Society has written deep into each strand of tissue of every living person on earth. What it writes into the heart muscles of five star generals is distinct from what it writes in the pancreatic tissue and intestinal tracts of Black single mothers in Detroit, of Mexicana migrants in Fresno, but no body stands outside the consequences of injustice and inequality. *O man, this alone believe.*

These words are the lyrics to a creative collaboration across time between late 19th and early 20th century Japanese feminist poet Yasano Akiko and Naomi Weisstein, born in 1939, feminist psychologist, neuroscientist and founder of the Chicago Women's Liberation Rock Band, and it was the soundtrack to my awakening as a young feminist in Chicago in the late 1960s and early 1970s. I saw it silkscreened onto posters by members of the Chicago Women's Graphics Collective with whom I lived after I dropped out of high school in 1970. *All sleeping women now awake and move.*

All women whose muscles ache with permanent inflammation, all women who find lumps, all women whose babies miscarry one after another, whose life expectancy is stunted by malnutrition, who, because of industrial farming and "free trade" no longer own plots of land to grow food, who work in dangerous factories or sell sex in urban slums. My body and your bodies make a map we can follow.

We are connected to every jobless reservation and scarred, stripped tract of rainforest, every factory takeover and vacant lot community garden, every malaria death and clean water project, every paramilitary gang and people's constituent assembly. Our bodies are in the mix of everything we call political.

What our bodies, my mother's and yours and mine, require in order to thrive, is what the world requires. If there is a map to get there, it can be found in the atlas of our skin and bone and blood, in the tracks of neurotransmitters and antibodies. We need nourishment, equilibrium, water, connection, justice. When I write about cancer and exhaustion and irritable bowels in the context of the treeless slopes of my homeland, of market driven famine, of xenoestrogens and the possible extinction of bees, I am tracing that map with my fingertips, walking into the heart of the storm that shakes my body and occupies the world. As the rising temperature of the planet births bigger and more violent hurricanes from the tepid seas, I am watching the needle of my anger swing across its arc, locating meridians, looking for the magnetic pulse points of change. When I can hold the truth of my flesh as one protesting voice in a multitude, a witness and opponent to what greed has wrought, awareness becomes bearable, and I rejoice in the clarity that illness has given me. As my aching body and the storm-wracked body of the world tumble and spin around me, I enter the clear eye at the heart of all this wild uprooting, the place our sick bodies have brought us to, where light breaks through, and we can see the pattern in the broken forests and swollen waters and aching flesh—the still and shattered place where transformation begins.

II: LETTER FROM QWO-LI DRISKILL

Dear Gloria,

I am writing this on el día de l@s muert@s. A deep chill has come to central Texas, not only because of the shift to autumn but also because of a rise in reactionary conservatism that is reflected in state elections. I am wondering what you would say about all of this. I'm wondering what kind of offering we can make to all of our ancestors to, in your words, "let us shift" to a place of "conocimiento" to change this world.

I am writing this despite the aches in my shoulder blades, a growing headache, hips that feel they could pop from their sockets at any moment, and a deep exhaustion. Sickness moved into my body seven years ago. And since the morning I woke up sick and never recovered, I've been thinking about what the body tells us, how our bodies are ignored, how the bodies of those of us marked with chronic illness, physical difference, and extraordinary minds deeply disturb people. We unsettle the landscape, the cityscape. We remind people that bodies are fragile, that they transform. We remind people that bodies are temporary.

I first encountered your work, Gloria, as an undergraduate student in a violently conservative town in Colorado. Those of us who were brave enough to present our queer selves to the world did it with huge risks to our lives. I knew of only a few other Indians there. So, *Borderlands/La Frontera* was a lifeline to me. I read it over and over again. Even though our experiences were vastly different, I recognized my own mixedblood queer Cherokee self in your work, and it was transformative.

And so I return to your work to think about transformation. This time, as someone with disabilities. I didn't read your work as disability theory when I first encountered it. I didn't even know that disability theory and disability studies existed, even though they did. I thought very little about disability as a place of radical community and transformation. And I didn't think that I was disabled at the time, even though the trauma I survived before that point and was surviving was, in fact, disabling. But I'm returning to your work again to read it as a radical disability text. As someone whose disabilities mean that I spend a lot of time in bed and in pain, I'm drawn to your idea of the *Coatlicue state* to think about work of stillness, of listening, of pushing through flare-ups and mental fogs. To think about pain and illness a space of radical transformation and decolonial potential.

Ableism is colonial. It is employed to maintain an ideal body of a white supremacist imagination. This ideal body is heterosexual, male, white, Christian, non-disabled, and well-muscled. It is an ideal with a long and troubling history inseparable from racism, genocide, misogyny, and eugenics. I'm not sure that we can talk about race, gender, class, and sexuality without talking about disability. Disabled people and our struggles become erased by the ableist tropes that insist on looking at us with pity or fear or disdain. It is difficult to call for a radical disability justice analysis when we are only beginning to have people acknowledge "disability" along with other locations of oppression, when we have to push against ableist discourses that refuse to even list disability along with other oppressions. When we still can't get to the conference or the direct action or the performance, and when we're there we can't stay because of the toxic products people wear, or can't get inside in the first place, or find that our concerns are simply not present. Or perhaps we don't even try to go because we know that the most basic access will not occur. There will be no ASL interpreters. There will be no transcription of materials. There will be no personal assistants. Our bodies are not even present within the imaginations of a supposedly radical future.

If we are to take your words and the words of other scholar-artists-activists like you, Gloria—if we are to commit to radical transformations of our collective consciousness, if we locate our bodymindspirits as central to transformation—then we must push towards a critical consciousness about ableism.

Ableism—the systemic marginalization and oppression of people with physical and psychological differences that are constructed as "abnormal"—cannot be extricated from other systems of oppression. I don't think we are doing a very good job talking about race, gender, sexuality, or class if we're leaving out discussions of ableism. The construction of race in this country—and elsewhere—is irrevocably tied to the constructions of disability. Race, as a concept, is in fact the construction of a "normal" body with "normal" features, skin color, hair color, eye color, etc. Racism is rooted, in part, on the idea that those who are constructed as "non-white," including Ashkenazi Jewish people, have mental, spiritual, and physical pathologies that are made manifest through physical characteristics.

Roxanne Dunbar-Ortiz traces the discourse of blood and race, for instance, to the Spanish doctrine of *limpieza de sangre*, "purity of blood," that was used to assert racial differences between Christians, Jews, and Muslims during the "reconquest" and Inquisition. Dunbar-Ortiz writes, "What we witness in late fifteenth-and early sixteenth-century Spain is the first instance of class leveling based on imagined biological racial differences, indeed the origin of white supremacy, the necessary ideology of colonial projects in America and Africa." (Dunbar-Ortiz, "The Grid of History"). These ideologies were employed in genocidal settler-colonial projects in Iberia, Ireland, Africa, and the Americas.

Discourses of blood and race are also rooted within the construction of Western medical knowledge. In his book *Seeing the Insane,* Sander L. Gilman traces histories and images of "madness" in Western European discourses. The ancient Greek concept of "the humors," he explains, gave rise to the idea that mental and emotional states could be detected through physical symptoms. An imbalance of "black bile" was seen as the cause of what was constructed as emotional and psychological disorders. The outward symptoms of an imbalance of "black bile" were dark skin, hair, and eyes. In the history of U.S. slavery, the medicalization and pathologicalization of African bodies was used as a justification for slavery. Vanessa Jackson points out: "Benjamin Rush, MD (1746–1813), signer of the Declaration of Independence, Dean of the Medical School at the University of Pennsylvania and the 'Father of American Psychiatry,' described Negroes as suffering from an affliction called Negritude, which was thought to be a mild form of leprosy. The only cure for the disorder was to become white" (4). She continues to describe Dr. Samuel Cartwright's 1851 creation of two mental disorders unique to slaves: *drapetomania* and *Dysaethesia Aethiopica.* Drapetomania, Dr. Cartwright explains, "…induces the Negro to run away from service, is such a disease of the mind as in any other species of alienation, and much more curable, as a general rule" (qtd. in Jackson 4-5). The treatment for this disorder was whipping. *Dysaethesia Aethiopica,* Cartwright defined, was a "hebetude of the mind and obtuse sensibility of the body—a disease peculiar to Negroes called by overseers—Rascality" (5) and had the physical symptom of lesions. Whipping was also recommended as a treatment.

Within the construction of dominant Western medical knowledge, race and gender are, in fact, not separate. Race is a pseudo-scientific construction of bodies that is inseparable from medical discourse. And much of the medical knowledge that is used today is, in fact, deeply rooted in the abuse and torture of people of color. While the Tuskegee experiments often come to mind, and many people of color are well aware of histories of genocidal medicine in their communities, other practices are rarely talked about. The recent *Anarcha Project* reminds us through performance and archival work of the stories of three enslaved Black women—Anarcha, Lucy, and Betsey—who were experimented on by James Marion Sims, considered the father of American gynecology. Feminists of color, working-class feminists, and disabled feminists remind us that Margret Sanger—the founder of Planned Parenthood—was an active and vocal eugenicist who was not concerned with reproductive rights, but with controlling the population of poor people, immigrants, and people of color as a part of a plan for social engineering. Andrea Smith's scholarship and activism has pointed out that controlling the birth rate of Indigenous women and other marginalized women through forced sterilization is part of ongoing genocide. Natalia Molina's work traces how Mexican immigrant bodies were medicalized and constructed as a health threat to the United States in the early twentieth century. And scholars of the history of the Freak Show in the United States have shown how the racialized discourses around physical differences were put on display in a process of what David Hevey calls *enfreakment* (53), a process that the medical model of disability gradually took over, turning those constructed as "abnormal" into oddities through what Foucault calls the "medical gaze."

Radical disability rights activists such as Stacey Milbern and Leah Lakshmi Piepzna-Samarashinha have already started articulating what is being called a "disability justice" movement that distinguishes itself from white-dominated disability activism by articulating the relationship between disability, race, gender, sexuality, and class and calling for a shift in consciousness around disability (Kouddous). Your work, Gloria, can help inform this movement through your articulation of the body as a site of resistance and transformation, by your rejection of the ideas of "normality" in favor of a queer, "abnormal" politic that articulates the potential of nepantla to shift the consciousness of the world. Of the borderlands, you write, "*Los atravesados* live here: the squint-eyed, the perverse, the queer, the troublesome, the mongrel, the mulato, the half-breed, the half dead; in short, those who cross over, pass over, or go through the confines of the 'normal'" (25). Passing over the confines of the "normal" defines disability. It is within and against this context that I return to your work in order to think about how you articulate resistance to these ongoing histories and argue for disability as a location of radical transformation and decolonization. Robert McGruer employs your work to articulate what he calls *crip theory*, a radical disability critique. He writes, "crip experiences and epistemologies should be central to our efforts to counter neoliberalism and access alternative ways of being" (42). Your work articulates a crip epistemology through articulating states of stillness, silence, and struggle as necessary for artistic and activist work to take place that you call *Coatlicue* states: "We need *Coatlicue* to slow us up so that the psyche can assimilate the previous experiences and process the changes. If we don't take the time, she'll lay us down with illness, forcing us to 'rest'" (*Borderlands* 68).

A capitalist and ableist culture only values bodies through what they can *do,* what work they can contribute to the wealth of the powerful. But in order to create change through art, writing, scholarship, activism, and radical consciousness, you argue that we cannot rely on paradigms of capitalist production: "By keeping the conscious mind occupied or immobile, the germination work takes place in deep, dark earth of the unconscious" (69). What is considered as "inactive" by dominant culture is actually "active." And yet, those of us with chronic illnesses and disabilities often internalize the concepts of a production-oriented culture that only values us for our labor. Gloria, your words resonate for those of us who try to live up to ableist expectations: "Now she beats herself over the head for her 'inactivity,' a stage as necessary as breathing" (*Borderlands* 71).

Your disruption of the idea of normativity has been taken up widely in discussions of race, but not enough has been articulated about the relationship between your critique of normality and what it can offer to shifting consciousness about disability. Disability is articulated quite explicitly when you write, "But there is a magic aspect in abnormality and so-called deformity. Maimed, mad, and sexually different people were believed to possess supernatural powers by primal cultures' magico-religious thinking" (41). While the second part of this last sentence gives me pause because I—like many Native people—worry that you sometimes romanticize indigeneity, what strikes me here is your privileging of the radical potential of disability and queerness in transformation.

In your essay, "now, let us shift…the path of conocimiento…inner work, public acts" the *Coatlicue* state is more explicitly tied to disability. You describe being thrown into a deep state of depression after being diagnosed with diabetes. You articulate your own journey out of this depression as part of a transformative resistance. This discussion is important in light of your correspondence with AnaLouise Keating's students about disability studies and disability identity. "I don't identify as disabled or as a diabetic," you write, " …disabled would reduce me to an even more partial identity than Chicana, feminist, queer, & other genetic/cultural slices-of-the-pie terms do. … Diabetic would make a victim. But neither do I deny nor reject that I am disabled in some manner and suffer from diabetes & its complications. … I feel an in-my-face, up-front-and-personal relationship with diabetes & its disabling complications." You continue, "When marginalized groups fall back on defending identity as a strategy of resistance, when we cling to our identity as 'disabled,' 'immigrant,' or whatever and use identity as a basis for political mobilization, we inadvertently enforce our subordination" (Keating 302). Even though you speak about your disabilities, at first glance, your stance here unnerves me. Yet, perhaps I want too much from you. You were a brilliant writer, artist, scholar, and activist—to be sure—but no santa anymore than any of us are. As influential as your work is, it is not perfect. Nor should we expect it to be. Taking your work seriously means grappling and arguing with it. I doubt you would disagree.

I wish I could sit and talk with you in person to ask you questions about this. I think what you are arguing for is a shift away from identity labels in order to think beyond oppression and towards what you call "holistic alliances." I think that these alliances can be thought of in relation to Andrea Smith's call for "unlikely alliances," that do not completely reject identity politics, but instead, argue for identity politics as part of tactical alliances that can bring about social change.

The *Coatlicue* state asserts disability—particular experiences with chronic illness—as part of the development of a larger radical consciousness. Even while you grapple with internalized ableism through your story, you reject the victimhood that ableist thinking projects onto disabled bodies. Instead of seeing disability as a place of suffering, you look to the *Coatlicue* state in order to argue for illness as part of a larger process that can bring about *conocimento*. Disability becomes a place of power—one that does vital work even when our bodies are still and silent—rather than a place of victimhood. It is during, and because of, the most difficult struggles with pain, depression, addiction, and illness that radical and transformative change is brought about. People with disabilities, then, may be able to more easily access the *Coatlicue* state—along with *la facultad* and *Nepantla* because our bodyminds require and experience constant crossings between consciousness. Crip bodies and crip consciousness are part of a larger "healing of the wound."

Dear Gloria, I write this to you just as the student government at the university I work for is trying to pass legislation that would revoke in-state tuition for undocumented students. This is a time of deep shifts, and the shifts are frightening. I doubt they will be easy. I wish I could talk to you in the flesh. I have so much to ask you about your own experiences with disability and chronic illness. I want to hear more from you about how you were able to enter into these sweet dark places in order to transform yourself and your work in the world. I want to talk about how exhausting it is to try to do this work, how we forget our bodies and minds, how we forget to take care of ourselves. *Coatlicue* hisses, *listen.*

Gloria, our experiences are different. You, a patlache Chicana/Tejana who lived with diabetes and its resulting impairments. Me, asegi aquadanto Cherokee mixedblood who lives with fibromyalgia, chronic fatigue immune dysfunction syndrome, and multiple chemical sensitivities. We dwell on different sides of the bridge that spans this life and the next. And yet, what brings us together is our hope for transformation, our place within the bright matrix of the universe.

What your work offers me, offers all of us, right here and right now, is an understanding of the radical and resistant work of disability and forging an intersectional disability movement and how a crip consciousness works for our mending. Your words help me understand my own body, my own days in bed in pain or too weak to move, as necessarily contributing to *conocimiento*. Our bodies—you remind us—remember everything.

Dendagohoyu,

Qwo-Li

III: LETTER FROM LEAH LAKSHMI PIEPZNA-SAMARASINHA

So much time spent in bed: Gloria Anzaldúa, chronic illness, Coatlicue and disability.

Another fibromyalgic queer coloredgirl morning

Dear Gloria,

Dawn. Sunrise floats through the window slats of my shack, the little EI-safer house in the back of the queer collective house I inhabit. Some days, I will rise now. Some days, I will hit the snooze alarm for three hours. I will turn over and over in my big bed. I will shift. I will get up oh, so slowly. How damp is it out, how bad is my pain, how shaky is my balance and my cognitive ability today?

Yet another fibro morning. Dawn creeps past my eyelids and I shove her away. Not yet! My fatigue—the deep fatigue of chronic illness, untouched by days and weeks of good sleep, not the fatigue of a night staying up too late—has not been touched today. I turn over and down. I drift back to sleep. My life is bookended by library books, vibrator, and baths. Something more than simple self care, and something other than a life of a lazy, privileged girl. It is a crip life, a chronically ill life. It is a life of dreamtime.

I am a chronically ill, disabled writer. I am a queer woman of color writer. I have a shelf full of anthologies with my words in them. I have been able to pursue the path of red and black ink.

I am a queer woman of color writer. I am a chronically ill woman.

My entire adult life has been marked by illness. It's hard for me to tell when the pain, butterfly balance, fatigue and immune transparency I name as fibromyalgia really started. A childhood filled with abuse, terror and a need to sleep as much as possible bleeds into chronically tired yet overachieving college years, bleeds into the early 20s when I walked back into my incest memories, got sick and spent a lot of time on my futon, struggling with fatigue, pain and shakiness.

Fibromyalgia is a name I choose for the constellation of repeating cycles of fatigue, muscle pain that does not have an organic source, immune system meltdowns, shakiness, balance problems and cognitive delay that hit me when I am stressed or doused with chemicals. Yoga, a regular bedtime, flextime, herbs, quitting smoking, kale and protein and quinoa all helped, but there is no cure for this body. This is my body. This syndrome is new/old and ongoing, unfolding. It changes as we find new ways to think about trauma, our bodies, embodiment, environmental racism, and sickness.

Chronic illness sucks. But, oh, there is the secret bliss of bed! Chronic illness may not have made me a writer, but it illuminates my writing life. I can't work a 9-5. The times I tried left me winded in bed after three days—but bedtime means lots of dreamtime. Sometimes it's low-quality dreamtime—dreamtime where I am zonked on half a Soma, watching *Caprica* on Sidereel, using my vibrator and alternating soaking in hot baths with laying on a big ice pack to manage my pain. But whether it is high or low quality dreamtime, being a sick girl means I have more dreamtime than most 9-5ers or movement organizers could ever dream of!

It is so difficult to write both of what sucks about disability—the pain, the oppression, the impairment—and the joy of this body at the same time. The joy of this body comes from crip community and interdependence, but most of all, of the hard beauty of this life, built around all the time I must spend resting. The bed is the nepantla place of opening.

Capitalism says that disabled, tired bodies that spend too much time in bed are useless. Anyone who cannot labor to create wealth for owners are only valued for the wealth they labor to build for capitalism; crips are useless to capitalism. That's why social programs are cut, why Hitler referred to us as "useless eaters"—we often are not able to be fast, assembly line workers who produce wealth for someone else.

I am a chronically ill queer woman of color artist and so much of my time is spent in bed. I joke that my bed, heaped with cushions, is my office, my world headquarters. My life is arranged around my bed. There is good art to look at, a window, my vibrator plugged in, a stack of books within easy reach. I lie in it thinking of all my other crip poet friends who spend most of their days in bed too. Draped in pillows, red and plum sheets, surrounded by good art to look at, curtained by plum sari fabric. This is my place of power, the fulcrum, place everything emerges from.

I dream here. I write here.

What I know is that Gloria Anzaldúa and I meet in bed. Not like you think. Maybe like you think. Gloria and I meet in bed. It's sexy. And it's just life. Gloria and I meet in bed, in the chronically ill sickbed heaped with pillows where we both spend so much time. Gloria, we meet in bed. You never said you were disabled, that I can find, every inch of evidence you left resisted that label. But whatever you felt about that world, this is where you dreamed and lived too. This place of bodily difference, a tired body that comes in pain and suffering, that allows us to work part-time weird jobs, to rest, to fly.

1938: Gloria is born in Hargill, Texas. At three months, her mother sees tiny pink dots of menstrual blood on her diaper and freaks the fuck out. The doctor says "Don't worry, she's a throwback to the eskimo—eskimo girls get their periods early." Is she intersex? Would she call herself that now? She calls herself jota, mita y mita, half and half, the way lesbians are called in South Texas. Her breasts develop at 8, there is a secret, a folded rag pinned to her underwear, in grade school, her breasts bound down tight with bandages by her mother. "Keep your legs shut, Prieta." In her twenties and thirties, fibroids and 104 degree fevers rock her body monthly. In her 40s, she develops diabetes. During the week of May 15, 2004, Gloria Evangelina Anzaldúa transitions to the ancestors/ died of complications related to diabetes. She is 61.

She is marked by physical difference all her life, from the blue spot on her butt at birth, the mark of African blood and the ability to see beyond, to pain, the need for rest.

1979: Gloria decides to devote life to writing, takes series of part-time lecturer and writer-in-residence jobs to buy as much time to write as possible.

1991: Gloria wins NEA grant, uses it to buy house in Santa Cruz by her beloved ocean, Yemaya, so she can visit it daily.

A quote from *Borderlands*: "It is dark and damp and has been raining all day. i love days like this. as i lie in bed i am able to dive inward. perhaps today i will write from the deep core."

She writes while other people sleep. She writes of getting up, sitting down, looking for, and always, the writing. The path of red and black ink.

Gloria, the written record I have access to is often silent about how sick you were, how much those knife-like fibroid pains, those energy drops from diabetes that stole your life early, affected your life. But on the record is how you stole dreamtime. Stole time to write and dream. You stayed up all night, slept all day. You joked about how you would do anything, anything to avoid the writing— clean house, make nopalitos, take a bath, burn candles. But you knew the writing was always there, waiting, your constant lover and companion. The toad inside that makes poems open to you. You chose writing over lovers, over others. You wrote of being a bridge, drawbridge, sandbar or island—identifying finally as a sandbar, a natural formation that could be connected or isolated as the tides turned. Like the tides of our bodies—our sick, in pain, in less pain bodies that resist a boxed-in life that an ableist world demands.

Queer women of color never say we are disabled if we have any choice about it. We come from families who believe in being tough, in sucking it up. We do not want any more identities than we already have to wrestle with. Our bodies are already seen as tough, monster, angry, seductive, incompetent. How can we admit weakness, vulnerability, interdependence and still keep our jobs, our perch on the "thin edge of barbwire" we live on? Why would we join crips who are all white in the mainstream rights movement?

How do we claim this body—broken, beautiful—as not a liability but a gift? To know that interdependence is what has saved us time and time again—as queers and trans people, people of color, women, broke folks. How my lovers and friends help each other survive—passing $20 back and forth across the movement, driving me to groceries when I can't make it down the stairs.

How do we say that my hurting body in bed sucks and is also a beautiful ability to write for hours because I can't hold down a 9-5 even if I wanted to?

And part of the beauty is our access to dream time. Time for the stories to grow. Time that is not logical, rational, clock time, punch the clock time. Thirty-five, I am surrounded by people who say, how do you have time to write those poems and stories, co-create those projects? How are you so productive? I am so productive because when my gut tells me to take a day off, I do. I lie, say I have a family emergency. When I was a kid I knew that I was supposed to grow up and work a 9-5 job but I didn't ever understand quite how it would happen. I follow the words out my belly. I give in to the bed, to the dreams, to the long long sleeps and times curled up. The words curl close to me because of it.

How can I say that being chronically ill is a gift? That maybe I would not have become a writer if I had not been too sick and tired to work? That I had to figure something else out? My illness opens the door to write, be in the Nepantla place. Takes me to the path of red and black ink, to where the stories go.

Says AnaLouise Keating, "Although Anzaldúa had been living with diabetes for over a decade, many of her readers were unaware of the disease's ongoing, debilitating effects on her life. Even those of us who knew her well were shocked by her sudden death. As Kit Quan, one of Anzaldúa's oldest friends and writing comadres explains, "Gloria always told me that she was going to stick around for 20 more years. She struggled with diabetes and all its complications daily... but she was so well read on the disease... and worked so hard at managing her blood sugars that I believed we still had more time." (Keating, *Entre Mundos* 9).

If I say all this story, maybe no one will be surprised at my death. Maybe someone will know when I get really sick. Maybe I will have enough time. Maybe my sick, dreaming, flying, writing body will have enough people around it who recognize that place for its strength and weakness, too.

But when I roll over onto my pink t-shirt fabric sheets on another disabled woman of color artist day, feeling the bliss of the cotton on my sore body, when I sleep late and stay up late typing, I feel your body brushing me. We brush sick bodies that hurt and also fly. Our sickness a road out from the 9-5, trading labor for cash life. Our bodies can't work like that so they dream instead. Steal time for dreams, poetry, world changing, on that thin edge of barbwire. We dream away through the teeth of the dragon of whitecapitalistpatriarchal amerika. Turn over, write another line. Poems flying in our teeth.

"Caminante, no hay puentes, se hace puentes al andar. *Voyager, there are no bridges, one builds them as one walks*" (Anzaldúa, *Bridge* 352).

WORKS CITED

Anzaldúa, Gloria E. *Borderlands/La Frontera: The New Mestiza.* Third Edition. San Francisco: Aunt Lute, 2007. Print.

---."now, let us shift… the path of conocimiento… inner work, public acts." *This bridge we call home: radical visions for transformation.* Gloria E. Anzaldúa and AnaLouise Keating, eds. New York: Routledge, 2002. 540-578. Print.

---.Foreword. *This Bridge Called My Back: Writings by Radical Women of Color.* Berkeley: Third Woman Press, 2002. Print.

Dunbar-Ortiz, Roxanne. "The Grid of History: Cowboys and Indians." *Monthly Review: An Independent Socialist Magazine.* 55.3 (2003). Web. 27 June 2011.

Foucault, Michel. *The Birth of the Clinic: An Archeology of Medical Perception.* New York: Vintage, 1994. Print.

Gilman, Sander L. *Seeing the Insane*. Lincoln: University of Nebraska, 1996. Print.

Hevey, David. *The Creatures Time Forgot: Photography and Disability Imagery*. New York: Routledge, 1992. Print.

Jackson, Vanessa. "In Our Own Voice: African-American Stories of Oppression, Survival and Recovery in Mental Health Systems." *Mind Freedom*. Web. 27 June 2011.

Keating, AnaLouise. ed. *Entre Mundos/Among Worlds: New Perspectives on Gloria Anzaldúa*. New York: Palgrave Macmillan, 2008.

---. *The Gloria Anzaldúa Reader*. Durham: Duke University, 2009.

Kouddous, Sharif Abdel. "Disability Justice Activists Look at 'Ways to Maintain Ablism' and Counter "How Our Bodies Experience Trauma in the Medical-Industrial Complex.'" *Democracy Now!* 23 June 2010. Web. 27 June 2011.

Kuppers, Petra. *Anarcha Project*. University of Michigan. Web. 27 June 2011.

McGruer, Robert. *Crip Theory: Cultural Signs of Queerness and Disability*. New York: New York University, 2006. Print.

Molina, Natalia. "Medicalizing the Mexican: Immigration, Race, and Disability in the Early Twentieth-Century United States." *Radical History Review*. 94 (2006): 22- 3 7 . Print.

Smith, Andrea. *Native Americans and the Christian Right: The Gendered Politics of Unlikely Alliances*. Durham: Duke University, 2008.

DEFINING AN ALTERNATIVE DISCOURSE: A LOOK INTO CHICANA/O SPACES CREATING IDENTITY, RESISTANCE, AND HEALING THROUGH ART AND MUSIC

SUNSHINE MARIA ANDERSON

"...Or perhaps we will decide to disengage from the dominant culture, write it off altogether as a lost cause, and cross the border into a wholly new and separate territory. Or we might go another route. The possibilities are numerous once we decide to act and not react."

—Gloria Anzaldúa, *Borderlands: La Frontera*

INTRODUCTION

Communication through creative expression has been associated with all cultures for centuries. In current times, this type of communication continues. This is a study of creative expression in the context of a Chicana/o[1] community in East Los Angeles (ELA), specifically the areas east of the Los Angeles River. I am looking at the various modes of communication that exist through performance art, poetry, theater, music, and all mediums of visual art. I suggest that they act as an alternative discourse that provides opportunities for gaining knowledge that is culturally relevant but rarely available in traditional K-12 education. What brought me to investigate this topic is my own experience in attending and participating in various events in my neighborhood and surrounding areas. I gained knowledge of the term Chicana/o and connected to this identity through attending these various events, which I call community cultural events. In this study, I look at various events that have taken place since the 1990s, integrating a methodology of Critical Race Theory explained by Tara J. Yosso.[2] This lens values experiential knowledge and utilizes methods of storytelling, family histories, biographies, scenarios, parables, *cuentos, testimonias*, chronicles and narratives.[3] Through interviews, discussion, and four examples of community cultural events, I hope to create an understanding of the importance of the arts in relationship to education. Through my discussion and descriptions of these community cultural events, I provide a narrative that shares the experiences and knowledge gained by these events: *Café Caliente, Farce of July*, the *Anti-Mall*, and *Mujeres de Maíz*.

I personally remember having to confront the question of identity for the first time, in fourth grade. During class, we were penciling in basic information on a test sheet. When I came to the question of ethnicity, I had these choices: Caucasian, Hispanic, Asian/Pacific Islander, African-American, Native-American, or Other. I was not quite sure what Hispanic meant. Many thoughts came to mind. I knew my grandmother spoke Spanish; however, I did not grow up with my Mom speaking Spanish, and she was born here in Los Angeles. My Dad grew up in ELA, was fluent in Spanish but spoke to us in English. I did not know much about his father, but his mother was from New Mexico, and my name did not offer much help. Confronted with the question of my identity, I raised my hand to speak with the teacher. She asked me questions about where my parents and grandparents were born, and we finally decided Hispanic was the best choice versus "Other." No other listed answers seemed to fit.

In relationship to cultural identity, the discussion of "What am I?" never came up at home until later that day, and the answer was "American-Mexican." Added to that were stories of mixed marriages in past generations that included French, Irish, and various Native American communities. Those discussions added to my uncertainty. Eventually, I understood my identity to be a third generation American-Mexican. I did not see much representation of this identity on television, or in the textbooks at school. The junior high I attended, El Sereno Junior High used to be Wilson High School, which I now know as one of the participating schools in the 1968 ELA High School Walkouts. Why was I not aware of this history until after high school? Public education, in a sense, left me ignorant about my environment and the community in which I lived.

My consciousness and understanding of a Chicana/o community and identity evolved out of attending backyard shows with local bands on the Eastside of Los Angeles. Many of these bands eventually began playing at various collectively run community spaces located on the Eastside of L.A. in the later 1990s. Some of these spaces I attended include: *The Aztlán Cultural Arts Foundation* (Lincoln Heights), *Arroyo Books* (Highland Park), *Peace and Justice Center* (Downtown L.A. (DTLA), *Luna Sol Café* (near MacArthur Park), "*The Loft on San Mateo*" (DTLA), *Troy Café* (Little Tokyo), *Art and Commerce* gallery space (DTLA), *Regeneración* (Highland Park) and *Self Help Graphics and Art* (ELA). The bands that played at these venues included: *Ollin, Quinto Sol, Aztlán Underground, Calavera, Quetzal, Ozomatli, Sol, Yeska, Sugarskull, Cactus Flower,* and many others. With their names in English, Spanish and/or Náhuatl,[4] they all offered a Chicana/o sensibility through their music and lyrics, and at these locations there was a sense of community and inclusion, different from the experience in a mainstream environment.

I gained awareness of an identity that I felt connected to from being present at these events, which provided me with culturally relevant expressions that I had never seen anywhere else. I began participating in some of these events with an opportunity to display artwork in the gallery of *Self Help Graphics and Art* (SHG)[5], and I eventually became one of the regular vendors for their annual arts and craft sales and have participated in many other community cultural events since then.

Many art spaces were created such as those that I previously mentioned. The events were often benefits/fundraisers for the space and for various social and political causes; they took place in public and private spaces such as rented halls, community gardens, and parking lots of community spaces. What was and is always present are the cultural and political references. In my research, I uncovered the role that the arts play to raise consciousness and facilitate an understanding of cultural and political awareness through its alternative discourse.

The guiding questions for my research are: Does art in a Chicana/o community serve as an alternative discourse and vehicle toward gaining cultural awareness? Do these cultural events provide opportunities for members of the community to gain and access valuable knowledge? Does this knowledge allow for healing and how does it translate into social change? Along with experiential knowledge, my research is informed by interviews, observation, and participation in community cultural events.

My social location, a term defined by Patricia Zavella, helped me in being able to connect to an identity. Zavella explores the reality of varied experiences and looks at how it plays into identity. Zavella focuses on women specifically, explaining that there is diversity among Chicanas. She points this out immediately in describing how the terms we use for identity vary. She writes, "When speaking among ourselves, we highlight and celebrate all the nuances of identity—we are Chicanas, Mexicanas, Mexican-Americans, Spanish American, Tejanas, Hispanas, Mestizas, Indias, or Latinas and the terms of identification vary according to the context."[6] With this understanding of diversity, it can be understood why Chicana/os sometimes face challenges in terms of identity. Zavella further points out that while there are common issues, there are also differences in histories, settlement patterns, sexual preference, and cultural practices. However, Zavella reminds us that there are connections in history and that the legacies of colonization provide a sense of solidarity among Chicanas.

An article by Michelle Habell-Pallán confirmed that ELA has a wealth of cultural history with its music and art scene worthy of documentation. With accounts of the autobiographical narratives of Chicanas in ELA who were part of the 1970s and 1980s punk scene, Pallán draws a connection to expressions of a political awareness. She describes the experience and concept of being on the East side of Los Angeles and crossing the L.A. River to get to the West side of L.A. Her argument is "Chicanas as producers transformed punk and new wave aesthetics into sites of possibility for transnational conversations concerning violence against women and the effects of the shrinking public sphere."[7] Relevant to my research is Pallán's notion of "sites of possibility for transnational conversations." Through creative expression, such as the music of bands from ELA, they have been able to communicate ideas related to cultural experience, political, social awareness, and identity. Furthermore, the venues where ELA bands perform could be seen as "sites of possibility for transnational conversations." In Pallán's discussion of the club Vex[8] at SHG, she notes a response from the singer of *The Brat*, a band during that time: "Theresa Covarrubias remembers, 'The Brat did a show there with local artists...it was through the Vex that I realized there were a lot of artists and poets in East L.A.'"[9] Covarrubias found a community of artists and musicians that she may not have known existed in such abundance. *Vex* offered a space for this community in ELA. Pallán also points out that although various artistic mediums were being used, there were common themes that ran through the expressions, such as "themes of sexuality, antiwar protests, and antiracism."[10] Similar to Pallán's analysis of the shows at *Vex,* I explored a continuum of cultural events that have taken place after the 1980s, throughout the 1990s and through the 2000s, that have revolved around music and art with themes responsive to social and political issues and that specifically contribute to a Chicana/o cultural identity. Although in this essay I am making a claim that the music and art of ELA contributes to the construction of a Chicana/o identity, it is important to note that within the identity politics of Chicana/o culture there is a continuous shift in how this identity is defined and expressed. Throughout the 1960s, 1970s, 1980s, 1990s and today, the term Chicana/o as a cultural and/or political identity continues to change and evolve.

While I propose the idea of an alternative discourse, I also value the scholarship and work of previous scholars including: Alicia Gaspar de Alba, Gloria Anzaldúa, Chela Sandoval, Laura E. Pérez, Dolores Delgado Bernal, Tara J. Yosso, Judith L. Huacuja, Karen Mary Dávalos, Daniel Solórzano, and Paulo Freire. All of their works stem from and contribute to a Chicana/o studies framework, which has also been influential in my research.

Gaspar de Alba's theory of "Alter-Nativity" has been influential. In her theory she acknowledges the situation of being part of American culture but also an "other." Alba explains it as "both indigenous and alien to the United States, an *alter-Native culture,* whose identity has been carved out of a history of colonization and struggle."[11] She also notes that Chicana/o identity has often been placed into the category of a sub-culture in relation to the dominant culture. An *alter-Native culture* is one that was native to California but at the same time different, influenced by but can change the dominant culture. My idea of an alternative or new discourse is not to criticize traditional discourse but rather to confront the fact that often communities of color lack the access to culturally relevant discourse within their K-12 education that can inspire and lead to a path of higher education.

The community cultural events that I will discuss as an example of an alternative way of gaining knowledge are also informed by the theoretical framework of Gloria Anzaldúa's important work *Borderlands: La Frontera.* Her work has also been influential in my research, especially the notion of a new consciousness. Anzaldúa uses the term *mestiza consciousness* to describe consciousness as a way to acknowledge the social location of being in the U.S. while having Mexican, African as well as indigenous roots. She explains how there is a feeling of straddling the border while also facing a situation of assimilation. Anzaldúa explains: "The new *mestiza* copes by developing a tolerance for contradictions, a tolerance for ambiguity. She learns to be an Indian, in Mexican culture, to be Mexican from an Anglo point of view. She learns to juggle cultures."[12] In ELA there are various stages of generations of Chicana/os who may or may not identify with this term, but it is the first, second, and third generations who were born or grew up in the U.S. who might relate to a Chicana/o consciousness along with Anzaldúa's idea of a *mestiza consciousness.* In the community cultural events that take place in ELA, I examine how these ideas all become relevant.

Resistance to oppressive conditions and injustices can develop from a critique and understanding of these conditions. This can lead to a desire to make change in such an environment. Daniel Solórzano and Dolores Delgado Bernal provide an explanation on transformational resistance within the context of critical race theory and in relation with two examples of student resistance.[13] One, the East Los Angeles School walkout in 1968 and two, the 1993 UCLA Chicano/a Studies Protests.[14] Utilizing methods of qualitative research and counter-storytelling or testimonies, Solórzano and Bernal expand on the idea of resistance as being a transformative experience through internal or external methods. Within the spaces of community cultural events that I look into, resistance is end xpressed in ways that can also be transformative. Through my research, I have found that there are transformational experiences and that there is also a connection to identity and healing in the transformational process.

In one of the more recent books published on the topic of Chicana/o art titled *Chicana Art: the Politics of Spiritual and Aesthetic Altarities* by Laura E. Pérez,[15] I found themes that connect to the idea that healing is an integral part of experiencing, producing, or viewing the elements within the events that I describe. Pérez looks at Chicana art as an offering or an altar. Her analysis of various examples of Chicana art connects to the idea of spirituality and healing. In my study, I also suggest that the art present at community cultural events contributes to a healing environment.

My influence in defining an alternative discourse stems from Paulo Freire's theory on education. Freire proposes abandoning the idea of "deposit-making" or the banking method in education and favors a "problem-posing" system of learning where communication is a key element and the teacher-student roles become mutual.[16] I see the creative expressions in community cultural events as a tool for promoting a "problem-posing" system of learning because at these events there are many references to political issues. This promotes an exchange between the viewer and the artist.

LOCATION: EAST OF THE RIVER

Although segregation is supposed to be a reality of the past, Los Angeles is a segregated city. Los Angeles is divided up into many neighborhoods and Latinos are part of all of these areas; however, there is a majority on the Eastside that consists of people who are Mexican-American, undocumented or documented, and who may identify as Mexican, Chicana, Chicano, or Latino. Segregation seems to be occurring in different ways. As a native of Los Angeles, I realized that there is an invisible, informal, border-like, symbolic division between the east side of Los Angeles and the west side echoed in the term "east of the river," a reference to the Los Angeles River. Michelle Habell-Pallán refers to this geographic situation in her article about the music scene of the 1980s in East L.A. She writes:

> …punk's international sensibility also appealed to Chicana/os…perhaps because of the city's history of physically and economically segregating Chicanos apart from the wealthy West side, thought to be by Los Angeles's dominant culture the place of important 'worldly' cultural invention.[17]

This history of segregating plays out in different ways. If you happen to live in East or Northeast L.A., accessibility to a quality education that contains culturally and socially relevant pedagogy is most often out of reach within the Los Angeles Unified School District. This is evidence of the economic injustices that are continually taking place in Los Angeles.

In many ways, the development of the Chicana/o movement began in response to economic divisions evident within Los Angeles communities such as the inequalities within the schools that resulted in the historic East Los Angeles high school walkouts of 1968. The Chicana/o movements' labor and commitment has paved the way for many Chicanas/os today who continue to face systematic racism and injustices. Zavella's theory on *social location* explains that amongst Chicanas there are various factors that exist in connection to identity and one's position in society by systems of power that play a part at the individual, community, societal and global level. These aspects of social location are at the same time indications of social inequality that are reflective of power relations within the dominant mainstream society.

DIY: NON-TRADITIONAL FORMS OF DISCOURSE

Artists and musicians, along with organizers, have historically communicated their resistance to the dominant culture against injustices. An example of this is seen in the work of "El Teatro Campesino," a theatre group directed by Luis Valdez. Valdez organized California farmworkers into El Teatro Campesino in an effort to raise funds, support, and awareness to the unfair and dangerous working conditions of the farm workers. Another example is *The Great Wall of Los Angeles*, a mural by Judy Baca, created in 1974-1981 with a continuous group of collaborators ranging from at-risk youth to other artists. *The Great Wall of Los Angeles* depicts the history of Los Angeles that is not in textbooks, beginning with a scene of Native Americans and continuing through the 1950s.

My focus is on the art and music within community cultural events, which I define as an independent collective-production created in various locations of the producers' community, including rented halls, art studios, youth centers, parks, community gardens and in the streets all in a do-it-yourself (DIY) fashion. These events are open to anyone and provide an accessible space for artists, poets, musicians, and members of the community; some of these events have a specific theme and take place annually. Common factors present at these spaces include themes of resistance, consciousness, and a Chicana and Chicano identity in various multimedia expressions.

Eddie Ayala, musician, former singer of ELA bands *Los Illegals, OddSquad*, and co-producer/promoter of *Café Caliente*, describes his inspiration for creating an event:

> Café Caliente was a Chicana/o multimedia underground event inspired by the rave and underground club movement. Events would take place in warehouses in downtown of the eastside area with music, art, dance and performance...exposing younger Chicana/o artist and musicians to an expression and environment, which encouraged independence from the constraints of galleries and the lack of opportunity and a place to be free creatively. [18]

The concept of *Café Caliente* (See Fig. 1) described by Ayala embodies the overall ideas that exist behind the inspiration in creating these events. This particular event was not annual or monthly but took place throughout the later 1990s. According to Ayala, the first one took place in Lincoln Heights at The Women's

Building.[19] Some of the participating artists and musicians included at this particular event included Chicana/o artists such as Tito Lariva, Gronk, John Valadez, Patssi Valdez, and Diane Gamboa, integrated with new and upcoming bands like Cactus Flower, Quetzal, and Sol. Ayala explains that the talent of ELA should also be heard in mainstream media outlets but does not receive any airplay. In his opinion, the music business excludes this genre of music he refers to as *Chicana/o Alternative*. Because of his experience with exclusion and racism in the music-business he decided to create a compilation CD, released in 1997 titled: *Barrios Artistas Vol. I. Chicana/o Alternative*. The compilation included the following bands: Quetzal, Lysa Flores, Calavera, John Vatos, Cactus Flower, Jabom, Marble, Motita, and Announcing Predictions. All of these bands have played at many community cultural events. The do-it-yourself or DIY concept stems from the punk scene, and there are similarities in the idea of *Chicana/o Alternative* in the way that the punk scene rejected the mainstream culture and took on an attitude of working independently without having to conform to mainstream U.S. society.

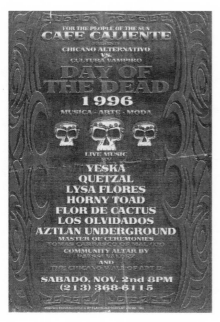

Figure 1: Original Flyer, *Café Caliente,* 1996. From the collection of Eddie Ayala.

Part of what sparked a reawakening of the Chicana/o movement in arts and activism in the 1990s was the reaction to the political climate affecting Chicana/o communities. In 1994, Proposition 187 targeted towards undocumented immigrants, would restrict them from rights to education and healthcare. In

1996, Proposition 209 would end affirmative action, affecting the number of Chicana/o students that would gain access to higher education, and in 1998 Proposition 227 sought to end bilingual education.[20] This contributed to the anti-immigrant sentiment aimed at Mexican immigrants and felt by Chicana/os. This anti-Mexican-immigrant sentiment has continued since then, and artists, activists, and scholars continue to respond. In 2010, Arizona passed a Senate bill known as SB1070 that would require proof of citizenship and the right of an officer to ask for proof based on suspicion. This bill has gotten much attention in the Chicana/o community. Consequently, artists have created work in solidarity with Arizona residents and supporters opposing SB1070.

The Anti-Mall (See Fig. 2) is another example of a community cultural event. It takes place every December in various locations with a focus on independent DIY style crafters, designers, and artists who are also activists. Music performance

and non-profit organizations are also included in this event along with healthy food options, creating an environment of consciousness. The phrases used in promoting this event are "Invest in your community" and "People before Profit." Laura Palomares, the primary organizer of the *Anti-mall*, refers to participants as "artivists" because eligibility to participate in this event is dependent on the artist being involved in political and social activism. *Uprising*, a show on KPFK, describes the mission of this event: "The idea behind *Anti-Mall* is to enable people of conscience to 'recycle' their money by investing in its local artists, cooperatives and independent businesses that are committed to social justice."[21] The purpose is to create a space and outlet for creating an independent economy and to encourage consumers to support

Figure 2: Flyer, Anti-Mall, 2009 Graphic Design by Joel Garcia.

local artists instead of going to a mall and supporting corporations that usually outsource their products to sweatshops. The *Anti-Mall* makes an effort to cultivate conscious consumers.

Figure 3. Flyer, Farce of July, 2007.
Graphic Design by Manuel Torres

Farce of July (See Fig. 3), another example of a community cultural event, has taken place annually for the past thirteen years. This event was created by "Xicano Records and Film"(XRF), a grassroots collective of musicians, organizers, visual artists, poets and performers. The title is a reference to the actual holiday of the Fourth of July or Independence Day. "Farce" implies an absurdity – the absurdity of the idea that we all have complete freedom and independence in America. According to XRF in a press release found in *American Renaissance*, "The Farce of July* was created in order to use art and music as an instrument of community empowerment, education, and celebration while bringing to light the experience of historically oppressed peoples throughout the world."[22] While the notion of "community empowerment" tends to be generally used, it is an important concept as it can aid in the prevention of the various negative effects of an inner city environment. One example would be prevention of youth involvement in gang activity.

Often at these events, there are marketplaces, areas where vendors or local artists can set up and offer their items for sale, similar to the idea of the *Anti-Mall*. This also contributes to the environment created in these various locations. Some of the items for sale include handmade soaps, oils, incense, purses, paintings, prints, jewelry, books, ceramics, home décor accessories, and a variety of silkscreened t-shirts with original designs. Popular images have included Frida Kahlo, Che

Guevara, Zapatista images, Pre-Columbian symbols, Virgen de Guadalupe, and Día de Los Muertos-Calaveras.

By creating and transforming various locations with art and music, these spaces become environments that become inclusive of culturally relevant discourse that is outside of traditional academic discourse. Alicia Gaspar de Alba documented one of the first major gallery exhibitions of Chicana and Chicano art. She writes, "Embedded in the images of the brown-skinned Virgin and the black thunderbird on the red United Farm Workers flag…of resistance to dehumanization, colonization, and assimilation as well as the politics of the mestizo/a heritage whose roots were Toltec as much as Spanish."[23] It is through the various creative visual expressions that the Chicana/o movement has been able to sustain visibility and a continued awareness of the need for a movement that acts in resistance. Through the content in the community cultural events that take place in ELA, identity, consciousness, resistance, and healing are being fostered and are somewhat of an extension of the Chicana/o movement.

Gloria Anzaldúa describes having to find a new way of thinking and finding a change in the way we perceive reality. She acknowledges this as a new consciousness. She explains, "The work of *mestiza* consciousness is to break down the subject-object duality that keeps her prisoner and to show in the flesh and through the images in her work how duality is transcended."[24] Anzaldúa brings to light the identity politics that exist for Chicana/os. The acknowledgement of this duality is confronted in the spaces where community cultural events take place. Through images that make reference to indigenous cultures of Mayan, Aztec, Mexica, and Native Americans, and sometimes in hybrid representations, the viewer of these representations can begin to gain another way to perceive reality through this *mestiza consciousness*. In an interview with a participant who has been part of many of these events as a spoken word artist, she reveals what she has gained through attending and participating in community cultural events:

> If I had not gone to all these events, I would not have ever heard Náhuatl. I wouldn't be who I am, I wouldn't have this strong sense of rebellion, I wouldn't critically look at colonialism, I mean all of the gigs, the events,

the workshops the women's circles, all of that stuff, the writing that I did back then all was because of these events. That was like central to it and it wasn't only something I did, it was who I was. My whole network of best friends those are the people that were a part of that and we didn't just observe we actively participated.[25]

It appears that her experience in attending and participating in these various events has made a positive impact on her life and that there were things that she learned such as Náhuatl which were influential to her identity. She also suggests that she gained many valuable friendships, which is a way of creating community. When I interviewed her she was a student at Cal State Los Angeles, and she also said that she did not think she would be going to school and majoring in English if it was not for her experience in writing poetry and performing at these events. In a sense, she was empowered through her experiences, and this is a form of social change.

In connection to *mestiza* consciousness, Allegra Padilla, an activist/organizer who is an attendee of many of these types of events, offered her opinion:

> The arts become that gateway, that entrada, for other messages to get across the messages of resistance, and I think if it wasn't for that role that the arts play in the community now and in the past, people would not be aware of certain things and how that manifests into action is challenging to measure.[26]

Padilla agrees that the arts are important in being able to communicate messages and provide information; however, she does suggest a question that may need further investigation. How does all of this exposure to the arts actually manifest into action, and how can this be measured? In some ways, I am asking the same question. The communication and expression through the arts is valued and speaks sometimes with a stronger impact to the viewers. The actions one takes, whether it be in one's personal life or in solidarity with a movement or cause, is where the action can also be taking place. Through a gained consciousness of spirituality, political awareness, advocacy, and community, the action one takes is in different levels and stages but always evolving.

TRANSFORMATIONAL RESISTANCE

Within the context of education, Dolores Delgado Bernal and Daniel G. Solórzano introduce the concept of transformational resistance that includes internal and external resistance. They explain: "Transformational resistance framed within the tenets of critical race theory allows one to look at resistance among students of color that is political, collective, conscious, and is motivated by a sense that individual and social change is possible."[27] They further explain the two types of transformational resistance: external and internal. Internal resistance is explained as being aware and involved in a conscious critique of oppression; the resistance is in a form that is not as obvious such as pursuing a higher education with hopes of creating social change. External transformation, for example, is participating in and organizing a protest in an effort to create social change or having written research dedicated to social justice published. Relating this idea to transformation of space, I found similarities to this theory of transformational resistance in an interview with Felicia Montes, a performer, artist, activist, organizer and co-founder of *Mujeres de Maíz*.[28] Montes explains:

> A lot of the circles or events that we put together are kind of about coming together, yeah about resisting but also about what's good about our community, what's positive about ourselves specifically what *Mujeres de Maíz* has been more about [is] finding an alternative but not only resisting but living. So, not only surviving but actually flourishing or living in some good positive way holistically.[29]

This statement places resistance into a positive action and speaks to the idea of an alternative way of living with the DIY attitude, creating the vision that you want to see in your community and in yourself. Montes has an academic background with a B.A., an M.A. and an MFA, and she has integrated her knowledge into these events, allowing for information to reach others who may not yet have access to an academic environment. She explains in her own words: "So basically since college, I've tried to connect my classes and anything that I learned either from family or street knowledge back to the community in some way." One of the ways she has done this is through *Mujeres de Maíz*. She describes *Mujeres de Maíz* as "a women of color, art and poetry, multimedia art collective…it's a real

Figure 4. Flyer, Mujeres de Maíz, 2008. Graphic Design by Joel Garcia and Mujerez de Maiz. Compiled with images of various artists

open collective, so people have come in and out and really, we say anybody can be involved." The performance group eventually began hosting an annual event (See Fig.4) that takes place every March to commemorate Women's History Month with different themes annually; it is now in its fourteenth year. In addition, with these events they publish a "zine" that includes submissions from artists, poets, and authors. Montes also points out that part of the major influence that took place was from "the 1997 encuentro that happened in Chiapas with a lot of Chicana and Chicano artists." She is referring to the Zapatista[30] movement in Chiapas when many artists, organizers, and activists took trips in support of their movement and brought back a lot of inspiration and ideas.

HEALING

The visual empowerment available in Chicana/o art that is often only visible within community cultural events is significant in the process of understanding and healing from internalized oppression. Laura Pérez expresses the element of spirituality within Chicana art. She writes:

Conjuring and reimagining traditions of spiritual belief, traditions whose cultural differences have been used by discourses of civilization and modernization to justify subjugation and devaluation, are conscious acts of healing the cultural *susto*: that is, the "frightening" of spirit from one's body-mind in the colonial and neocolonial ordeals, the result of which is the "in-between" state of *nepantla*, the post conquest condition of cultural fragmentation and social indeterminacy. Put in more familiar terms, these conscious acts work toward the reintegration of the psyche fragmented by the internalization of loathing of the native self, which Franz Fanon described as vital to decolonizing practice...[31]

Pérez references Chicana artists' use of traditional indigenous spiritual beliefs depicted within the art as a form of reclaiming an existence in the quest for acknowledgement and validation specifically within modern society, which perpetuates what society's spiritual beliefs should be and devalues other spiritual beliefs. She explains that by "reimagining traditions" Chicana artists are engaging in "acts of healing from the cultural *susto*" (a Spanish word that translates as "scare"). She suggests that the spirit has reacted to the events that took place in the acts of colonization and in learning of this history the spirit continues to respond sometimes in the feeling of "loathing of the native self"[32] or self-hatred, both related to internalized oppression. Through experiencing community events that contain culturally diverse and socially relevant perspectives, there is opportunity for entering into a path of healing and transformation.

At some events, there are often opening *ceremonias* performed by local *danzante* groups (Aztec dancers) dressed in Aztec style and decorated with images of day signs from an Aztec calendar complete with various types of feathers. A smell of copal or sage burns, while the sound of the a drumbeat plays in the background. The audience of all ages, performers, and organizers are all gathered in a circle as part of the ceremony. They are guided through a blessing or prayer and turn to face each of the four directions, east, west, north, south; each direction is connected to an element: fire, water, earth, and spirit. Through this informal experience, the idea of "reimagining traditions" is being performed. The visuals of a culture from a distant past offer new knowledge in a holistic manner.

Learning about practices and ceremonies of the Mexica in a classroom would be a different experience. The opportunity to learn in a participatory way is facilitated through this type of activity while also providing a sense of spirituality that is potentially healing.

In the narratives of the interviews I conducted, this is the response I received when asked if there has been any healing experiences through attending and/or participating as a performer. Alejandra Sánchez a participant and attendee said:

> Definitely, I think that healing is a major part of it…the Personal is political. I think that becoming empowered and finding your own voice and expressing yourself through creative avenues there is a major healing that takes place. Not only do you see your capacity for creativity and beauty but you have this sense of shared community that I don't know if a lot of Americans feel, I think that we're kind of disjointed folks a lot of times, so that sense of power and strength and shared resistance and shared vision and community is so important, and I think that that heals in profound ways. And I don't think that it's a mystery either or anything new because I think that our people have done this ever since and it's about ceremony. So it's kind of like the new ceremony, I think that it's in our blood to be ceremonial people, so by creating events is also a part of tapping back into that energy and getting in touch with the sacred. It's highly personal but in order for it to reach a higher level it has to be attached to community.[33]

Alejandra emphasizes the value and importance in the idea of shared community. It is through this environment that she felt she was able to find her own voice and express herself creatively. Through the act of spoken word and performance in a space that is welcoming and familiar, the sense of empowerment can offer moments of healing. Additionally, she brings in the idea of ceremony, suggesting that in the spaces where the events take place creative expression is a form of ceremony; she links it to being something that is in our blood, suggesting that ceremony of the indigenous is something that happens instinctively. In my previous description of the opening *ceremonias* with *danzantes*, I see a connection with this idea discussed here. There is a necessity to connect with community in order for action to take place. She also speaks on the idea of the sacred and getting in touch with this through community. This is similar to what Montes talked about in her discussion on resisting in a good and holistic way and finding the positive in yourself and your community. The reimagining of traditions that Pérez talks about is also at work here; the artists and audience can collectively navigate through what she calls the "in-between state of *Nepantla.*" Allegra Padilla shared her thoughts when I asked her if she has had any experiences of healing through attending these events:

> I definitely think that participating in these events there are some ways of healing and for me, specifically through relationship building with different individuals…I can't name one specific experience that has been healed by one particular event but I just know that it feeds my soul. When you're constantly facing these challenges and you're looking at all the bad things that are going on, like health and housing and… another person gets killed by the police. I think that in every event that people come together to talk about it to share about it and that people are there to be with one another and give that gift of time and attention it has been really healing, especially through something like building community altars for Day of the Dead.[34]

In a very different but slightly similar way, the ritual of attending church every Sunday, comes to mind. There are altars present, music playing, and instead of performance and art there is shared prayer and community. In attending these events, Allegra reveals that it is something that feeds her soul, these spaces of shared community offer a sanctuary-like experience from dealing with many challenges that exist. Felicia Montes also talks about the element of healing with *In Lak Ech*[35] (another performance group that includes some members of *Mujeres de Maíz*). They perform on a regular basis at various spaces, such as schools or conferences. After each performance, they always get feedback; people in the audience reveal to them that they were able to see themselves and they related with a story or a song. Montes, stresses the fact that it is not about them performing but it's about sharing and expressing; she encourages others to feel that they can and should be expressing in some way too because, Montes explains, "our voices have been silenced for so long."

In relationship to discourse and education, Paulo Freire reminds us that "Education is communication and dialogue. It is not the transference of knowledge, but the encounter of subjects in dialogue in search of the significance of the object of knowing and thinking."[36] The encounter of subjects in dialogue, explained by Freire, is central within these community cultural events. The audience and participating artists are the subjects in communication and dialogue.

In my interviews I found narratives that speak about learning, sharing, and community. Allegra Padilla shares her experience:

> I think that it's much easier for you to reach a mass amount of people using the arts and creativity. Sure, a pamphlet and a flyer can be creative and original and all that but you're just able to reach so many more people through things like posters and mass communications, radio... public art, things like murals, and the music; the music has had a huge impact on me personally. And I feel that's where I got a lot of my education in terms of, you know, what's been going down historically. How to articulate, you know, some of the challenges that we face in the community, but music was able to really give some words to that along with some visual imagery, So I think you have to have creative avenues to get your message across and to build a community in resistance.[37]

In her narrative, it is evident that the arts and especially the music, has had a positive impact in her life. She specifically says, "I got a lot of my education" referring to history as she says, "what's been going down historically." While it may not point out the specifics, my analysis is that what she means by "going down historically" is in reference to the histories that are excluded in schools. She makes another statement regarding things she has learned: "A lot of my knowledge in terms of say a topic like aromatherapy or herbal remedies comes from this desire to heal and resist I don't know say colonization through medicine, so I think that there's a very intentional effort put behind a lot of these events to develop a community in resistance, and a community." In this statement there is a suggestion regarding the idea of gaining knowledge on topics that are often looked at as alternative, such as aromatherapy and herbal remedies that are considered to be alternative medicine. Gaining this awareness and knowledge is a form of resisting, because it is in contrast to Western medicine, so this idea is the same concept of resisting mainstream society. The idea here is similar to what Felicia explained earlier regarding resisting but not in a negative way; it is about finding a balance through positivity. The arts and music in these spaces are integrating these ideas through the images and lyrics. The intentional effort Allegra speaks about in developing a community in resistance suggests again the importance of community coming together to share, and exchange. It may be that it turns into resistance because in this community there are a number of social and political challenges.

Through this alternative discourse, these spaces become counter spaces. They reject the mainstream galleries, museums, radio stations, malls, movie and music industries and theaters that tend to exclude Chicana/o artists. In these spaces, there is a cultivation of community and in this community the artists and musicians are teachers, while the audience is composed of students and these roles are interchangeable; the audiences become the teachers and the artists become the students. The creative expressions and narratives of a community are being shared, and dialogue through a variety of creative expression becomes discourse.

Unlike the Chicana/o movement in the past, current representations have come to be more inclusive and accepting of women and gender politics. Judith L. Huacuja credits such groups as *L.A. Coyotas, Mujeres de Maíz,* and *Las Comadres Artistas.* These groups are found in the context of community cultural events similar to the ones I have described; the groups themselves, Huacuja explains, organize many of the events:

> For these Chicana artists, group processes always link art-making with education and political activism. In so doing their work performs new notions of cultural citizenship defined as "a range of social space for Latinos in this country," a space where difference is seen as a vital resource producing new cultural forms.[38]

It is through their productions, performances, and installations, in a space or location, that their work is given life and becomes praxis. This idea echoes Freire's theories that education is the practice of freedom and that both the educator and the student can teach each other through dialogue, communication, critical thinking and praxis.

I thought about these performances mostly outside of the classroom because this is where they began and in a sense, the community cultural events I have talked about can be thought of as alternative classrooms. They are spaces that exist with the intention of teaching, sharing, and creating an outlet for independence, inclusive of diversity and political consciousness. All of this was done out of necessity to fill in the missing gaps in textbooks, movies, TV, theaters, radio, and museums, with the hopes of creating change through art and awareness. The images and words that exist in the diverse Chicana and Chicano arts contribute to the creation and confirmation of a relevant place in history. Miguel León-Portilla, a Mexican anthropologist historian who has studied the history and language of Pre-Columbian cultures tells us that the cultures who spoke Náhuatl believed "that perhaps the only possible way to speak truthful words on earth was through the path of poetry and art, which are 'flower and song.'"[39] Within the community cultural events that I have discussed, I see a connection to this concept. The creative expressions are like offerings; they are the flowers and songs of the generations that have contributed to creating these alternatives, that in reality are not only an alternative but they exist parallel and outside of mainstream media while creating their own clothes, jewelry, herbal remedies, spirituality, music, art, performances, discourse and a community towards healing, empowerment and consciousness.

ENDNOTES

[1] The term Chicana/o is generally defined as a person who is of Mexican descent but at the same time is from the United States. There is also a political consciousness inherent to this term and identity. I use the spelling Chicana/o as an abbreviation for Chicana and Chicano; this is inclusive of both genders.

[2] Tara J. Yosso, "Whose Culture Has Capital? A Critical Race Theory Discussion of Community Cultural Wealth." *Race, Ethnicity and Education* 8, no. 1 (2005): 69-91.

[3] Ibid, 74.

[4] Náhuatl is an indigenous language of the Mexica/Aztec culture.

[5] SHG has a long history that goes back to the 1970s, where many Chicana/o artists got their start and contributed to the creation of the genre of Chicana/o art. The arts were a vital part of the early days of the Chicana/o movement. See Kristen Guzmán, Self Help Graphics & Art: Art in the Heart of East Los Angeles (Los Angeles: UCLA Chicano Studies Research Center, 2005).

[6] Patricia Zavella, "Reflections on Diversity Among Chicanas," in *Challenging Fronteras: Structuring Latina and Latino Lives in the U.S.: an Anthology of Readings*, ed. Mary Romero, Pierrette Hondagneu-Sotelo, and Vilma Ortiz (New York: Routledge, 1997), 187.

[7] Michelle Habell-Pallán, "Soy Punkera, Y Que?: Sexuality, Translocality, and Punk in Los Angeles and Beyond," In *Beyond the Frame: Women of Color and Visual Representation,* edited by Neferti Xina M. Tadiar and Angela Davis. (New York: Palgrave Macmillan, 2005), 219-41.

[8] A club that took place at Self Help Graphics and Art. More information can be found in David Reyes and Tom Waldman. *Land of a Thousand Dances: Chicano Rock 'n' Roll from Southern California*. Albuquerque: University of New Mexico Press, 2009.

[9] Ibid, 232.

[10] Ibid, 232.

[11] Alicia Gaspar De Alba, "A Theoretical Introduction: Alter-Native Ethnography, a Lo Rasquache." In *Chicano Art Inside/Outside the Master's House: Cultural Politics and the CARA Exhibition* (Austin: University of Texas Press, 1998), 1-28.

[12] Gloria Anzaldúa, "Towards A New Consciousness," In *Borderlands/La Frontera* (San Francisco: Aunt Lute Books, 1999), 99-120.

[13] Daniel Solórzano and Dolores Delgado Bernal. "Critical Race Theory, Transformational Resistance, and Social Justice: Chicana and Chicano Students in the Urban Context," *Urban Education* 36, no. (3) (2001), 308-42.

[14] Solórzano and Bernal described these events in the same article. They explain, "In March of 1968 over 10,000 students walked out of the predominantly Chicana and Chicano high schools in East Los Angeles. To protest the inferior quality of their education…As a result of the poor educational conditions and the fact that numerous attempts to voice community concerns were ignored, students

boycotted classes and presented an official list of grievances to the Los Angeles School District's Board of Education. Twenty–five years later in 1993, a multiethnic group of students occupied the UCLA Faculty Center to protest the Chancellor's decision to not support the expansion of the Chicano Studies program to Departmental status. The occupation of the Faculty Center ended when over a hundred students were arrested and taken to jail. In the aftermath of the arrests, a second protest was planned. Students organized a hunger strike at the center of the UCLA campus."

[15] Laura Elisa Pérez, *Chicana Art: the Politics of Spiritual and Aesthetic Altarities*. Durham: Duke University Press, 2007.

[16] Paulo Freire, "Chapter 2," in *Pedagogy of the Oppressed*. (New York: Herder and Herder, 1970), 66-67.

[17] Michelle H. Pallen, "Soy Punkera,'Y Que?': Sexuality, Translocality, and Punk in Los Angeles and Beyond," 223.

[18] Eddie Ayala, interview by author, Los Angeles, 2010.

[19] The Women's Building was previously a feminist artist run space that closed in 1991. (http://womansbuilding.org)

[20] Detailed information on these Propositions and their effects can be found in Juan Carlos Gonzalez and Edwardo Portillos, "The Undereducation and Overcriminalization of U.S. Latinas/os: A Post-Los Angeles Riots LatCrit Analysis," *Educational Studies* 42, no. 3 (2007): pg. #252-253.

[21] "Attention conscious consumers, 2005," www.uprisingradio.org.

[22] American Renaissance, Farce of July, http://www.amren.com (accessed April 07, 2011).

[23] De Alba, Alicia Gaspar, Chicano Art Inside/Outside the Master's House: Cultural Politics and the CARA Exhibition (Austin: University of Texas Press, 1998), 41.

[24] Gloria Anzaldúa, "Towards a new consciousness," in *Borderlands La Frontera* (San Francisco: Aunt Lute Books, 1999), 80.

[25] Alejandra Sánchez, interview by author, Los Angeles, 2010.

[26] Allegra Padilla, interview by author, Los Angeles, 2010.

[27] Danial G. Solórzano and Dolores D. Bernal, *Critical Race Theory, Transformational Resistance, and Social Justice: Chicana and Chicano Students in the Urban Context*,10,14.

[28] Mujeres de Maíz, A community event that takes place annually and during the month of March for women's history month.

[29] Felicia Montes, interview by author, Los Angeles, 2010

[30] For further reading see, George Allen Collier and Elizabeth Lowery Quaratiello, *Basta!: Land and the Zapatista Rebellion in Chiapas* (Oakland, CA: Food First Book, The Institute for Food and Development Policy, 1994).

[31] Laura Elisa. Pérez, *Chicana Art: The Politics of Spiritual and Aesthetic Altarities* (Durham: Duke University Press, 2007), 21.

[32] Ibid, 21.

[33] Alejandra Sánchez, interview by author, Los Angeles, 2010.

[34] Allegra Padilla, interview by author, Los Angeles, 2010.

[35] In Lak Ech is a Mesoamerican word meaning you are my other me.

[36] Paulo Freire, *Education for Critical Consciousness* (London: Continuum, 2007), 126.

[37] Allegra Padilla, interview with author, Los Angeles, 2010.

[38] Judith L. Huacuja, "Borderland Critical Subjectivity in Recent Chicana Art," *Frontiers* 24 (2003): 119.

[39] Translation by Laura E. Pérez, in notes to chapter one, *Chicana Art: the Politics of Spiritual and Aesthetic Altarities* (Durham: Duke University Press, 2007), 314.

WORKS CITED

Anzaldúa, Gloria. "Towards A New Consciousness." *Borderlands/La Frontera*. San Francisco: Aunt Lute, 1999. 99-120. Print.

Collier, George Allen, and Elizabeth Lowery Quaratiello. *Basta!: Land and the Zapatista Rebellion in Chiapas*. Oakland, CA: Food First Book, The Institute for Food and Development Policy, 1994. Print.

De Alba, Alicia Gaspar. "A Theoretical Introduction: Alter-Native Ethnography, a Lo Rasquache." *Chicano Art Inside/Outside the Master's House: Cultural Politics and the CARA Exhibition*. Austin: University of Texas, 1998. 1-28. Print.

Freire, Paulo. "Chapter 2." *Pedagogy of the Oppressed.* New York: Herder and Herder, 1970. 66-67. Print.

Freire, Paulo. "Chapter III. Extension or Communication." *Education for Critical Consciousness.* London: Continuum, 2005. 126. Print.

González, Juan Carlos, and Edwardo Portillos. "The Undereducation and Overcriminalization of U.S. Latinas/os: A Post-Los Angeles Riots LatCrit Analysis." *Educational Studies* 42.3 (2007): 247-66. Print.

Guzmán, Kristen. *Self Help Graphics & Art: Art in the Heart of East Los Angeles.* Los Angeles: UCLA Chicano Studies Research Center, 2005. Print.

Habell-Pallán, Michelle. "Soy Punkera, Y Qué?": Translocality, and Punk in Los Angeles and Beyond. *Beyond the Frame Women of Color and Visual Representation.* Ed. Neferti Xina M. Tadiar and Angela Davis. New York: Palgrave Macmillan, 2005. 219-41. Print.

Huacuja Pearson, Judith L. "California Chicana Community and Cultural Praxis." *Chicana Literary and Artistic Expressions: Culture and Society in Dialogue.* By Maria Herrera-Sobek. Santa Barbara, CA: University of California, Santa Barbara, 2000. 137-61. Print.

Pérez, Laura Elisa. *Chicana Art: the Politics of Spiritual and Aesthetic Altarities.* Durham: Duke UP, 2007. Print.

Solórzano, Daniel, and Dolores Delgado Bernal. "Critical Race Theory, Transformational Resistance, and Social Justice: Chicana and Chicano Students in the Urban Context." *Urban Education* 36. (3) (2001): 308-42. Print.

Yosso, Tara J. "Whose Culture Has Capital? A Critical Race Theory Discussion of Community Cultural Wealth." *Race, Ethnicity and Education* 8.1 (2005): 69-91. Print.

Zavella, Patricia. "Reflections on Diversity Among Chicanas." *Challenging Fronteras: Structuring Latina and Latino Lives in the U.S.: an Anthology of Readings.* Ed. Mary Romero, Pierrette Hondagneu-Sotelo, and Vilma Ortiz. New York: Routledge, 1997. 187-93. Print.

EDITORIAL CONOCIMIENTOS: GLORIA ANZALDÚA'S IMPACT ON CHICANA FEMINIST PUBLICATION AND MENTORING PRACTICES

TIFFANY ANA LÓPEZ

All of us are theorists and practitioners with a significant reservoir of ways of knowing the world that has been cultivated from experience, yet this foundation is such a given aspect of Chicana identity that we do not name this as epistemology, we do not view it as theoretical, nor do we understand it as infusing us with a sophisticated lens of critical acumen. It takes a visionary like Gloria Anzaldúa to articulate for us that each and every person is on some level a theorist and practitioner.

In *Borderlands / La Frontera,* Anzaldúa archived the conversations—monologues as well as dialogues—that had transformative personal impact on her life, and in the form of a book written across genres, she staged that conversation on a public page. Her work set forth a groundbreaking invitation to use the personal as a springboard for critical engagement by so frankly and poetically writing about the spectrum of violence—inclusive of historical, cultural, physical, and representational violence—that she viscerally understood as definitively shaping her sense of identity on multiple fronts. It delivered a call, but it also offered a model for how to process what trauma theory terms the unspeakable or the unsayable, the resultant aftermath of traumatic experience in the struggle to articulate simultaneously the shattered sense of self and the sense of self necessarily under reconstruction. As I have written elsewhere, the form of Anzaldúa's work is intimately connected to the meaning of her work. *How* we tell stories is bound to the content of the stories being told.

Given that my pedagogy, creative projects, and scholarly engagements focus on matters of trauma and violence and the ways that theater, literature, and art provide avenues for personal healing, community building, and social change, Anzaldúa's writing has been incredibly influential on my work. As a scholar and creative artist (professor, editor, dramaturge), I have followed her model of working across genres to produce work about trauma and violence that is fueled in very large part by a personal grappling with what it means to survive traumatic events.

In 1999, while I was completing the final working draft of a book project about representations of violence in U.S. Latina drama, I received news that my brother had murdered our father. Without a doubt, there are events that leave a person broken and without the ability to see beyond the scope defined by trauma. The events of a family homicide have the potential to do just that. The only way for me to heal—but also to advance in my work—was to find a way to give language to the unsayable so as to make sense of horrific events, to name and identify in order to find understanding not only for myself, but also for others. Being able to articulate the complexities and contradictions of one's personhood is absolutely foundational for personal healing, creative work, and professional productivity. The scope of Anzaldúa's work exemplifies this. It helped me to ask a very significant question: How do we write about traumatic events from within the vortex of trauma?

I often credit the act of reading with saving my life because it introduced me to writers and inspired me to seek them out as mentors on the page with the power to usher me onto a path of survivorship. Notably, in her *Prietita and the Ghost Woman*, Anzaldúa spotlights the role of the mentor in the form of the Ghost

Woman who guides Prietita out of the forest and into her community. In my introduction to the short story anthology *Growing Up Chicana/o*, I write, "For many of us, literature was our salvation. It told us what others would not and gave us permission to realize our dreams." Books showed me that my home life was not the norm and that it was, in fact, highly toxic. At the age of fifteen, I was forced to leave home in fear for own my life as well as the lives of my siblings. School became an ever increasingly important space, ranging from haven to hospice. I am here today because of support programs, such as affirmative action, and the work of deeply committed Chicana mentors. My education, but especially my readings in Chicana/Latina studies—grounded in the foundational works of Anzaldúa and Cherríe Moraga—along with my collaborative projects with Chicanas/Latinas in the arts, has dramatically changed my life by enabling me to understand how my experiences with violence and trauma are not something to be stoically endured and deeply tucked away in the vault of personal memory. Rather these wounds constitute an important archive of knowledge, what Anzaldúa identifies and explores as *conocimientos* and *la facultad*. Articulating our personal and collective wounds, but most importantly showing how they are generative, is necessary to making transformation. This process of coming into an understanding that our stories of violence are stories of hope is what I call the "alchemy of blood."

Beginning with the landmark anthology, *The Bridge Called My Back*, Anzaldúa and Moraga distinguished themselves as foundational theorists of trauma and violence. Both together in *This Bridge Called My Back* and later in their separate projects (*Borderlands/La Frontera* and *Loving in the War Years*) Anzaldúa and Moraga speak in clarity and detail about the ways our bodies have been constructed as contested geographies, the existence of borders of all types as scarified contact zones, and the necessary embrace of the spirit and psyche as core spaces to be honored and protected. Their work dares to name and touch the most painful of wounds and, in the process, show how our wounds can be transformative. Anzaldúa provides us with some very potent vocabulary, such as her oft-quoted description of the border as a "1,950 mile-long open wound," a location where the "first world grates against the third and bleeds" (2). Her graphic phrasing signals the physical and emotional trauma that results from the forces of violence historically involved in both the establishment and maintenance of borderlands spaces. She strategically crafts a vocabulary for grappling with matters of violence and trauma, offering keywords, such as "una cultura mestiza," to describe a space dedicated to personal and cultural healing where one's voice and agency are actively fostered. Such vocabulary empowers us to read and think differently, and therefore to act differently. It teaches us to define our wounds—historical, cultural, personal, physical, and emotional—and to speak both clearly and frankly in documenting our struggle.

Very simply stated, Anzaldúa's work affirms that we are seldom alone in our experiences, and this in and of itself is a major touchstone in the legacy of her work. The ultimate quest for survivors is to see themselves—and to thus have others see them—as much greater than the events of violence that inform but do not solely define identity. In Anzaldúa's words, writing is "an endless cycle of making it worse, making it better, but always making meaning" (73). Significantly, such confrontational work can debilitate at the same that it energizes. As Anzaldúa recognizes, "Knowledge makes one more aware, but also more uncomfortable" (48).

In my work, I have coined the term "critical witnessing" to describe the process of being provoked or inspired by a creative work to the point of refusing apathy in favor of actively resisting participation in behaviors or systems that create climates or cycles of violence. Just as there is a spectrum of violence, so is there a spectrum of critical witnessing that includes survivors and their allies. This is the lens that filters my reading of Anzaldúa's work. For me, from *Borderlands/La Frontera* to her two children's books, Anzaldúa's writing is intensively invested in cultivating an arena of critical witnessing by exploring the force and impact of violence, particularly the two strands of wounds inflicted from the dominant culture and from within Chicana/o culture—the braid of historical violence of the borderlands terrain that defines Chicana/o identity. I interpret Anzaldúa's work as a primer about how to name and process those wounds by using the personal as a springboard for critical engagement, offering her own story as a model for how to process trauma in a way that yields both personal healing and social change. If we do not clearly understand the sources of our wounding, how are we to discern the sources of our healing and proclaim the strengths we might share with others? Developing and fostering editorial *conocimientos* requires this.

Throughout my work, but most especially in my position as an editor, the goal has been to remain brave, to work through the unsayable, if not for myself, for my colleagues and most especially for my students, many for whom I serve as a mentor and public parent in the extended *familia* they are working to build from scratch. In my role as co-editor of *Chicana/Latina Studies: The Journal of Mujeres Activas en Letras y Cambio Social*, I strive to practice editorial *conocimientos* through the staging of difficult and necessary conversations at our various meeting places, from the pages of our publications to the platforms of our conferences. An editor, as Anzaldúa was (*This Bridge Called My Back* and *Haciendo Caras / Making Face, Making Soul: Creative and Critical Perspectives of Feminists of Color*), vows that there are no sacred texts: "nothing is thrust out, the good the bad and the ugly, nothing rejected, nothing abandoned" (79); "a new mestiza consciousness comes from continual creative motion that keeps breaking down the unitary aspect of each new paradigm" (80).

Anzaldúa's *Borderlands/La Frontera* set a benchmark in the definition of Chicana feminist scholarship that clearly resonates throughout our field, including in the structure—the form—of the conversations we stage, not just in what we publish but also in how we publish it. In the seven years I have been co-editor of *Chicana/Latina Studies*, I have noted several significant ways Anzaldúa's work resonates throughout the pages of the journal. To begin, we publish creative work alongside academic essays; additionally, we select cover images not merely to showcase artists, but for the ways they visually represent the scope of the collected work in each volume. Within the pages of the journal, one finds a range of writing, with creative pieces alongside academic writing and contextualized as part and parcel of the staged conversation of each issue. For example, in an issue devoted to the theme of "Life Paths," (Volume 9, Issue 2, Spring 2010) one finds Tanya Gonzalez' essay on *Ugly Betty* and representations of Latina sexuality hinged to Adelina Anthony's *Bruising for Besos*, a solo play about the impact of violence on formations and expressions of Chicana/Latina sexuality. In our role as a flagship publication and the only interdisciplinary and feminist Chicana/o or Latina/o studies journal of a professional scholarly organization, we follow Anzaldúa's imperative to understand the creative voice and the critical voice as integral in the production of Chicana feminist writing in its entirety, for the work performed in both theory and practice.

In addition to the attention we bring to fostering, developing, and publishing writing in the journal, the editors of *Chicana/Latina Studies* are further committed to a Chicana/Latina feminist editorial practice. Each year at the MALCS Summer Institute and Conference, we hold a variety of creative and scholarly writing workshops and participate in scholarly panels and professional development roundtables. In our expansion of the colectiva editorial support network to include the editors' home institutions (presently the University of Texas, San Antonio and the University of California, Riverside) we seek to expand and fortify well into the future the meeting ground of Chicana/Latina community building that is facilitated by the journal.

Part of my initial goal in proposing a session devoted to editorial *concimientos* at the Mundo Zurdo Conference was to discuss the impact of Anzaldúa's oeuvre on editorial work and mentoring practices within the journal by offering specific examples represented by the collaborative work taking place through the journal. Joining myself and Josie Méndez-Negrete (Lead Editor, *Chicana/Latina Studies*) were two of our graduate students, Lisette Lasater and Sandra Garza, both of whom are our mentees and members of the UC Riverside and UTSA editorial staff colectiva who help run and manage *Chicana/Latina Studies*, and are themselves mentors to others through their own Anzaldúan-influenced pedagogy and critical practice. Our focus to fulfill the mission of *Chicana/Latina Studies* directs us in very specific ways born from a shared commitment to the brand of personal leadership, public pedagogy, and creative activism that Anzaldúa's work outlines. Because of the fiscal realities of the journal, all of us are keenly aware of the fragility of this project and conduct our work with a fierce sense of responsibility to the organization of Mujeres Activas en Letras y Cambio Social and to the field of Chicana/Latina studies itself.

Lately, in reflecting on seven years of work with the journal and my own career-long investigations into matters of trauma and violence, I've been thinking a lot about the fragility of our work and the importance of not losing sight of what we are ultimately working towards with the totality of our individual and shared efforts. Some points of reflection: While *Chicana/Latina Studies* is the only flagship interdisciplinary journal of Chicano and Latino studies, submission patterns indicate that the journal still faces a challenge in being fully acknowledged as the primary publishing destination for those working in the field of Chicana/Latina feminist studies. (See Karen Mary Davalos's "Journal Report, 2003-2009," *Chicana/Latina Studies,* Volume 9, Issue 1, Fall 2009, pp. 14-22.) These submission patterns give the appearance that writers feel more intellectual capital is gained from publishing their work in mainstream journals. On one hand, this illustrates an understanding of the great impact journals have in our professional lives. On the other hand, from an editorial perspective, this risks sending problematic and mixed messages within the field, i.e., that the specialized conversations we wish to stage within Chicana/Latina studies matter more when they are vetted outside the field and held for other voices. As editors, we also face the challenge of responding to work that gets submitted merely because it thematically addresses the subject of Chicana/Latina studies; such work displays a truncated reading of the field because it is not written primarily for a Chicana/Latina studies audience. These essays tend to be characterized by citational footprints that quote Derrida or Foucault while eliding foundational Chicana and Latina scholars; such work purportedly engages in Chicana/Latina feminist studies as a field but, significantly, does not speak from within the heart of the field because it is not conversant with the evolution of the critical terrain the writing seeks to traverse and because the writer does not actively signal entering a discussion between and among Chicana/Latina scholars. Notably, universities cite editorships of flagship journals as a significant indicator of national reputation because of the impact journals have on a field; and scholarly organizations regularly invite editors of their flagship publications to lecture to membership. An important question for us to then ask: How do we support Chicana/Latina studies work, from our reading practices and publishing activities to our encuentros, platicas, teaching, and leadership? Here, I think it is very important to note that nearly all of Anzaldúa's writing was published with independent presses committed to advancing writing by feminists and people of color. Imagine if Anzaldúa had been motivated by acquiring intellectual capital rather than speaking for and to the communities that she perceived as grounding her work.

In thinking through the lens of my research in preparing for the Mundo Zurdo conference that gave rise to this paper, I could not help but also consider the ways we are propelled by loss. We come to emotionally celebrate and critically honor Anzaldúa and her work. By having a regularly scheduled conference, we insist on the vital role her writing and life plays for all of us. We cast a spotlight on her oeuvre that we then direct onto an international stage. We recognize the full scope of her writing, life and career, in the process adamantly insisting on its merit beyond question and without rationalization or concern for the mainstream, the academy, or whatnot. (In many ways, the Anzaldúa conference is a giant communal teach-in.) In thinking about what it means to organize around loss, I find myself asking, do we have to lose something or someone in order to be propelled into a state of appreciation, preservation, or enlightenment? Our present moment of crisis as exemplified by the case of Arizona very much shows the dual fragility and urgency of our work. How ironic is it that Anzaldúa's writing is so widely anthologized in composition textbooks and survey volumes on American literature but is now being banned from such curriculum with Chicana/o studies positioned by some as a discipline of harm rather than the critical exploration of healing that is exemplified by Anzaldúa's work.

When we celebrate Anzaldúa, we must also articulate what it is about her work, inclusive of its form and content, that we strive to honor not just in theory but also in practice on the pages and stages of our lives and work. This is a line of inquiry that we at the journal *Chicana/Latina Studies* take most seriously in our commitment to practicing editorial *concimientos*, that specific combination of scholarship, poetics, sobrevivencias, and witnessing, the legacy of Anzaldúa's work as an intellectual and creative visionary, critic, poet, children's author, and, not to be forgotten, editor.

WORKS CITED

Anzaldúa, Gloria. *Borderlands / La Frontera: The New Mestiza*. San Francisco: Aunt Lute Books, 1987.

-----. *Prietita and the Ghost Woman*. San Francisco, Children's Book Press, 1996.

Anzaldúa, Gloria E. and Cherríe Moraga, eds. *This Bridge Called My Back: Writings by Radical Women of Color*. Berkeley: Third Woman Press, 1981.

López, Tiffany Ana. *Growing Up Chicana/o*. New York: William Morrow and Company, 1993.

-----. "Emotional Contraband: Prison as Metaphor and Meaning in U.S. Latina Drama." In *Captive Audience: Prison and Captivity in Contemporary Theater*, edited by Thomas Fahy and Kimball King, 25-40. New York: Routledge, 2003.

-----. "Reading Trauma and Violence in U.S. Latina/o Children's Literature." In *Ethnic Literary Traditions in American Children's Literature*, edited by Michelle Pagni Stewart and Yvonne Atkinson, 205-226. New York: Palgrave Macmillan, 2009.

López, Tiffany Ana and Phillip Serrato. "A New Mestiza Primer: Borderlands Philosophy in the Children's Books of Gloria Anzaldúa." In *Such News of the Land: American Women Nature Writers*, edited by Tom Edwards, 204-216. Hanover: University Press of New England, 2000.

MARFITA: A TOLTEC METHODOLOGY

JOSH T. FRANCO

Invoking Art: In the ethno-poetics and performance of the shaman, my people, the Indians, did not split the artistic from the functional, the sacred from the secular, art from everyday life.

—Gloria Anzaldúa

To investigate daily life in order to translate it into thinking is a dangerous venture, since it is necessary, particularly here in América, to make the grave mistake of contradicting the frameworks to which we are attached.

—Rodolfo Kusch

INTRODUCTION/KEY

Maps and mapping are themes running throughout this writing. They operate at multiple registers: as metaphor for visualizing and grouping modes of expressing thought, as organizational tool of the text itself, and as a method for making political and aesthetic interventions where called for. While the ultimate aim is to delineate a methodology of the Toltec, so named following the work of Gloria Anzaldúa and Laura E. Pérez in concert, "(re)mapping" is a way to name the primary activity of that figure. The figure and the activity are inextricable. The figure of the Toltec is aligned with Walter Mignolo's "fractured subject," and through this alignment and others, it is conceived as a figure whose daily constitution happens by activating a desire to be always involved in a remapping of the world *and* to the modes of expression given to the thoughtwork aimed at capturing and articulating that activity. Gestures as to how this operates in concrete terms are provided in the process of describing and rethinking the installation project MARFITA.

ON MAPPING ME MAPPING MARFITA

I am currently involved in a large scale installation project entitled MARFITA. This is the Spanish diminutive of the name of Marfa, a semi-rural town in far west Texas, population approximately 2,100. Founded in the late 1800's, the town has served as a center for the many ranches in the area, as home base for generations of migrant farmworkers moving between Texas and California as the seasons dictated, as the site of the U.S. Army's Fort D.A. Russell, and most popularly today as home to canonical American artist Donald Judd's permanent installation of his own works and select others, under the guardianships of the Judd Foundation and the Chinati Foundation. "Most popularly" because this collection draws over 10,000 visitors a year to what has become a pilgrimage site of sorts for minimalist, post-modern, and contemporary art lovers from around the globe. It has yet one more attraction, however, a pilgrimage site proper, in all the religious and sacred implications that come with the use of the term.

In 1994, the Virgin Mary appeared to Hector Sánchez in his backyard. The Sánchez family live in the last residential home one passes before entering the long driveway up to the Chinati Foundation's main office. Here, less than half a mile from Judd's famous cement blocks, Sánchez erected an altar to honor the apparition. Complete with a hand painted statue of the Virgin overlooking a lovingly dug and cemented shallow grotto, and housed within an upturned bath tub, this installation stands resplendently *rasquache*, and is positioned so that Chinati is always in her sights. She too draws pilgrims, and these are accounted for in the log kept by Sánchez's wife, Ester. These two groups are largely unknown to one another, though their itinerant paths surely cross frequently at the auspicious, gravelly roundabout that swings pilgrims decisively toward one site or the other.

In Summer 2009 I visited a friend during her internship at the Chinati Foundation. One day, I was wandering around town alone and found myself in the gallery BALLROOM marfa. Notebook in hand, I took in the exhibit[1] deploying the vocabularies provided by my Art History and Philosophy degrees. Then other terms crept onto the page. These came from further back in my memories; they too were inspired by the site of Marfa, but from outside the gallery walls.

While this was my first visit to BALLROOM marfa, it was by no means my first visit to the town of Marfa. As a child and a teenager, I visited there to pay respects to ancient *tías y tíos*, the brothers and sisters of two of my grandparents. My maternal grandfather, Hipólito Hernández, grew up in the house where the Sánchez family still lives, and where the Virgin Mary appeared to Héctor. During those visits, Marfa was a space of Tejano Spanish, dark brown skin, local roots, low income, and familial happiness. In the more recent visit, Marfa became a space where I was read as English speaking, well-educated, worldly, and convivial in that way that puts one at home in the austere artspaces of contemporary hipsterdom. My friends would probably not recognize the child that I was; my family often has difficulty discerning the person I am now. I cannot disown either of these, nor do I want to. Nor do I want to perpetuate this "'either' between selves" but rather seek out the historical ingredients of their complicated relevance. Walking the path alongside Judd's cement blocks, then up to *La Virgen* (Fig. 1) behind my grandfather's childhood home, from one side of the renovated military wall to the other, I faced the enduring question: What is art? Now, I also question my desire to ask this question. *It itself comes from the same structures that exclude the bathtub altar from the realm of the cement blocks and vice versa.* It is this entire structure that I want to undermine by going for decoloniality and by practicing and furthering methodologies for doing so.

Fig. 1. Hector Sánchez, untitled (altar to La Virgen), 1994-1997. Photo credit: Frances Franco

This experience is bound by the organization of space through salient aesthetic markers. Some of these markers are authorized as 'Art'; others are not. So (un)authorized, how are they organized in relation to one another? In organizing art and its spaces amongst effervescent conversation with mainstream U.S. and international curatorial practices and theories, how are spaces like BALLROOM marfa and the Chinati implicitly re-organizing and aestheticizing the unauthorized, pre-Judd spaces and markers of the small West Texas town in which they are situated? What is the nature of the complicated conversation between those cement blocks and *la Virgen* who resides just outside the walls that authorize their spaces differently and meaningfully? What would a show look like that put these questions at its heart?

I want to explore the notion that Marfa was taken as a sort of "frontier" by Judd, et al. The metaphor of a blank canvas is more than apt here to assume in the imaginations of these art world denizens when they decide to move to Far West Texas. Of course, the canvas was never blank, but the imagination of it as such is a direly familiar one. In the same spirit, contemporary artists seem eager not only to create works in the grassy landscape, but particularly works premised on the reproduction of habitats from elsewhere there. Two examples are *PRADA Marfa* and the installation/dwelling *hello meth lab in the sun*. Both projects were commissioned by BALLROOM marfa. These call for extensive analyses on their own; I point to them here as a beginning of evidence-collecting for calling out the exploitative aspects implicit in the mainstream art world's desires to take up space so permanently and prominently in Marfa. At the same time, whatever critiques might be launched in this vein are immediately and significantly tempered by the sheer amount of thought and creative production that has resulted—indeed, if one has access, Marfa can feel like the cutting edge. Ostensibly, its appeal is that one finds oneself in the welcome shadows of Judd, Dan Flavin, Claes Oldenburg, Roni Horn, et al, while also having the space, literally and conceptually, to grow ideas to an exceptional fullness. Not to mention the economic sustenance that the overlaid (now integral) cultural matrix springing form Judd's presence brings to the area. It is my own fascinations from both within *and* outside of this world that drive me to think so extensively about it. I do not assume my own innocence or distance from those desires, even as I am critical of them.

The Situationists' theory of the *derive* further shades the account of wandering that led me to BALLROOM marfa in the account above, and to the multiple paths that cross uncomfortably in Marfa between galleries and remodeled homes and Spanish-speaking restaurants, convenience stores, and yards with *rasquache* altars:

> In a *derive* one or more of the persons during a certain period drop their usual motives for movement and action, their relations, their work and leisure activities, and let themselves be drawn by the attractions of the terrain and the encounters they find there. The element of chance is less determinant than one might think: from the *derive* point of view cities have a psychogeographical relief, with constant currents, fixed points and vortexes which strongly discourage entry into or exit from certain zones. (Debord)

I want to add to this, based on mine and my family's ongoing relationship with Marfa, the interplay of race and ethnicity with the "currents, fixed points and vortexes" of a given city or town. I plan on making more trips to Marfa with my grandparents, cousins, and other family members in order to explore how these operate. There are certainly feelings of discomfort and alienation with the artspaces that edge up against places of great familiarity for my family. My mother will eagerly visit her father's childhood home, but is loudly uncomfortable walking the path alongside the cement blocks; these are just yards away from one another geographically, but apparently worlds apart "psychogeographically." For myself, I am at ease walking the path alone, less so with family members, and I have anxieties, particularly linguistic ones, when meeting with people from the Marfa where my grandparents are most at home. Exploring these phenomena has been key in the production of MARFITA, a work that explores the fraught landscape of Marfa.

INSTALLATION DESCRIPTION: MARFITA, 15-29 OCTOBER 2011, CO-LAB, AUSTIN, TX

MARFITA is a collaborative project. The artists involved are Alison Kuo, Joshua Saunders, and me, with *teatrista* Natalie Goodnow who will make her contribution at the opening. It is comprised of four main components:

Film - Kuo will direct this part. It incorporates the extant, remarkable film footage of the original apparition (white shadowy figures of Mary and Christ in a tree trunk), as well as filmed interviews with local Marfa residents, and film documentation of the three main artists' "double pilgrimage" motivated as our journeys west now are by an active interest in both the altar and the artworks by Judd and his associates. Film will be projected on multiple surfaces and at multiple scales on the grounds of Co-Lab.

Miniaturized Architecture and Objects – I am currently constructing miniature (approx. 1:12 scale) reproductions of the artillery sheds of Fort D.A. Russell renovated by Judd's own hand and direction. These will be laid out on the outdoor grounds of Co-Lab according to their situation in Marfa. They will contain miniatures of the 100 untitled works in milled aluminum. Also included will be miniature versions of the iconic cement block groupings arranged by Judd on the grounds of Chinati.

Home Interior Simulation - Saunders will take over the interior of Co-Lab with a loose reproduction of the interior of the Sánchez (formerly Hernández) home where the original altar builder Héctor Sánchez lived prior to his untimely death a month after the altar's completion. Some film and original collaborative works by the artists will be incorporated as well as Saunders' "live looped" reenactment of Hector's walk from inside to backyard, beer in hand, on that auspicious night.

The Larger-Than-Life Altar - Composed of a renovated arbor, film, and found objects, this 8-10 foot reproduction of Sánchez's altar will be situated behind the Co-Lab building beneath a tree, as it is arranged in Marfa. During the first night of its installation at Co-Lab, Goodnow will lead an interactive procession through the East Austin neighborhood where the space exists, culminating in a ceremonial, participatory prayer at the altar itself.

The multimedia and collaborative nature of this large-scale endeavor is a result of shifts in my approaches to ideas and materials, largely as part of sustained study of Anzaldúa's writing, particularly when she thinks explicitly about these same things. I have realized recently that the ingredients for my desire to take off from her writings have been gathering for some time.

"MIND MAPPING": DISPLACING TEXT ON THE AESTHETIC FIELD

When I was in the sixth grade I learned a new way to take notes. Our teacher demonstrated with different colored chalks, outlining a paper—introduction, thesis, body paragraphs, and conclusion—on the board. Each section was written in a different color and then circled in a different color according to how important it would be to the paper. Less important thoughts during brainstorming could be cut in the final version. None of the pieces of the paper were written linearly, but floated on the gray-green backdrop of the board. Different colored lines signaling different kinds of connections were drawn between each item;

this was the last step before ordering the pieces into a standard formatted essay. I was less concerned with the final product and more fascinated with the colorful imprint of the "rough draft" left on the board. What resulted was a constellation of circles, ovals, dashed and complete lines; our collective thoughts in pastel greens, pinks, blues, and yellows. We were given this method as an option, along with a box of colored pencils and unlined paper, when required to turn in rough drafts of papers. The teacher called it "Mind Mapping." I silently called it art and continue to practice it today. Almost a decade later, I would encounter the work of Anzaldúa, a creatrix who would "feed, bathe, and dress" her writing. Not art, not a sign or representation, but a live being in the world in itself, she cared for her writing, grew and nurtured it. I was, and remain, enthralled with both of these relationships to writing, that is, to thought and the materials available for expressing it, with the possibilities of generatively joining our thoughts on the aesthetic field.

More than enthralled, I am inspired and motivated. How have I actively taken up what so sticks with me from these moments in the formation of an approach to my own work? What methodologies might they reflect or engender? And the task I have given myself here, how do I articulate a fascination with these methods and logics that is already operating in the work I have done so far? By what names do I call my own in-formation methodology? It has something to do with resisting the distinction between writing and making. For instance, one never says "I am creating a paper" as we might say "I am creating an artwork." It also has to do with the already widely thought and resisted distinction between "Art" and "craft." It is interesting that "*crafting* a paper" is a familiar notion. However, the "*art* of writing" is equally familiar. Ultimately this semantic game does not go so far, but it points to the ambivalence around writing and the production of art in a cosmology that, at least nominally, takes "writing" and "art" as given, discrete categories, even when evidence sometimes points to the contrary.

Importantly, the distinction is more pointed when the categories are embodied in the persons of the Academic and the Artist. I take these figures as elements of a cosmology particular to a people, against its having been violently universalized within a much larger colonial project over time: the university, the museum, the disciplining of knowledge in the west. The methodology guiding this research is what I am attempting to work out here, as both academic and artist, but more to the point, as neither. This is a cosmological "neither." It is the "neither" that I imagine Anzaldúa to inhabit, one that does not aim at cynical rejection or nostalgic recovery, but at tediously working through the contradictory cultural conditions in which we find ourselves through multiple venues and practices continuously. Other figures like Amalia Mesa-Bains, *altarista* and academic, come to mind. Likewise Norma Cantú, poet and scholar. There are many who have already broken and tilled this ground, for which I am grateful. Mignolo describes this activity as that of the "fractured subject," particularly in the introductory essay, "On Describing Ourselves Describing Ourselves." I understand his articulation of the "fractured subject" here as follows:

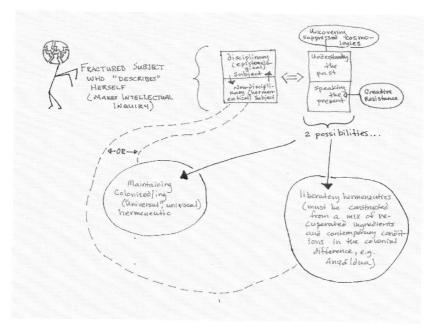

The "neither" I am thinking of resides most saliently in the Liberatory Hermeneutic region of the preceding map. It is from the underneath of the modernity-that-became-postmodernity. It is from beneath the cosmology that supports their construction, from understandings of the world that (post) modernity's other face, coloniality, attempted to obliterate, and successfully brutalized and suppressed for hundreds of years. The postmodern "neither" is also a "both." If I go for this, I am going for being *both* Artist and Academic, while also being neither, which leaves me afloat. While this has been an undeniably generative position for some particular concerns, it does not fundamentally trouble the categories, or the violent epistemological histories that provide the conditions of their possibilities.

The "neither" I invoke is markedly different. It is not a floating, but a grounded triangulation (the same triangulation, I think, Chela Sandoval is working out between coloniality/modernity, its critiques of itself from within, and critiques from Chicana and Third World feminists). Its ground is the ground of the colonial difference, where I attempt to think from. Why a triangulation rather than a flat-out refusal? Because this "neither" is also not a romantically induced attempt at re-inhabiting or reconstructing the past, but a politically charged attempt to "speak the past in the present" (Mignolo). This entails a difficult, often painful accounting of many selves' histories of oppression and resistance *together*. I call it a triangulation because of its accounting for two sets of conditions, modernity and coloniality, towards creatively producing a third social reality, decoloniality.

ORIENTING MULTIPLE SELVES

This is an account limited by my relationship to the terms "art," "Aesthetics," and "gaze." And even then, it is only a snapshot from that ongoing struggle marked by welcome and unwelcome conflicts and uncomfortable familiarities. The struggle is amongst multiple selves, selves that have wholly and happily bought into the delimitations and sanctions of what is and is not worth looking at by a mainstream art world and a canonical discipline, Art History, and the selves that have been pushed to exclude or cut off from familial and communal worldviews by those same sanctions and investments.

As an undergraduate I eagerly immersed myself in the histories of 18th, 19th and 20th century art in Europe and the U.S. (particularly the U.S. art scene with its nexus in New York City). I also concerned myself with the (proto)Greek milieu that Europe cast as its intellectual ancestor during its process of becoming *Europe*. I wrote two senior theses. One involved a close reading of Thomas Crow's *Painters and Public Life in Eighteenth-Century Paris* with a particular goal of furthering an investigation for which Crow opens the door, the historical conditions that made possible the homosociality amongst men in that time and place. The other was a reading of Hellenistic representations of "sex" (sculptures, mosaics, and paintings) against what the contemporary "West" designates as 'sex acts' today. My desires to take on these projects I now understand as largely constructed by the academic institution and the discipline of Art History. Both required an understanding of my self as constituted from—or desire to be constituted from—a Eurocentric trajectory of history, which though not untrue, is a disproportionate understanding to say the least. It does not take into account the crucial colonial disruptions that it took for me to end up with this in my constitution in the first place. These disruptions are far from innocent, and I am indicting them and the institutions that uphold them as much as the fact that they were ignored by that student who was so immersed in histories that were his/mine only through a highly complicated and violent relationship.

Following graduation, I took a position at a university in San Antonio, Texas. During my two years there, I was exposed to multiple, rich histories of Chicanos/as. This was a transformative time for me, and I began to read my own experiences growing up Chicano in semi-rural West Texas as lived results of this history. And during this time, I had the opportunity to work closely with multiple arts groups. I had various roles with each, from artist and collaborator to community and university liaison, event coordinator, discussion panelist, and activist against public assembly and city arts funding discriminations. I also taught contemporary art and performance at Por Vida Academy, a charter school for "beyond risk" high school students. Additionally, I participated in non-institutional collaborations with artists in San Antonio and Austin. It was during this time that I began to understand the profound depth to which the way I *looked* at the world, literally, had been formed as a collusion between multiple institutions and coloniality/modernity to keep me from seeing otherwise, from seeing the histories of violence that congeal in my body, and from inhabiting the visions of the world that accord with the suppression of the memory of those histories, down to my own internalized notions of what is beautiful and desirable.

MAPPING CHICAN@S MAKING

As a result, it has become increasingly striking to see (while I participate in) historical shifts of Chicano/a self-making and self-understanding through our art from the early and mid-twentieth century to today. For instance, in our earlier mid-twentieth century history, playwright Luis Valdez insisted on an essential and unique Chicano aesthetic and demonstrated this aesthetic through the works of his company *El Teatro Campesino*. In contrast, today one reads essays accompanying an exhibit like the Los Angeles County Museum of Art's travelling 2008 show, *Phantom Sightings: Art After the Chicano Movement,* and finds them saturated with explicit references to the body of works which were my primary concern as an undergraduate, the works of the mainstream U.S. and European twentieth century. These references are also in the works themselves, e.g., Ochoa's and Marco Ríos' *Rigor Motors* riffs sculpturally on Rene Magritte's painting *One Fine Late Afternoon* transforming its meanings as it does so. Chon A. Noriega exposes and explores this riffing in depth in his curatorial essay in the catalogue, "The Orphans of Modernism."

As Chicano/as of my generation and our recent predecessors are and have been educated as artists and Art Historians in the U.S., we shift the disciplines and their practices while we ourselves are shifted in return. This interplay is then evidenced as we self-make through a now prolific and still rapidly growing body of art. *Phantom Sightings* aimed at the momentary capture of this activity. Noriega reads the openness to influences outside of Chicanismo—that is, outside of the "identity art" that Valdez created, for instance—as taking part in the production and constant undoing and reassembling of elements drawn from what he calls the "white noise" of postmodernity: "In short, this new generation operates outside either a social movement or a viable notion of the public, and it does so within the intensified 'white noise' of global media and a multiracial, multilinguistic urban street culture" (González, Fox, and Noriega 30). While much of his writing throughout a long career certainly operates within an always politicized historical chain of Chicano/a thinkers, something about this phrase and this formulation is alarming. In partitioning off this "new generation" from any and all social movements, including, we can assume, *El Movimiento*, and further closing off possibilities of understanding them in relation to rural Chicanos/as by identifying them solely with "urban street culture," Noriega leaves little room for artists now to engage with those histories, much less be read by historians and would be theorizers as continuous (if markedly different) with them.

His reading fosters a selective amnesia—he is quick to read the works with their many allusions to European and Euro-American works, and rightly so—within readings of current cultural production by those who would desire to read those works as imbricated in the work of previous generations of Chicanos/as, even if their aim is a radical resistance to many of our predecessors' tenets, organizations of the social, and cultural and national priorities. Indeed, to figure these acts of resistance comprehensively, it is of the utmost importance that the fits-and-starts of the historical flow between "then and now" be all the more open for investigation, not precluded on the basis of contemporary conditions.

Thus Noriega points too closely toward the erasure of historical difference that postmodernity as a notion tends to engender without being critical of that operation. In Noriega's curatorial writing for the show, the artists' pictorial and conceptual allusions have little other reason than the fact of the globalized conditions we currently live. It is these conditions he calls the "white noise." The artists in the show partake in it, they float in it, and in this reading in which they float, they are tacitly moved slowly away from the politics at Chicanismo's inception and into the sonorous, homogenizing ether of the postmodern. This is precisely the understanding I want to resist, while also definitively refusing to claim any essentialism or solidly bounded identities for Chicano/a artists and their works as many other Chicano/as, past and present, are compelled to do. Rather, I want to go for a rigorous account of differently weighted ingredients, where they come from, and how they come to be there. In place of white noise,

I offer the setting of the cacophonous symphony, a multitude of instruments, and a textured imbalance of loud, silenced, unruly, and generally discordant players. This heavily historical work then does not take the "white noise" of our postmodern global conditions for granted, but goes for re-membering through the histories from which it results. Shifts in interpretive tools brought to bear on reading the visual, the performative, and so on would be but one set of results.

So accounted for, what is to be asked of these histories? For the purposes of interpreting and producing creative works, I expect to find in them the story of how our visions and our deployment of our visions as we create have come to be colonized. For instance, in materials on Chicano/a art, Daniel De Siga's *Campesino* is often brought up as one of the more striking examples of art invoking the ongoing farmworker struggles. But no one as far as I have read has noted its undeniable formal affinities with Jean-Francois Millet's work in both *The Sower* and *The Gleaners*: the striking similarities in scale, composition, use of light, and the lionization and posturing of the figures against the landscape. There are at least two moves to make in order to read this relationship. The first is a groundclearing: an acknowledgment that I, the Chicano art historian in the US in 2010 see, and have difficulty seeing around *The Sower* as I look at *Campesino*. And in fact, that when first encountering De Siga's work, I saw Millet's work first, before seeing De Siga's painting for itself. Besides being suspicious and critical of my own gaze, this first move also requires an investigation as to how De Siga came to paint this piece that so strikingly recalls works by the French Realist. Coincidence? His own training? Something else?

After rooting out the plays of power that brought De Siga to paint *Campesino*, the second move would involve building useful and resistant meaning from De Siga's move and my reading, and doing so at the colonial difference. After the groundclearing, articulating the geopolitics and Eurocentrism at work, there is interesting positive work to be done that resists stopping here.

What is De Siga doing in taking visual cues from Millet? Can it be seen as a subversion? A cross-political invoking of workers and political allies across spacetime (the radicality of Millet's project in his own milieu should not be ignored)? During the 70's and into the 80's other Chican@ artists like Ester Hernández and Xavier Viramontes deliberately relied on icons, symbols, and techniques from *within El Movimiento* (even when radically subverting their heteronormativity and nationalist patriarchy as in the case of Hernández). How did De Siga, their contemporary, come to paint *Campesino,* which depicts a figure that could be a farmworker anywhere? Admittedly, there are two tiny clues that work against anonymity: on the figure's left hand a tattoo of a cross emanating light, and more to the point, on his right hand, a small "c/s" tattooed where the bases of his thumb and forefinger meet. But these are available only upon very close inspection, whereas the cultural investments in the other two artists' works are bold and forthright. Indeed, their images depend on this display of cultural signals, while for De Siga they are more incidental to the image than crucial to its portrayal of labor.

Does *Campesino* do resistant work, if differently than, for instance, Hernández's *Libertad* and Viramontes' *Boycott Grapes*? And if so, how? As works by Chican@s, as well as our readings of these works, increasingly evidence and even embrace the many geopolitical lines that cross our bodies, how do we take up these works and our interpretive frameworks for them in ways that both account for and resist complying with the colonial modernity (and postmodernity) these lines are meant to maintain? How do we decolonize our vision?

Active in the account I have just given are the selves of my undergraduate days who persist, eager to make hermeneutical moves with works and theories of art validated by the Western-rooted discipline of Art History and its institutions of residence, the museum and the university, in order to read works that lie outside and have been actively excluded for racist and colonial reasons, from those spaces. *As* active are the selves that are conscious of these operations and seeking out possible resistances, the selves seeking to enact a decolonized, decolonial gaze.

MARFITA is an attempted inhabitation of these fractures. I attempt to inhabit them with the goal of practicing a methodology suited to responding to the question of how I/we might go about the decolonization of our vision, rigorously, and without taking up a postmodern attitude toward identity, *nor*, certainly, an essentialist one. The gaze that results from this work and the mode of interpretation rehearsed above is not a passive one; it is and will be actively guiding our movements in the material world, from the subtle to the grandiose, from how we move to greet a friend, to how we manipulate metal, wood, film and so on in large scale "artistic" endeavors.

THE TOLTEC APPROACHES THE TERRAIN

In approaching such endeavors now, I do so with Anzaldúa, and many more elders and *compañero/as*. The ground of my triangulation—modernity, coloniality, decoloniality—is the border, particularly the one known geopolitically as the Texas-Mexico border, described as a constitutive open wound by Anzaldúa. I choose to think, to *look*, from here in light of the histories that inscribe my own body. With Anzaldúa and other Chicano/as, I join in the *mythos* of this border as also between a Nahua-speaking ancestry and a Spanish one, and a *mestizaje* of much more that is reconfigured with each generation. We imagine and enflesh this *mestizaje,* reproducing ourselves as protean beings who forge new terrain with ancient and new mangled ingredients as we move, step by step. As Anzaldúa puts it, "I write the myths in me, the myths I am, the myths I want to become. The word, the image and the feeling have a palpable energy, a kind of power" (Anzaldúa 93).

Like Anzaldúa and other Chicano/as, I work in the re-membered Aztec cosmology that the *tlamatinime* and the *tlacuilo* inhabited, transformed and fraught by modern colonial conditions. Following Mignolo's posing and exploration of the question "Was the *tlamatini* also a *tlacuilo?*" (254), Laura E. Pérez ventures her own response:

> While the crucial question of cultural differences Mignolo is mindful of does not seem to have been lost on writers like Anzaldúa and Cherríe Moraga…interestingly, they have appropriated these concepts in ways that suggest the return of what may have been lost in Eurocentric translations. More often than not, they conflate the Nahua concepts of the *tlacuilo* and *tlamatinime* in their reimagining of writers, visual, and

performance artists as glyph-makers, that is, as makers of signs that point beyond themselves, to significations that are spiritually and politically interdependent and simultaneous, and that hold ancient but relevant alternative knowledges. Chicana/o artists' collapse of glyph-makers and their sage readers, the *tlamatinime,* operates through their perception of both through metaphor of the divinely attuned artist as "Toltec," wise beyond technical mastery to a deep sense of the sacred purpose of her or his material practices, and therefore able to assist those who hold the work in the lifelong process of 'making face, making soul.' (Pérez, 27-8)

Inhabiting the Toltec—or allowing its possession of oneself—signals a striving for a decolonial vision of the world that guides the mutually constitutive acts of interpreting and producing it. The "sacred [read political, following Pérez] purpose" of MARFITA is largely to respond to my grandmother's command to me over the phone once to write about our family. It is also motivated by something in a letter she once wrote me, responding to a question I asked her: "Nana, what are our indigenous roots?" She responded (to my English with her Spanish): "*Lo siento mijo. Lo unico que yo se es que creo nosotros los mexicanos benemos de los Astecas y Spañoles* (sic). / I'm sorry, son. The only thing that I know is that we Mexicans come from the Aztecs and the Spanish." With others who think modernity and coloniality as the two sides of a coin, I see this loss of access to one's own memories as a violent colonial imposition required for modernity's success. More directly, MARFITA is a response to impositions by the same art world indicted earlier, much closer to home in West Texas, indeed, at the very edge of my grandfather's childhood backyard. In what might be defined by that world, and the cosmology in which it resides, as an "aesthetic" project, I am claiming here as a political and spiritual launch against those very terms, even with its own materials and in its own venues (reclaimed and radically repurposed though it, CoLab, will be during and afterward). At stake are my own face and soul, and those of my families, then those of Chicano/as, then those of all fractured beings living in/as the open wounds of borders and colonial legacies. I am "reimagining" myself resistantly as glyph-maker rather than artist. Again, I am not only choosing not to choose "artist" (or "academic") in the postmodern sense, but have sought out, and joined in the imagining of a grounded decolonial option, and am going for *tlacuilo-tlamatini,* Toltec. My methodology has the germ of its logic here.

CONCLUSION: "AUTOTOPOGRAPHY"

In the introduction to *Subject to Display: Reframing Race in Contemporary Installation Art*, Jennifer A. González re-introduces her term "autotopography":

> The production of an autotopography is a spatial practice, but also a semantic practice that produces a grammar of juxtaposition that follows its own narrative logic. Existing as a collaborative prosthesis or skeletal armature to a life story, it has in common with public museums the imperative of archiving and preservation. Unlike museum displays, however, autotopographies generally do not produce rational taxonomies or categorical frameworks. Like an autobiography, an autotopography can be uneven, ambivalent, and by equal measures confessional or dissimulating, but it is also always a practice of claiming ontological rights through the preservation and display of personal objects: the right to exist, the right to a story, and the right to a territory, whether imaginary or actual, where the psyche of the subject dwells and leaves behind a physical trace. (González 19)

I take González's term as a further articulation of the creative agency I want to practice. I find it liberating that autotopographies "do not produce rational taxonomies or categorical frameworks." I include in my understanding of these "frameworks" those of the mainstream art world that, whatever claims it may make, still accords to a "virtuous" aesthetic as Anzaldúa describes it, "The aesthetic of virtuosity, art typical of Western European [Euro-American] cultures, attempts to manage the energies of its own internal system such as conflict, harmonies, resolutions and balances" (Anzaldúa 89-90). As Anzaldúa does, González also makes room for ambivalence, and furthermore, reads it as inherent in autotopographical projects. I take this as part of a methodology for thinking from the colonial difference, allowing modernity and coloniality to come through together in all their conflicting characteristics (though with the same aims).

González because she formulates her term in a reading of [installation art]—which, from a Toltec perspective, must be bracketed as a term pointing away from the decolonial in participating in the framework of "virtuous aesthetics"—while Anzaldúa is thinking particularly about [writing] which must also now be bracketed. With autotopography, I can reconsider the materials we take up in MARFITA against the grain of the "virtuous aesthetic." It is the aesthetic, and its cosmology, that I resist. I look forward, with some anxiety but without hesitation, to working out whether or not we will fall into its traps, which are admittedly desirable, or maintain the spiritual, political, and communal inspiration and approach of the *tlacuilo-tlamatini;* whether or not I/we can inhabit and practice a Toltec methodology.

ENDNOTES

1 *Two Face: Aaron Curry and Thomas Houseago*, May 14 – August 1 2009, Ballroom Marfa.

WORKS CITED

Anzáldua, Gloria. *Borderlands/La Frontera*. San Francisco: Aunt Lute Books, 1987. Print.

Crow, Thomas. *Painters and Public Life in Eighteenth-Century Paris*. New Haven: Yale University Press, 1987. Print.

Debord, Guy. Internationale Situationniste #2, Dec 1958.

González, Rita, Howard N. Fox, Chon A. Noriega. *Phantom Sightings: Art After the Chicano Movement*. Los Angeles: Los Angeles County Museum of Art, and Berkeley & Los Angeles: University of California Press, 2008. Print.

González, Jennifer A. *Subject to Display: Reframing Race in Contemporary Installation Art*. Cambridge: MIT Press, 2008. Print.

Kusch, Rodolfo. *Indigenous and Popular Thinking in América*. Trans. Maria Lugones and Josh M. Price. Durham and London: Duke University Press Books, 2010. Print.

Mignolo, Walter. *The Darker Side of the Renaissance: Literacy, Territoriality, & Colonization*. Ann Arbor: University of Michigan Press, 1995. Print.

Pérez, Laura E. *Chicana Art: The Politics of Spiritual and Aesthetic Altarties*. Durham and London: Duke University Press, 2007. Print.

Sandoval, Chela. *Methodology of the Oppressed*. Minneapolis: University of Minnesota Press, 2000. Print.

CHALLENGING THE ACADEMY ONE NOPAL AT A TIME

MARCOS DEL HIERRO

It is a typically hot Sunday afternoon in Bryan-College Station. My partner and I are in the produce section of HEB. If you know anything about this area, you know that the HEB in Bryan is where you go for tortillas, bulk-dried chiles, productos Bimbo, Marinela, Choco-Milk, and nopalitos. If you need certified organic, aloe-vera-infused products, and want to pay extra money for sleek packaging, rather than keep a plant at home like our mothers taught us, then you go to the College Station HEB. Wear your flashiest name-brand running gear too.

Every week I pick out my bag of fresh nopalitos out of the large ice bin. This moment always reminds me of the markets in Juárez and El Paso, where you always find nopalitos pre-sliced or whole. It is normal to see people removing the spines and bagging them in the store, ensuring freshness. I love nopalitos in all forms: in a liquado with pineapple, raw as a snack food, with scrambled eggs, and sautéed with beans.

On this particular March afternoon, two elderly white women stop next to me. The one with the bluish cotton candy hair asks, "Have you actually eaten those?" She points at my bag of nopalitos like a dare. Something foreign, strange, and uncanny.

I smile. "All the time. They're delicious."

"Really?" she says.

I smile wider. "Really."

"How do you eat those?" she asks, still pointing. When people ask this question, I imagine that they imagine I'm eating the spines in a bowl as if they were cereal: *Nopali-O's! Part of a balanced breakfast!* I also imagine they think I am participating in some eating fad or new, adventurous, and sexy cuisine—as if Bobby Flay will serve nopalitos in some sort of chipotle concoction with acai-infused salsa at his signature New York and Las Vegas restaurants. People in *couture* and chunky glasses will sample the food and usher the next wave of *haute cuisine* by furiously waving a nopal paddle in the air. Maybe the next *Iron Chef* challenge will be nopalitos, and as soon as the host unveils them, the chefs will break into feverish sweats, declaring instant forfeit. Of all the exotic ingredients in the world, this one truly stumps. Meanwhile, the kitchen staff in the back—the actual cooks—shake their heads and laugh, deciding whether they want nopalitos con chile colorado or in a salad with radishes.

But this woman's wonder at how I prepare my nopalitos seems genuine, and I remember Gloria Anzaldúa's urge that we need white allies and that "[t]hrough our literature, art, *corridos*, and folktales we must share our history with them" to bridge communities and recognize a mutual desire for social justice (107). So I finally reveal my ancient culinary secret, one passed down from generation to generation: "Usually sautéed with some olive oil, onion, and tomato. Makes a healthy meal."

I hold the bag out to her, but today is not for leaps of faith. She stares at the green bag and laughs uncomfortably. "Maybe some other time." Both ladies walk away, marveling at what people consider food. My partner looks at me in disbelief. She scoffs at the way these women looked at our dinner and at us. Their attitude towards our food reflects their views of our community and culture.

She shakes her head. "How convenient that we serve as entertainment."

"I know. White people be trippin.'"

A week later, I'm sitting in a course on Native rhetorics taught by Qwo-Li Driskill where we learn and discuss ways of knowing that actively challenge assumptions that the only valid ways of understanding the world come from the heteropatriarchal European system that dominates how many think within our society. We also learn how many of our practices, from the everyday to the formation of government institutions in the United States, are tied to indigenous practices. We discuss how there are stories, knowledges, and memories taught, stored, and communicated through the body. The class feels like a breath of fresh air because for once, I feel validated as a person, scholar, and thinker. Whereas in other classrooms people dismiss me when I challenge Western ways of thought, in this classroom I feel enabled. As a matter of fact, there are others like me just as angry and frustrated from their other classroom experiences.

Knowing that this safe space allowed for my own contributions without fear or ridicule, I shared that I made nopalitos on a regular basis and that they were "Off the hook!"—especially when *I* made them. I also told the class that the act of making them, like my grandmother and mother taught me, "did" something for me that I felt in my spirit. My mother and grandmother made them often because along with fideo, beans, and jalapeños, they are relatively cheap, nutritious, and filling. During my busboy days at Rita's Mexican Fiesta Café in San Antonio, Texas, Leo, one of the cooks, would make nopalitos with pinto beans for the kitchen staff because that's what he and his brothers ate back at his family's ranch in San Luis Potosí. Leo would send someone to the nearest supermarket for some nopalitos. As soon as the owner went into her office, Leo's nod told us dinner was ready. A belly full of nopalitos, beans, and tortillas fed us much better than anything on the menu.

In my apartment, gently stirring my nopalitos as they sauté on the cast-iron skillet makes me feel good. This is an act of communion. The green aroma, my motions, and the fire from the stove create a culinary-meditative state that protects me and nurtures my spirit. The anticipation of the meal infuses my entire body with happiness. I place two warm corn tortillas on a plate and carefully fill each one with the nopalitos. Sometimes I add beans, other times I add cheese. Next to the plate, I place my plastic container of salsa next to it. How I plate my food belongs to the entire process. Eating them with corn tortillas and spicy chile reenergizes my body and spirit. For the duration of the preparation and meal, I am no longer in College Station, Texas. I am in my own, private space. I'm reminded of how Anzaldúa thinks of the connection between food and memory:

> There are more subtle ways that we internalize identification, especially in the forms of images and emotions. For me food and certain smells are tied to my identity, to my homeland… Even now and 3000 miles away, I can see my mother spicing the ground beef, pork and venison with chile. My mouth salivates at the thought of the hot steaming tamales I would be eating if I were home. (83)

Makes your mouth water, right? Similar to Anzaldúa, I often remember those dishes unique to my family, especially those always-available staples that I took for granted as a child, but now beg for on the daily. Food scholar Meredith Abarca talks about temporality as an important aspect of cooking and eating because "the aesthetics of the moment as generated by culinary artistic creations are an engagement in a participatory relation" to our surroundings, environment, and each other (*Voices…* 101). Recognizing that these moments call for our bodies, minds, and spirits to collectively experience food also calls to mind the power of the ordinary as a radical way of challenging Western notions and assumptions about knowledge and aesthetics. Over-privileging textual-based knowledges, as the West does, makes us ignorant of how other knowledges and conversations, such as those provided by food, create different and important pathways to greater understanding and agency.

I wanted to share this with my classmates because it is one of the most important ways I prevent losing my mind in a social and academic atmosphere not friendly to people of color even though we often receive emails and invitations to events filled with slogans claiming the promotion of diversity, the value of perspectives, and the virtues of cross-cultural dialogue. They provide diversity reports, scholarships, and events programming funding, and it all feels so disingenuous considering the poor retention rates of Chican@ students. Within my close-knit circle of friends, we all agree we feel unsafe, unwanted, and ignored. Growing up in Juárez-El Paso, I always felt I belonged. When I moved to Central Texas, the Brazos Río Valley, and the academy the label of "atravesado" was imposed on me. Like Anzaldúa warns us, "The only 'legitimate' inhabitants are those in power, the whites and those who align themselves with whites" (26). When I hear professors and classmates make hurtful, ignorant, and racist statements with so much freedom, sometimes obliviousness, and always privilege, I strain every muscle in my body to keep from screaming. I considered keeping a running tally of racist moments on campus, but I am afraid of confirming numerically what I already know.

For me, the preparation and consumption of nopalitos functions as a moment where out of memory and the kitchen, I create a sense of belonging. This practice informs my work because the ability to create roots exists in my family, community, and traditions. Abarca details how she had this realization one day while teaching a course she created, entitled, "Women Philosophers in the Kitchen." Memories of smelling her mother's "freshly made refried beans with *chorizo* or *papas con chorizo y huevo* (sic)" and helping her mother make flour tortillas vitally inform her pedagogy and academic work because these moments continue nourishing her "spiritually, emotionally, and intellectually" (*Mi Fronteridad...* 277). Our work should create safe spaces for those who are in equal search of comfort, and our work should provide nourishment for others seeking change and transformation. As part of her kitchen-based methodology, Abarca defines the rhetorical concept of the "sazón" as "the sensory-based logic of cooking, which is highly personalized but socially changed" (*Voices* 11). In other words, two people making the same dish will yield different results based on varieties of interconnecting factors because "[e]ach person's sazón [...] carries personal, cultural, and social messages that exceed the preparation of a meal" (71). Abarca applies this methodology to her pedagogy and academic work explaining that two people may teach in the same field, but each will also yield different results. And it is in the ways that we prepare and season our particular works that will make our messages palatable and interesting to others.

Diana Taylor asks the question, "How does expressive behavior (performance) transmit cultural memory and identity?" (xvi). In asking this question, she also wonders how dominant methods of storing and transmitting knowledge exclude people and communities, especially those systemically marginalized from access and availability. In *The Archive and the Repertoire,* she states, "If performance did not transmit knowledge, only the literate and powerful could claim social memory and identity" (xvii). As someone working in academia, it is easy to forget our hyper-dependence on alphabetic writing as the preferred method of conducting research, creating conversations, and establishing scholarly credibility. It is easy to forget that our heads belong to bodies equally important to our work and that when we walk into the classroom or the conference panel, we are not heads floating into rooms.

Helena María Viramontes recognizes that the ability to write is "a privilege limited to a certain sex, race, and class" that often excludes Chicanas from being able to exercise their imaginations on the page (34). She credits part of her creativity to the inventiveness her mother exercised when cooking for a family of eleven with a limited budget. She states, "Time and time again, I saw her cut four pork chops… and miraculously feed all of us with a tasty guiso [or] the nopales she grew, cleaned, diced, scrambled with egg, or meat, or chile…" (34). While admitting she never has "been able to match her [mother's] nopales," she has "inherited her capacity for invention." If we are to recognize the privileged space those of us inside the academy inhabit, while remembering Meredith Abarca's call to recognize that intellectual labor occurs in our kitchens, we may also recognize how the academy works to separate us from our families, traditions, and cultures by convincing us through elitism that we should ignore the knowledges with which our communities blessed and armed us, and follow the path of the Western scholar. When my sister graduated from college five years ago, I remember sitting in the audience with my entire family, cheering the heck out of our section because she was the first in our family to graduate from a far-away college. When they recognized all the *summa cum laudes* in the room, my mother said, "¡Ah que no pueden cocer una holla de frijoles!" My mother, Gloria Del Hierro, is hilarious, insightful, and brilliant. We value certain kinds of "academic" work while ignoring other kinds of work that inquire, perform, critique, and respond to the academy and the conversations it contains.

Food philosopher Lisa M. Heldke argues that Western thinkers like Plato have ignored and discredited food growing and making because they see both activities as primarily bodily labors. Heldke goes so far to declare that had he "taken foodmaking seriously… Plato would not have developed that particular craft/art distinction… nor would he probably have distinguished as he does between knowledge and opinion, theory and practice" (203). To dominant Western thought, everyday work, like foodmaking, takes time away from the "higher" labors, which privilege passive, contemplative activities. These "higher" forms of work also privilege removal from one's object of study/work because it allows for a distance Plato felt allowed for objectivity. Foodmaking involves a direct, personal relationship with the tools, measurements, raw materials, and emotions of the cook. Foodmaking privileges sensory knowledges of the body that determine taste, style, presentation, and method that make the practice highly subjective and difficult to classify and control according to Plato's preferences. Thus, in the academy, where Plato still reigns as one of its cornerstones of thought, foodmaking receives little thought and attention as a tool for inquiry and knowledge-making. Heldke explains how these ideas still root themselves beyond the academy and into contemporary society:

> Plato's hierarchy of kinds of human/parts of the soul makes its way into present-day life in the way that certain kinds of 'manual' labor are ranked below certain forms of 'intellectual' labor. This ordering can be seen in the way that the work of farmers, homemakers, and other such 'manual workers' is subordinate to the 'knowing professions' like bio-chemistry, genetics, and other sciences. (211)

In addition, when food does receive attention, it occurs in an elitist fashion. Heldke writes that when food-making receives the scholarly treatment, as a "theoretical activity," the practitioners are "middle- and upper-class cooks who invest enormous amounts of money in equipment and ingredients, to produce food that is 'innovative' and 'artistic'" (213). My earlier allusions to the Food Network Stars' would-be treatment of nopalitos speak to this phenomenon. When food becomes an aesthetic status symbol denoting Western notions of high art, all the food-makers, such as my mother and grandmother, who make food as a daily practice, find their experiences silenced and erased. As a Chicano male, who firmly roots his development and growth as an academic scholar in the teachings of two Glorias Del Hierro (my mother and grandmother), Meredith Abarca, and Gloria Anzaldúa, I find little use for Plato's definitions of valuable people and labor, as they have been used to beat me, while it is in strong, brilliant Chicanas that I have found the sustenance to survive.

I start with heating the olive oil. The wispy lines of smoke tell me when to add the carefully chopped onion. I breathe the aroma in while I give the bright green nopalitos a quick rinse, and I steal a few because I like their crunch. As the water runs through them, they release some of their viscous nutrition. I imagine the elderly woman with the cotton-candy hair wretch at the thought of slimy nopalitos. When the onions bits brown, I add the nopalitos to the heat. Next I chop a tomato and garlic clove, which I add towards the end of the process. Whenever I reach this step, I transport back to the home of Maria Camacho, my partner's grandmother, in Harlingen, Texas. In early January of 2010, we all stood by her bed as she resisted her cancer until it was too much. Family from all over both sides of the border traveled to say goodbye, and I remember her cousin telling me that she used to walk to Maria's house with a bag of nopalitos and tomatoes because that's the way she preferred to eat them. They spent afternoons eating, catching up on family gossip, and talking about their lives. Rather than a phone call, they preferred seeing each other over meals. Although I never shared a plate of nopalitos with her, as I make them, I think of her. We make communion this way.

As I write this, I also transport back to the graduate program at the University of Texas at El Paso, where I stand inside of Meredith Abarca's office admitting that I had heard of that name, but I had never read any of her work. She looks at me surprised, that a young Chicano so interested in making change and riddled with hurt and anxieties about identity would not have encountered the work of Gloria Anzaldúa. I smile, embarrassed, but quick to point out that although my undergraduate academic experience seldom offered opportunities to study or read anyone remotely connected to my experience, I clumsily found some stuff on my own. I read Ricardo Sánchez, Lalo Delgado, and Sandra Cisneros while hidden from the classism, elitism, and racism prevalent on campus. She reached into her bookshelf and loaned me a copy of *Borderlands/La Frontera* and pointed at the door. I am not to talk to her again until I read.

Instantly, I am hooked. It is as if she walked with me the moment my immigrant parents sent me off to school on my own, knowing nothing about the school systems here, the Spanish I would abandon for English, and the assimilation we would be taught in the classroom. She speaks to me brilliantly without depending on the awkward and quite frankly boring academic language that the stuffy professors claimed made for the proper way to communicate important ideas. She explains to me how white supremacy creates and maintains exclusion. She says "*Los atravesados* live here: the squint-eyed, the perverse, the queer, the troublesome, the mongrel, the mulato, the half-breed, the half dead; in short, those who cross over, pass over, or go through the confines of the 'normal'" (25). I would like to add the nopal-eater to this list. I realized that the mere act of my existence within the university is already/always to be an atravesado because I was never meant to be here. I begin understanding why I struggled to finally walk the stage at Baylor University. Why after having been a model student for the first three years, I fell into a deep depression that caused me to fail and drop out. Why my parents looked at me, helpless, unable to understand why I lost all desire to finish what I started. Why it took years, and perhaps even the moment Gloria started talking to me, to acknowledge that what took me under was an oppressive system that makes you wonder about your own sanity when you question it. As a result, she explains that Chican@s engage in self-hate, self-blame, and self-terrorism that mostly "…goes on unconsciously; we only know that we are hurting, we suspect that there is something 'wrong' with us, something fundamentally 'wrong'" (67). When forces seek to discredit you, and when you lack a community willing to listen, explain, and bear your burden alongside theirs, what choices do you really have?

That is the moment when we must look to ourselves, our communities, and our traditions because those are the places where we find the nourishment we need to keep fighting and resisting. A semester before finishing my master's degree, Meredith Abarca and I talked about my desire to pursue a PhD. I admitted my fear of leaving Juárez-El Paso once again because the trauma I felt the first time as an undergraduate student led to the darkest times in my life. The idea of uprooting once again froze me. She wondered if one could establish roots in one place and learn how to maintain those roots while creating new ones in another location. The kitchen and cooking is one such avenue where I have found a place for solace and rest. A major ingredient in that process is a heaping portion of recalling those roots back home and enabling them to nourish me through my plates of nopalitos. Through keeping my family, ancestors, and community involved in my kitchen, I find myself resisting what often seems overwhelming. From there, I gain the strength to take my next step.

WORKS CITED

Abarca, Meredith E. "*Mi Fronteridad* in the Classroom: The Power of Writing and Sharing Stories." *Folklore: In All of Us, In All We Do.* Ed. Kenneth L. Untiedt. Denton, TX: U of North Texas P, 2006. 273-80. Print.

----. *Voices in the Kitchen.* College Station, TX: Texas A&M P, 2006. Print.

Anzaldúa, Gloria. *Borderlands/La Frontera: The New Mestiza.* San Francisco: Aunt Lute Books, 1987. Print.

Heldke, Lisa M. "Foodmaking as a Thoughtful Practice." Curtin, Deane W. and Lisa M. Heldke, eds. *Cooking, Eating, Thinking: Transformative Philosophies of Food.* Bloomington, IN. Indiana UP, 1992. 203-229. Print.

Taylor, Diane. *The Archive and the Repertoire: Performing Cultural Memory in the Americas.* Raleigh, NC: Duke UP, 2003. Print.

Viramontes, Helena María. "'Nopalitos': The Making of Fiction." *Breaking Boundaries: Latina Writing and Critical Readings.* Ed. Asunción Horno-Delgado, et al. Amherst, MA: U of Massachusetts P, 1989. 33-38. Print.

THE ROAD OF A *NEPANTLERA*: REMEMBERING BECKY

LINDA WINTERBOTTOM

I dedicate this essay to my friend Becky Cross who was, quite possibly, Gloria Anzaldúa's number one fan.

I came to Gloria Anzaldúa through the enthusiasm of my friend Rebecca Cross during the first year of our doctoral program at UTSA. A transgender woman living in silence about her true identity for many years, Becky's devotion to Anzaldúa's work was deeply personal. But I didn't know Becky then; I only knew her outward male persona, Ray. Then Gloria Anzaldúa came to town and everything changed. With Anzaldúa's visit to the Esperanza Center, Ray—the sanctioned outward person—and Becky—the yearning inward person—took bold steps in articulating her gender identity. As a source of theoretical power, Anzaldúa's ideas were crucial to Becky at this time. She began the process of declaring her female identity to others, a bold step that would lead to her eventual decision to undergo sexual reassignment surgery.

In our first year of the doctoral program, I knew Becky as Ray, a 50-ish graduate student, intelligent, funny in a wry sort of way, a father, a talented fixer-of-anything, and a terrific storyteller. We were reading Gloria Anzaldúa's *Borderlands/ La Frontera* in Sonia Saldívar-Hull's class. We were also taking Bridget Drinka's course The History of the English Language. We shared a routine of meeting at the library at the same time each week to study together. The week of Anzaldúa's visit to the Esperanza Center, Ray was enthused, carrying a stash of the colorful event invitation cards and doling them out to friends. I remember meeting at the library that day, Ray giving me an invitation and encouraging me to attend the lecture. It was clearly very important to him.

On the night of the talk, I climbed to the second floor at the Esperanza Center. At the top of the stairs stood a woman who looked just like Ray. "That *MUST* be Ray's sister," I remember thinking. Becky turned away and another friend of hers stepped forward to introduce us. "You might know Becky by another name," she said. But I was caught off guard with a crowd behind me, and unsure of what to say. It wasn't until after the lecture that I had the presence of mind to hug my friend and tell her it was good to see her. I returned home in shock and spent the weekend dwelling on this revelation of my friend's other side. In my ignorance, I worried there was "something wrong" with Ray, but I couldn't be more wrong. On the contrary, for Becky things were finally becoming right. I had a lot to learn.

Anzaldúa's writing supported Becky as she worked to interrogate some of the constructs—binaries in particular—that reinforced her imposed male gendering. From childhood, she felt female but was compelled to perform the masculine. Ray played the part of a son inheriting a paternal military tradition. He was a twenty-two year combat veteran and Special Forces medic. But in private, she was Becky. She tried to give her Becky-self some room to breathe, but that must have been hard. Becky's opportunities to leave the house were limited. I wonder—did she feel at times broken in pieces, like Coyolxauhqui? Or did she feel like a "fusion of opposites" (Anzaldúa 69) —always on the verge of "rupturing," as in Anzaldúa's "*Coatlicue* state" (7)?

But that semester, reading Gloria Anzaldúa filled her with energy and a sense of possibility. That first year of the doctoral program, Becky was laying critical groundwork—mapping out the theoretical framework she needed to make her move. By the end of that academic year, Becky transitioned openly and began preparing for a major journey—sexual reassignment surgery—which she would, ultimately, complete in 2005, right after attending and speaking at the First Pan-Asian Sexualities Conference in Bangkok, Thailand.

Becky died in July of 2006, on her way back from the Diné College in the Navajo Nation where she and a colleague journeyed each summer for creative and pedagogical work. During those visits, taken over five years, Becky and her friend collaborated on a writing pedagogy based on their experiences with Navajo student-writers. When she headed to Arizona that summer, she packed her draft dissertation chapters and notes. All that summer, when she wasn't teaching, or learning how to weave, Becky was hard at work, writing her dissertation. A few days before her death, she mentioned by email to a colleague that her manuscript was nearly complete. But Becky never returned to us. On the way home, she suffered a ruptured aorta. Maybe it was all those years of combat tours and narco-trafficking operations, the intense stress of running miles and miles through jungles under the weight of heavy gear and bullet-fire. Becky's heart had been through too much. The stitches would not hold. Her aorta could not be mended.

Becky wanted to live an honorable and productive life—and she was doing so. She was writing, reading papers at conferences, serving as an active member in several organizations. Her life was just opening up when she fell. With Becky's sudden disappearance from our lives, we, her friends and colleagues, mourned the friend we knew and loved, but also the scholar and writer whose bloom was cut short. To make matters worse, communications with her family grew strained. We waited and waited for word of the memorial service they told us would happen—but word never came. In death, as in much of her life, Becky was to be silenced and hidden away once again.

Finally, in August, we—her friends, other graduate students—held a memorial service for her at the Esperanza Center. Our department relayed words of caution:

the family had learned of our plans and they were angry. We were nervous, but we moved forward with our arrangements to honor and say goodbye to our friend. We gathered readings, planned a service, and decorated the Esperanza Center with flowers and a length of gauzy, shimmery orange fabric to symbolize a bridge. There was an iconic photo of Ray, in military gear, standing at the far end of a suspension bridge, looking back over his shoulder. A few of us considered that photo and the gesture it captured—the backward glance from the far side of a bridge—to be the quintessential image of Becky-in-transition. There had to be a bridge.

We had our service. It was beautiful.

* * *

For months afterwards, many of us dreamt of Becky. The gist was that Becky was at peace, even though the rest of us were not—not at all. We saw Becky everywhere: entering buildings on campus, striding across plazas, disappearing around corners in the library stacks—she even appeared at somebody's dissertation defense. Never content to take it easy while living, it seemed that Becky was maintaining a full schedule in the afterlife.

WHAT ANZALDÚA MEANT TO BECKY

Becky thrived on Anzaldúa's writing, which liberated and empowered her in her decision to begin coming out. AnaLouise Keating credits Anzaldúa's body of work with "giv[ing] courage and inspiration to many." Describing her writings as "complex, multidimensional," and "versatile," Keating calls Anzaldúa "one of the boldest feminist thinkers and social justice activists of our time" ("Remembering"). In "Reading National Identities: The Radical Disruptions of *Borderlands/La Frontera*," Beth Berila writes:

> Anzaldúa interrogates dominant conceptions of nation and identity, exploring whether and how it might be possible to develop a sense of

national identity that doesn't exclude and do violence to women and men of color and those who are poor or queer. The text's experimental form foregrounds the contestatory narratives of national identity, revealing the histories of colonization, exploited labor, and racism that make possible dominant national narratives. In doing so, it invites readers to enact a similar interrogation of national identities and their performances, offering us opportunities to critically locate ourselves in these narratives' formations and learn less violent ways to read national contestations. (121)

Becky deeply contemplated those national identities. She lived one for a long time, in a uniform. But as a graduate student, her journey was all about interrogating and deconstructing those hegemonic narratives. I will never forget the day she took a small box out of the cupboard over her desk, showed me the Special Forces beret inside, put it on and—striking a pose in her long skirt and stylish black boots—said: "Here I am! The army's worst nightmare!" In Berila's remarks above, she observes the "experimental form" of Anzaldúa's text and what that accomplishes; she claims that it "foregrounds" what is "contestatory" about those national narratives of identity. Did Becky's gender performance and her body take on an experimental form? Her juxtaposition of her Special Forces garb with her performance of Becky in high-heeled boots is nothing if not "contestatory."

In *Borderlands/La Frontera*, Anzaldúa describes a "validation vision" in which marginalized subjects "take back and uncover our true faces, our dignity and self-respect" (109). This possibility spoke to Becky. Anzaldúa's visit to the Esperanza Center emboldened Becky to take the first steps toward announcing her transition within our academic community at UTSA. Anzaldúa's writing offered a way forward where there had been none before. By transitioning from the performance of Ray to that of Becky, Becky asserted the identity she had always known to be her "true face"—and her right to express herself as Becky with "dignity." Part of Anzaldúa's visit to the Esperanza Center entailed a small group workshop prior to the evening talk. Becky attended that gathering, which gave her an opportunity to speak personally with Gloria.

Thereafter, Becky would study and write about notions of "performativity" and gender as a social construct. Bolstered by Anzaldúa's articulations of nepantla and mestiza consciousness, Becky undertook the major discursive and identitiary project of resolving painful ambiguity through the process of theorizing her experience of transgenderism.

NECESSARY RUPTURE

The painful state of ambiguity corresponds with what Anzaldúa, in *Borderlands*, calls "a constant state of mental nepantilism, an Aztec word meaning torn between ways" (100). AnaLouise Keating summarizes Anzaldúa's ongoing theorizing of nepantla in this way:

> Nepantla has multiple meanings that overlap and enrich each other. Nepantla represents liminal spaces, transitional periods in identity formation, or what she [has described in interviews] [...] as a 'birthing state where you feel like you're reconfiguring your identity and don't know where you are.' This in-between space facilitates transformation; as the boundaries break down, the identity categories that before were so comfortable—so natural, as it were—no longer work; they dissolve, compelling us to find new ways to define ourselves. Nepantla also functions as a metaphor for forbidden knowledges, new perspectives on reality, alternate ways of thinking. (Keating, *Interviews /Entrevistas* 5)

The concept of a nepantla state, a painful but necessary place of rupture, was crucial to Becky in her journey. During transition, her life was in a constant state of stress and upheaval; the concept of nepantla reminded her that the pain was only a stage and she was doing important work for her future.

Becky's involvement with the Esperanza Center and her direct engagement with Anzaldúa and scholars of Anzaldúan theory allowed her to be part of what Paul Gilroy has called a "communit[y] of interpretation, needs, and solidarity" (122). Becky was an active member of several groups and associations that promoted support and education around gender issues. In the year before she died, she was elected North American board member to the International Lesbian and Gay

Association and had attended the organization's world conference in Geneva, Switzerland. Becky was a transgender activist, a founding member of the San Antonio Gender Association, and a founding member of the Headwaters Coalition in San Antonio. Following Anzaldúa, she wanted to "creat[e] a new borderland space filled with a new meaning of self-in-community which bridges and balances two or more opposing worlds" (1).

Becky took an interest in Anzaldúa's ideas about developing "a subjectivity capable of transformation and relocation, movement guided by the learned capacity to read, renovate, and make signs on behalf of the 'dispossessed'" (Anzaldúa 7). This particular ability and skill Anzaldúa calls "la facultad" (Cross 5).

Becky explores Anzaldúa's description of la facultad as: "the capacity to see in surface phenomena the meaning of deeper realities, to see the deep structure below the surface. [...] It is an acute awareness mediated by the part of the psyche that does not speak, that communicates in images and symbols which are the faces of feelings, that is, behind which feelings reside/hide. The one possessing this sensitivity is excruciatingly alive to the world" (Anzaldúa 8) (qtd. in Cross 5).

In a 1983 interview with Christine Weiland, Anzaldúa claims that queer subjects "have access to this other world" that she calls "la facultad." She explains: "In Santería you call it 'having the capacity, the faculty to.' It's almost like cultivating an extra sense that straight people don't have, or that straight people who are insane or persecuted, or poor whites or creative people have." Queer subjects "have it," she notes, "because it's a matter of survival. You're caught between two worlds." [...] "we had to confront what other people repress: their sexuality, their fear, their racism. We had to confront everything—all the stuff in them—that they projected onto us [...] I call us 'divine warriors' because we have to fight" (Keating, *Interviews/Entrevistas* 122).

Becky did have to fight. She had to perform the exaggerated masculine role of the militarized man, the tough soldier, the brave and self-reliant boy who could survive in the woods alone. If she went out in public as Becky, she was sometimes attacked. She was once assaulted in a laundromat. Waiting for a load of clothes to finish, Becky was loudly confronted by a man and ordered to leave. Her clothes were still going in the machine. She offered to leave as soon as the cycle finished and she could gather her clothes. But the man wouldn't wait; he attacked her. Of all the transgender people in San Antonio the man could have targeted, I doubt he could have found one with more combat training. Of the two, only Becky left the laundromat on her own two feet that day. But it did not have to be that way. Becky did not go looking for fights; it was the intolerant, blind in their fear and hatred, who, by attacking, made her fight.

When Anzaldúa contemplates "divine warriors," she notes, "It takes tremendous energy, courage, and perseverance to keep that awareness awake. So you start tapping into your strength, your source of power. Some of us don't. Some of us go mad, get locked up, get knifed in the streets, kill ourselves, or pass for straight" (interview with Weiland in Keating, *Interviews/Entrevistas* 122). Anzaldúa shows how costly it is to inhabit such liminal positions, to straddle two categories, as Becky did. And Becky did it with such grace and composure. Only now, as I consider all the pressures she endured, do I wonder what it must have felt like to "tap into her strength" day in and day out. It must have been exhausting. But Becky had deep reserves, and she called upon them to persevere in the intellectual work she cherished, both for herself and myriad others who suffer quietly.

Becky's writing nourished her work in the community and vice versa. Advocating for others may have even been crucial to her own survival. Such work building solidarity promotes the coping strategy Anzaldúa names as subjects mediate the discomforts of hegemonic society "by developing a tolerance for contradictions [and] ambiguity" (Anzaldúa, *Borderlands* 101). "She learns to juggle cultures. She has a plural personality" (Anzaldúa, *Borderlands* 101). This must have resonated for Becky. Having spent many years "torn between ways," she must have identified with this description of living with ambiguity—negotiating the hegemonic culture's bruising blows, juggling cultures imposed and imagined, and in short, multiplying herself, because that was the only way.

Had she lived, Becky was scheduled to read a paper at the Western States Rhetoric and Literacy Conference in Utah. The title of her paper was: "Transgender Diplomacy: Translating Gender Identity for the UN Commission on Human Rights." Her collaborator, a valued friend and colleague, went to the conference and read the paper for both of them. Becky leaves behind many friends, and we go on, remembering, trying to extend her narrative, which is like a rope bridge connecting two impossible cliffs. We tremble as we fasten a few more planks. The bridge sways a little over the chasm. The distance is vast. We are afraid. But we see Becky, far away, on the other side. We can barely make her out. Then she looks over her shoulder. She comes into focus as her smile meets the sun. That is when we know her and she is gone.

WORKS CITED

Anzaldúa, Gloria. *Borderlands/La Frontera: The New Mestiza.* Second ed. Introd. by Sonia Saldívar-Hull. San Francisco, Aunt Lute Books, 1999. Print.

Berila, Beth. "Reading National Identities: The Radical Disruptions of *Borderlands/La Frontera.*" *EntreMundos/Among Worlds: New Perspectives on Gloria Anzaldúa.* Ed. AnaLouise Keating. New York: Palgrave Macmillan, 2008. 121-128. Print.

Cross, Rebecca. "Mestiza Spirituality: Community, Ritual, and Justice." Unpublished essay. 21 November 2004. Print.

Davies, Carole Boyce. "Black Women, Writing, and Identity." *Migrations of the Subject.* London and New York: Routledge, 1994. Print.

Garber, Linda. "Spirit, Culture, Sex: Elements of the Creative Process in Anzaldúa's Poetry."Keating, *EntreMundos/Among Worlds: New Perspectives on Gloria Anzaldúa.* Ed. AnaLouise Keating. New York: Palgrave Macmillan, 2008. 213-226. Print.

Gilroy, Paul. *The Black Atlantic: Modernity and Double Consciousness.* Rev. ed. Cambridge: Harvard University Press, 1993. Print.

Keating, AnaLouise, ed. *EntreMundos/AmongWorlds: New Perspectives on Gloria Anzaldúa*. New York: Palgrave Macmillan, 2005. Print.

----. "Remembering Gloria Anzaldúa (1942-2004)." *Women's Review of Books* (October 2004). 4 June 2010 <http://www.wellesley.edu/Womens Review/archive/2004/10/highlt.html/>. Web.

---. "Shifting worlds, una entrada." Introduction. *EntreMundos/Among Worlds: New Perspectives on Gloria Anzaldúa*. New York: Palgrave, 2008. 1-12. Print.

---. *Interviews/Entrevistas*. New York: Routledge, 2000.

Mohanty, Chandra Talpade. *Feminism Without Borders: Decolonizing Theory, Practicing Solidarity*. Durham and London: Duke University Press, 2003. Print.

"Rebecca Lynn Cross (March 10, 1953 – July 7, 2006.)" Obituary. Nepantlera.org. 2009. Memorial Website. Ed. *Guides Through Nepantla*. 2009. 28 November 2011 <http://www.nepantlera.org/childhood.html/>. Web.

Zaytoun, Kelli. "Theorizing at the Borders: Considering Social Location in Rethinking Self and Psychological Development." *Feminist Formations* 18.2 (2006): 52-72. Print.

LA GLORIA ERES TÚ: THE INFLUENCE OF GLORIA ANZALDÚA ON MY LIFE AND ART

DEBORAH KUETZPALIN VASQUEZ

EL CONOCIMIENTO

When I met Gloria Anzaldúa I was really excited. I had read *Borderlands/La Frontera* as part of my English literature at Texas Woman's University and was completely turned on by her writing. The chair of the English Department at that time was a Chicano, Dr. Frank Longoria, and I had met with him because I had avoided taking the literature classes that were required as part of my degree. He came up to me after I had spoken at a demonstration and asked if I had time to meet with him after my last class. The National Organization for Women chapter on campus and I had launched a campaign challenging the University's decision to integrate men into this historically woman's institution. We were in the middle of sit-ins, camp-ins, and happenings when Dr. Longoria approached me and asked if I was still attending classes. I replied that I was attending some of my classes, but not the classes where my professors weren't supportive of this issue. He said he thought he might be able to help me with that. Dr. Longoria was well respected by other professors, and his opinion carried a lot of weight with the administration.

When we met, he said he noticed that I hadn't taken any of my literature courses and that I was well into my program. I told him I was avoiding having to read all those boring English authors like Shakespeare and Vonnegut, and I didn't want to pretend to like it, to appear as an intellectual. He laughed and said that what everyone said about me was pretty much on the nose. He offered to give me independent studies for my English lit courses and loaned me books by Chicana and Chicano authors, beginning with Gloria Anzaldúa. My God! I loved it. I felt like she was writing about me. Finally, I embodied Roberta Flack's *Killing Me Softly*. She made me feel scared and secure all at once that with all my (what other closeted lesbians called) craziness. I could be out, Raza, hang in the barrio, and still be okay in academia, community, and with myself.

EL ENCUENTRO

When I was living in Madison, I heard Gloria was coming to the university. I couldn't believe I might have the chance to meet her, so I began to do a little research to find out who was bringing her. It was my first year at the University of Wisconsin, so I wasn't as connected yet. She was going to keynote the Mujer Latina Conference and present a workshop. Since I was one of those Chicana, not Latina, mujeres, I was not involved with this conference but I knew Diana, a young woman who was on the conference committee. When I was getting information on Gloria, she mentioned that she was picking her up at the airport and asked if I wanted to go with her. OF COURSE, I WANTED TO GO! As we drove up to our tiny airport, there she stood, a little brown unassuming woman. She could have been one of my tías, a younger cool tía of course. I looked in her face, and I was moved. I knew I was meeting someone who would be significant in my life. I had brought Gloria a huge bouquet of tropicals with a card that read, "From one Tejana, Chicana, Lesbiana to another. Bienvenida a Madison!" She loved it and asked for my digits just in case she needed anything.

Her keynote was amazing. She spoke with such ease, as if we were all sitting in her living room. I have seen many people present. They use such academic terminology that, even though I can comprehend it, the jargon is tiring to withstand. Upon leaving those lectures, I always feel agitated and annoyed rather than uplifted, like a sermon on homosexuality at mass on Sunday. Finally, I thought a speaker that can inspire like those sermons were intended (are they really?) to do. It appeared that the students had been disillusioned with the Latin@s that had visited the university. So when she was scheduled to present at her workshop, I rounded up all the Chicanitas (young women) that hadn't been to the keynote. The ones that liked to hang out at either the Chican@ Studies lounge or at the MEChA (Movimiento Estudiantil Chican@ de Aztlán) office, because nothing else on campus was about them. I talked them into going to her workshop. "She's the real thing," I assured them, "You have to come see her speak."

The room was packed with students and community who had gotten the message of the importance of this little brown woman speaking. The students, faculty, and staff from Women's Studies who were predominantly white sponsored her visit took and all the first few rows, and the Chicana students who had classes way on up on Bascom Hill arrived to find all the seats taken. Chican@ Studies had also co-sponsored this event, but no seats were reserved for this population. The Chicanitas were extremely upset. One of the faculty saw this and asked Gloria if she would "ask some of the women in the front rows to give their seats so that some of the Chicanitas, who were also Tejanas, so they could be closer to their paisana (someone from the same place you are)." Whew! I was so glad I didn't have to say anything. Two of the women in the front row immediately stood and offered their seats to the mujercitas, but after some serious murmurs and whispers no one else relinquished theirs. bell hooks had been there some years before and the same situation occurred. Without being asked, hooks asked the White women in the first row to give up their seats, so that Black women could sit closer and refused to begin her presentation until this was done.

Gloria very seriously stated, "I won't do that and let me tell you why." She went on to explain that when she was a young professor trying to present and get published, the White men did not publish her because she was a Chicana, Chicanos would not publish her because she was a lesbiana, the Chicanas and Latinas didn't publish her because she was not writing in what they thought was proper academic prose, and the only ones who did publish her were the White

Jewish women. So no, she would never ask her White sisters to give up their seats. Everyone was astonished. With bewildered looks on their faces, some the Chicanitas turned to me with flushed red faces that appeared as though they were going to burst into tears. I shook my head no, not to cry and signaled them to follow me. We walked up to the front of the room where Gloria was going to begin her presentation and stood up against the left wall of the small auditorium. The young Chicanas were right behind, some went to the left, others went to the right. Some sat on the floor in front of the women in the first row. In a quiet, quick, and orderly manner the Chicanitas, and a few of our Black and White allies filled the whole area around the podium where she was about to present. She watched as this happening and then turned to look at me. She gave a slight smile and went on to present. Once again she was amazing.

La Noche de Cultura was scheduled for that evening, and I was performing a work called *My Body Bound* along with other members of my Performance Art Class. After my performance, I stayed clear of Gloria. I felt I did what I needed to do at her workshop, but it was really difficult since I have a deep respect for her and her work. Real respect, not the forced respect children, women, and people of color are brainwashed and manipulated into having. I like the term conciencia more than respect. Later, Gloria asked one of the organizers to ask me to join her at her book-signing table. What could I do but humbly take whatever regaño (scolding) Gloria had prepared to give me?

As I approached Gloria's table, I could see her surrounded by mujeres getting their books signed and taking snapshots with her. Apparently everyone was as smitten with her as I was. When she saw me she patted the seat next to her motioning for me to sit. Sitting with her at the book signing was incredible. I could feel the energy flowing from her to the women and vice versa. She was so great with everyone, how angry could she be with me? I began to feel more at ease. As soon as there was a little lull in the book signing, she turned to speak with me. I quickly began to explain why I felt the need to urge the young women to take their space, no matter whom it was they were to go up against. She quieted me very gently with that beautiful smile, a firm hand over mine, and in a soft voice said, "I know you did what you needed to do. Just like I did what

I needed to do." After that we hugged and took a great photo with our heads butted up against each other and huge closed mouth smiles. With that visit, I learned that even if I don't agree with someone it doesn't mean they are wrong or I am wrong. It's just a different way of approaching a situation.

After the Noche de Cultura, my compañera (life partner) and I took Gloria to get sugar-free snacks since she had just been diagnosed with diabetes. I was telling her about my mother's diabetes and that she was on dialysis. She talked about the urgency in reforming our eating habits within our community and that we needed to look back at traditional culture for the answers. I agreed.

LA INFLUENCIA

Gloria influenced my life and work immensely. When I heard her speak to the audience, I knew that was the way I wanted to present. I wanted the participants to be at ease, until we reached an area when they weren't supposed to be comfortable. Her manner of simplifying complex subjects while other writers just complicated them further was a trait she shared with my jefita (Chicana slang for mother). Reading her was like home in the cold environment of university, and the other mujeres felt it also. Which is why they were dissatisfied to be stuck in the back when this woman with whom they identified was speaking. That's what we're supposed to teach our young Chicanas. To just not accept their situations, but challenge issues and oppressive situation as insignificant as they may seem to others. With that visit I also realized that our young women felt disempowered, even within our own gente (people), and that concerned me. In our communities we may be taught to speak out against injustice at the hands of the other but to remain silent when injustices are committed amongst ourselves for the sake of the familia and community. This is happening in San Antonio within our non-profit organizations at this time, and I'm sure it's happening in other places also. Gloria brought to light the injustices committed against her by our own people while she was presenting to our people. That was phenomenal to me.

The ability to speak my truth dio a luz (was birthed) by this little brown woman's words and actions. And I keep saying "little brown woman" because in the culture in which we reside, and even our own culturas y familias, we almost demonize the small, the dark, the woman. What we're afraid of is the power within the mujeres, the morena (dark woman), the small stature, so we refuse to go inside and concentrate on the outside and fall into the security of our colonized minds. We all do it, even those of us who embody those magnificent dark brown bodies.

After her visit, I couldn't wait to get in my studio, to paint, construct and release all the emotions, the tensions, the pure truth within. The following week I created, *How To Tame A Wild Tongue*, after her popular story in *Borderlands* that references la hocicona (the woman that talks back). Hocicona was my middle name growing up as I voiced issues that seemed unfair to me as a kid. I can still hear my jefita saying, "Don't be so hocicona with your teachers, 'cause they're not going to like you, and they'll fail you." She knew la onda (the way things are) in school even though she only went to the 5th grade.

How To Tame A Wild Tongue is a mixed-media painting on red, white, blue burlap. A big blue-toned, white soft cushy hand sculpture jumps off the canvas and holds a thick-noosed rope. The noose is tied around a woman's big red burlap tongue, which also juts off the canvas. The picture plane is a brown silhouette of the Alamo in front of a tattered, and re-sewn Texas flag referring to the unraveling and patching of Texas history. On the Alamo view as an icon within popular culture, there is an outline of a little girl. The outline contains a face with an open mouth from which the tongue protrudes. Also on the brown silhouette is a red, white, and blue hand with writing on the oppressive situation of our mujeres.

Shortly after, came the birth of Citlali, la Chicana Super Hero. She is the manifestation of a colectiva of mujeres' strengths and weaknesses, our histories and our realities. Conceived through the love of two diosas (goddesses), she reaffirms the idea of magnificent women conceiving powerful women through traditional and contemporary teachings, oral histories and art, and most importantly, example. Gloria's example of truth in the face of disapproval paved the path of resistance for my strong-seated opinions about Chicana culture and the manner in which we should proceed to fully support the development of youth.

Citlali is a highly spiritual visionary and slightly clairvoyant. She is guided through life by a pantheon of female Mexican indigenous deities, i.e. Koyolxauki, Tlazolteotl, Tonantzin, Xochiquetzal, etc. with whom she interacts metaphysically and secularly. Rooted in cultura (culture) Chicana, San Anto style, Citlali balances her life with the search for wisdom from the extraordinary gente of her pueblo and the challenging of institutional oppression on local and global levels. She acknowledges that our inner strength and wisdom come from our indigenous roots. Citlali realizes that justice must result by any means necessary, (brother Malcolm is one of her heroes), and combats oppression con la verdad (truth), limpias (cleansings), spirituality and chingazos (fighting). Please remember that this is a cartoon character. Gloria knew the importance of traditional culture for the development and longevity of our people.

Although the Citlali work is about one individual and her familia and friends, it speaks of traición (betrayal) and intrigue, erotica and innocence, love and responsibility, tradition and contemporary issues. In Queer culture, lesbians are just like heterosexual women and we all endure the one or all oppressive actions at the hands of our Chicano brothers, white men, and sometimes our white sisters. We are also the oppressors in many instances. We cheat, betray, love, sexualize… we're human. Gloria did not idealize our lesbianism, our indigenousness, our womanhood. She just presented it with all it's beauty and flaws, and let the truth present our magnificence. Ours is a universal story that can be embraced by all people if they allow their minds to open a little.

Gloria spoke of sexuality in the same matter-of-fact way she spoke about other subjects. I handle my erotica work in the same straightforward way in the paintings, ceramic tiles and various boxes. The lovemaking between women is a cherished personal moment. The viewer is allowed to enter that world and take a tiny glimpse of this beauty. In the paintings the colorful, raised headdress placed on the erotic figures defines them as Mexican indigenous. The lyrical contour black lines delineate the two women as they interweave on large blocks of gold, bronze and copper canvas representing the various tones of our majestic mujeres. Love exudes from their bodies in the form of flowering scrolls and vines as enlarged pulsating hearts unfurl the anticipation of climax. The concept of the two female figures intertwined is influenced by the clay pre-Columbian sculptures posed in various sexual acts and the paintings of the Kama Sutra. The concept of exhibiting a personal moment between two women breaks down the relegated categories of the mujer Mexicana as a non-sexual Virgen de Guadalupe or a sex worker. After all, aren't we all sex workers in some aspect or another? We are beautiful, sensual mujeres who fall within all positions of those two polarities.

CAFÉ CITLALI: NACIDO DEL PENSAMIENTO ANZALDÚAN

Café Citlali was established to bring light to delicious comida Chicana y Mexicana that is good for you or at the very least didn't kill you. I do not have a degree in nutrition, but I attained knowledge from my ancestors, particularly my jefita Chave, who received her knowledge from her mother, Amá Juanita. Both passed from complications of diabetes as did Gloria. This wisdom was passed down through plàticas around kitchen tables and verified through consejos (advice), from curanderas (healers), cocineras (cooks), and books. This method of passing down tradiciones, we shared with community and anyone who cared to learn. We conducted discussions, workshops, and exhibitions that brought awareness to this disease that so strongly affects mujeres in oppressed communities. The food was based on "Las Siete Guerrilleras" (The Seven Warriors) of our indigenous bodies, i.e. corn, cactus, squash, beans, chile, amaranth grain, and maguey, in the form of agua miel (honey water) which is a nectar. Other traditional superfoods of traditional culture were served at the café, like spirulina (blue green algae) and chia. The Mexica (Aztecs) were called the mud eaters because they would skim the blue green algae of the top of Lake Texcoco. They called it tecuitlatl (stone's excrement), and sold it in the form of little cakes. The Spanish were ignorantly passing up one of nature's most perfect foods and one of the highest, if not the highest form of protein on the food chain. We also had monthly Saturday Community Discussion groups on the power of healing, followed by limpias, readings, and consejos by Doña Luz and/or other curanderas and card readers. Doña Luz would share her remedies for diabetes and other illnesses and ailments, as would other mujeres and young queers. The discussions led to many connections of our food to our ill health. In addition, the pláticas (round table discussions) took the form of intimate discussions on the future of mujeres and queers in Chicano Art.

In 2009, the Society for the Study of Gloria Anzaldúa was asking for submissions for the First International Conference of the Work and Art of Gloria Anzaldúa. I was working on a mixed-media portrait of Gloria, and I was experimenting with crayon, pencil color, oil pastels and watercolor on paper. The elements placed in the work were representational of Gloria. The yolotl (heart) is the huge heart Gloria carried while the xochitl (flower) reflected her beauty and charm. The tletl (fire) represented the fire she lit in the hearts of her students and everyone who ever came in contact with her work. The koatl (serpent) was her rebirth, which signified her ability to admit that something she was doing might not be working and her courage to make the change. The ketzalkoatl (plumed serpent) symbolizes energy and her ability to turn people on to our issues and the embrace of our culture. All the images were handled in raw sketchy strokes that were almost childlike. And since Gloria created this childlike experience I titled the work *La Magia de Gloria Anzaldúa* (The Magic of Gloria Anzaldúa). My friend Rita had seen the drawing I was working on and suggested that the committee view the work. It was chosen, and I couldn't have been happier.

At this conference I was asked by Antonia Castañeda to present on a panel with Santa Barraza and Liliana Wilson on Gloria's influence on our art. At that panel, I introduced a music video entitled *La Gloria Eres Tú*. The singer in the video is Olga Guillot, a Cuban performer with an amazing voice that is reverberant and clear with a celestial quality that is difficult to duplicate. Filtered and colorized images of Gloria and the work she has influenced fade in and off the screen as the music plays. I also presented the video at this year's conference and NACCS (National Association of Chicana and Chicano Studies Regional Foco in McAllen, Texas.

Café Citlali hostted a small portion of El Mundo Zurdo: And International Conference on Anzaldúan Thought and Art and Performance held in November of 2010. El Mundo Zurdo means 'the world to the left.' The events involved community through art, pláticas, and the ability to feel at ease to experience the Anzaldúan concept of the events through the lens of artists and community. The Koyolxauki Art Exhibition invited artists to submit completed art or create work with the splendid moon as woman as the subject matter. Koyolxauki is the Diosa de la Luna (goddess of the Moon), and Gloria was considered the Koyolxauki of our cultura, taking our dismembered bodies and putting them back together through her words and vision.

The last event we hosted at Café Citlali was *La Lunada: Aullidos a La Madre Luna,* an evening of sharing stories, poetry, songs, music, and other methods of calling on the power of Koyolxauki, La Madre Luna. It was held right outside of the side doors of Café Citlali. With a makeshift stage, background curtains, and blue spotlights, we created a warm, nurturing environment for the participants to unleash their talent. It was a cold, crisp night and we warmed our guests with fire-burning chimeneas (fireplaces). We huddled together and served chocolate mexicano and our gente performed amazingly. Everyone performed as if they were on stage at the Majestic Theatre. As performers we have learned to adapt to situations and still emerge doing outstanding work.

Although I prepare my images, PowerPoints, videos and whatever materials I will use, I pretty much shoot from the hip when presenting. Without writing down the words to my presentation, I am able to include or exclude details to conform to time constraints or audience. Writing my experience with Gloria Anzaldúa has given me great insight to my art, and myself. She has impacted almost every aspect of my life, from my opinion on self-identification to the advice on the foods for our indigenous bodies. One of my proudest moments has been when Liliana Wilson said to me in passing, "You know, Gloria had a postcard of Citlali on her desk. She really loved your character."

I realize many have had long-lasting friendships with her and know more information than I can ever imagine. Others may have researched more about her life and work to write brilliantly long papers. But as I write these words I am in awe of just how much she has influenced my work and illuminated the path I walk through the world.

ANZALDÚAN LITERARY/ POLITICAL THEORIES

ANZALDÚA'S BACKPACK: NAHUALA INVENTORIES OF NEW MESTIZA INDIGENISM

GEORGE HARTLEY

As one way of clarifying the potential value of what I elsewhere call Anzaldúa's Coatlicuean appropriations[1] of Chicana Indigenism, I will engage in an extended critique of what has become an influential work for attacks on Chicana appropriations of indigeneity, María Josefina Saldaña-Portillo's essay "Who's the Indian in Aztlán? Re-Writing Mestizaje, Indianism, and Chicanismo from the Lacandón" (2001), an essay subsequently worked into her very important book on *The Revolutionary Imagination in the Americas*.[2] Her argument does several important things, such as (1) critique the ongoing legacy of Mexican state Indigenismo; (2) highlight the tendency for 20th-century revolutionary regimes of subjection to adopt the regime of subjection characteristic of modern capitalist developmentalism; and (3) recognize the need for alliances between the various decolonization practices throughout the Americas. Saldaña-Portillo's critical gestures *could* help in the construction of a strategic solidarity movement on the lines of Leslie Marmon Silko's network of tribal coalitions (1991) by providing guidelines for judging the efficacy and implications of the various mestizajes across the continent. And if Saldaña-Portillo's charges against Anzaldúa were true, then we should pay attention to avoid such mistakes ourselves. I will argue, however, that Saldaña-Portillo's critique in the end contributes to the further fragmentation of North American decolonization movements by erasing up front the radical potential of refigurations of mestizaje such as Anzaldúa's new mestiza.

SALDAÑA-PORTILLO'S CRITIQUE OF MESTIZAJE AS BIOLOGISM

The immediate framing context for Saldaña-Portillo's critique of Anzaldúa's indigenism in *Borderlands* is the former's attempts to move the concept and trope of mestizaje beyond the biologism and ultimately anti-Indian nature of Mexican *indigenismo*. Her overall goal is "to recuperate a more sophisticated concept of mestizaje: one that might possibly extend political enfranchisement or literary representation to the broad range of subject positions implied by a common Mexican heritage" (280). She suggests that Anzaldúa opens with a "moving" metaphor for mestizaje that promises just such a sophisticated recuperation: the border as the open wound that is constantly torn back open before it can heal. This metaphor, in its constant back-and-forth wounding/ healing/wounding movement, "unsettles the conventional usage of mestizaje by restaging the brutality of the initial colonial encounter between Spaniard and Indian in the neocolonial encounter between the First World and Third World" (280). In addition, it "unsettles the conventional usage of mestizaje for Chicanos, as well" as for Mexicans, by interrupting "the teleological drive of mestizaje" (280) in the "Raza Cósmica" imagination that sees the mestizo as the prefiguration of humanity's futuristic product of miscegenation. (I should note here that also Anzaldúa draws from this same teleology elsewhere in *Borderlands* by turning to José Vasconcelos's notion of the Raza Cósmica [99].)

The heart of the problem, as Saldaña-Portillo points out, lies in the following:

> I would like to refocus our attention on the residual effect of this era
> of Chicano nationalism: the continued use of mestizaje as a trope for
> Chicana/o identity and the presumed access to indigenous subjectivity

that this biologized trope offers us. Although the deployment of mestizaje in the Southwest is different from its historical deployment in Mexico, when Chicana / o intellectuals and artists appropriate the tropes of mestizaje and indigenismo for the purposes of identity formation, we are nevertheless operating within the racial ideology from which these tropes are borrowed. [. . .] Thus, in our Chicana/o reappropriation of the biologized terms of mestizaje and indigenismo, we are also always recuperating the Indian as an ancestral past rather than recognizing contemporary Indians as coinhabitants not only of this continent abstractly conceived but of the neighborhoods and streets of hundreds of U.S. cities and towns. (279)

The key problems of Chicana/o appropriations of Indigeneity that Saldaña-Portillo identifies here are biologism and erasure. These two procedural traps linger on as "residual effects" from Mexican appropriations of indigeneity in revolutionary mestizaje through Movimiento Chicano appropriations of this mestizaje to "postnational," "postrevolutionary" reappropriations by Chicana indigenists such as Anzaldúa.

Saldaña-Portillo is certainly right in part by pointing to a residual biologism in Anzaldúa's statements concerning "the Indian in her." Anzaldúa at times "proves" her indigenous roots by pointing out her "Indian" physical and personality features: "There is the quiet of the Indian about us" (86); "I am visible—see this Indian face—yet I am invisible. I both blind them with my beak nose and am their blind spot" (108). Yet it is through her distinctive physical features in contrast to her family—her dark skin, earning her the nickname Prieta—that Anzaldúa is first articulated or hailed as an "Indian." One of the crucial things this phenomenon shows is that identification with one's indigenous roots has only recently been encouraged among Chicanas and Chicanos, precisely through their articulation *as* Chicanas and Chicanos rather than Mexican-Americans or Hispanics.

ANZALDÚA'S BACKPACK

In preparing the reader for her critique of another layer of Anzaldúa's troubling indigenism in *Borderlands*, Saldaña-Portillo writes the following:

[I]ndigenous identity is not reducible to biology. Any person born an Indian, with all the genetic Indian features, can become Ladinized by refusing to practice his or her indigenous identity in the hopes of accessing the limited amount of power made available to poor mestizos. Indigenous identity, for Menchú and the Zapatistas, depends not simply on biology but on the rigorous practice of the thoroughly modern cultural, linguistic, social, religious, and political forms that constitute one as indigenous. And these are not forms that exist in a kind of pastiche grab bag of Indian spiritual paraphernalia, as they seem to exist for Anzaldúa. (286-87)

Saldaña-Portillo thus transfers us from the realm of *biologism*—"indigenous identity is not reducible to biology"—to the realm of *practice*: the "thoroughly modern cultural, linguistic, social, religious, and political" practice that constitutes Indigenous identity can be rejected through Ladinization or rigorously embraced through the performances that confer Indigenous legitimacy upon these practitioners. Anzaldúa's apparently "pastiche grab bag of Indian spiritual paraphernalia" has not been sanctioned through submission to such legitimating performances. I would suggest here that what Saldaña-Portillo does not make room for is the reverse: the turn from Ladinization to socio-political legitimacy. What is the mechanism whereby those who have been born into Ladinization might instead perform their Indigeneity? In other words, after centuries of genocidal detribalization, how does a people rejoin or reconstitute their tribe? It is precisely in an attempt to answer this question that Anzaldúa turns to her backpack trope, the difference between backpacks and grab bags being constitutive:

[The new mestiza] goes through her backpack, keeps her journal and address book, throws away the muni-bart metromaps. The coins are heavy and they go next, then the greenbacks flutter through the air. She keeps her knife, can opener and eyebrow pencil. She puts bones, pieces of bark, *hierbas,* eagle feather, snakeskin, tape recorder, the rattle and drum in her pack and she sets out to become the complete *tolteca.* (104)

Saldaña-Portillo elaborates on this passage:

> Ultimately, Anzaldúa's model of representation reproduces liberal developmental models of choice that privilege her position as a U.S. Chicana: she goes through her backpack and decides what to keep and what to throw out, choosing to keep signs of indigenous identity as ornamentation and spiritual revival. But what of the living Indian who refuses mestizaje as an avenue to political and literary representation? What of the *indígena* who demands new representational models that include her among the living?

I want to question various elements of this condemnation before moving on to Anzaldúa's actual indigenizing practice. To what extent is Anzaldúa's choice to reclaim her Indigeneity really a sign of her reproduction of "liberal developmental models of choice that privilege her position as a U.S. Chicana"? To what extent is the Coatlicue process—Anzaldúa's path to her Indigenous self—simply a consumerist collection of signs of Indianness? To what extent is the mestizaje of Anzaldúa's new mestiza really the same as the mestizaje posited by racist Mexican nationalism? Might the mestizaje that Anzaldúa constructs be desirable by some other "living Indians"? To what extent does Saldaña-Portillo's distinction between Chicanas and the living *indígena* reinforce the racist legacies of both the Spanish and the Anglo-American Conquests? What nationalist practices serve to police this rigid and racialized distinction, despite Saldaña-Portillo's claim to acknowledge indigeneity as a result of social performance rather than of biology?

Saldaña-Portillo positions the passage above as perhaps the greatest sign of Anzaldúa's apparent complicity in the Mexican nationalist uses of mestizaje (in Saldaña-Portillo's original essay) as well as her complicity in the developmentalist construction of the revolutionary subject (in the book version). Out of context, the list of items Anzaldúa chooses to keep in her New Mestiza backpack (bark, bone, feathers, drum) could appear to focus on the popular nostalgic images of the paraphernalia that would make one "Indian" and perhaps (but not necessarily) might contribute to the construction of Indianism as a parallel version of Edward Said's *Orientalism*—except, perhaps, because of the presence of the tape recorder, a "modern" object that disrupts the stereotyping work of the list of kept items. In her own response to Saldaña-Portillo's essay in a later interview, Anzaldúa acknowledges the danger here:

> I think it's important to consider the uses that appropriations serve. The process of marginalizing others has roots in colonialism. I hate that a lot of us Chicanas/os have Eurocentric assumptions about indigenous traditions. We do to Indian cultures what museums do—impose western attitudes, categories, and terms by decontextualizing objects, symbols and isolating them, disconnecting them from their cultural meaning or intentions, and then reclassifying them within western terms and contexts. (*SAIL* 14[3])

Rather than a mere decontextualized grab-bag list, the function of Anzaldúa's backpack list becomes radically transformed as she continues explaining the processes involved in this appropriative gesture:

> Her first step is to take inventory. *Despojando, desgranando, quitando paja.* [Stripping, shelling, removing straw—"separating the wheat from the chaff."] Just what did she inherit from her ancestors? This weight on her back—which is the baggage from the Indian mother, which the baggage from the Spanish father, which the baggage from the Anglo? (*Borderlands* 104)

To return to Said's notion of Orientalism, we should note the ways Said, following Antonio Gramsci, insists on the need to take inventory in order to come to just such an awareness of the historical roots that make up a person's identity. Said repeats this injunction, one version of which is as follows:

> The starting-point of critical elaboration is the consciousness of what one really is, and is "knowing thyself" as a product of the historical processes to date, which has deposited in you an infinity of traces, without leaving an inventory. The only available translation inexplicably leaves Gramsci's comment at that, whereas in fact Gramsci's text concludes by saying, "therefore it is imperative at the outset to compile such an inventory." (25)

The purpose of Anzaldúa's backpack, then, is not to serve as the presumed grounding gesture of bourgeois subjectivity—choice—but rather as the decolonizing site at which she can take inventory of the traces of the historical impressions on her very being.

I would argue that Anzaldúa's appropriations of mestizaje and indigenismo are not strictly *biologized* but rather *socialized*. Anzaldúa's primary notion of mestizaje does not refer to a biological given but rather to a socially-imposed existential condition resulting from life in the borderlands. The function of mestizaje in Anzaldúa's project cannot be reduced to the mestizaje/indigenismo binary that structures the mestizo as citizen of Mexico. This is primarily so because the location of Anzaldúa's "territory of mestizaje," so to speak, is not Mexico but the borderlands region of the United States. Whereas in Mexico the mestizo is the privileged figure standing in as the nation-state citizen, in the U.S. the mestizo is never recognized as such.

This becomes even clearer when we go on to read the passage that follows those above in *Borderlands*:

> *Pero es difícil* [but it is difficult] differentiating between *lo heredado, lo adquirido, lo impuesto* [the inherited, the acquired, the imposed]. She puts history through a sieve, winnows out the lies, looks at the forces that we as a race, as women, have been a part of. [. . .] This step is a conscious rupture with all oppressive traditions of all cultures and religions. She communicates that rupture, documents the struggle. (104)

In producing the inventory of her own historical positioning, Anzaldúa documents the struggle and, through such documentation, communicates the rupture that marks the new mestiza's rejection of all inherited, acquired, and imposed oppressive systems. Rather than "returning" to her Indigenous roots as some "nostalgic" or "romantic" escape to the past, Anzaldúa uses the knowledge she gains from her inventory as she "reinterprets history and, using new symbols, she shapes new myths." This is the subaltern process against hegemony,[4] the transformative Coatlicuean appropriation (deconstructing followed by constructing) of the new mestiza's nahual, shape-shifting nature in the molding of a new mode of being:

She strengthens her tolerance (and intolerance) for ambiguity. She is willing to share, to make herself vulnerable to foreign ways of seeing and thinking. She surrenders all notions of safety, of the familiar. Deconstruct, construct. She becomes a *nahual,* able to transform herself into a tree, a coyote, into another person. She learns to transform the small "I" into the total Self. *Se hace moldeadora de su alma. Según la concepción que tiene de si misma, así será.* [She becomes the molder of her soul. According to the conception she has of herself, so will she be]. (104-5)

Such is the potential power of her decolonizing appropriations at the site of various histories of competing colonizations.

ENDNOTES

1 See my "Coatlicue Appropriations and Transformations: The Decolonizing Strategies of Gloria Anzaldúa & Norma Alarcón."

2 Saldaña-Portillo's essay first appeared in *The Latin American Subaltern Studies Reader,* and has subsequently been integrated into Chapter 7 of her book. Page numbers refer to the 2003 book version.

3 This interview, first published in SAIL in 2003, is republished in *The Gloria Anzaldúa Reader* (2009). Because of the importance of the placement of this interview among the other SAIL contributions in that issue on "Indigenous Intersections," page references are to the SAIL version.

4 See Laclau and Mouffe.

WORKS CITED

Anzaldúa, Gloria. *Borderlands/La Frontera: The New Mestiza*, second edition. San Francisco: Aunt Lute, 1999. Print.

——. "Speaking Across the Divide: An Email Interview." *SAIL* (*Studies in American Indian Literatures*), Series 2, 15: 3 & 4 (Fall 2003-Winter 2004): 7-20. Print.

——. "Speaking Across the Divide." *The Gloria Anzaldúa Reader*. Edited by AnaLouise Keating. Durham, NC: Duke UP, 2009, pp. 282-94. Print.

Hartley, George. "Coatlicue Appropriations and Transformations: The Decolonizing Strategies of Gloria Anzaldúa & Norma Alarcón." Talk presented on October 8, 2009 at the 40th Anniversary of Ethnic Studies Conference at San Francisco State University. George Hartley's Blog, 11 Oct. 2009. Web. 1 July 2011. <http://georgehartley. blogspot.com/2009/10/my-san-francisco-state-talk.html>

Laclau, Ernesto and Chantal Mouffe. *Hegemony and Socialist Strategy.* London: Verso, 1985. Print.

Said, Edward. *Orientalism.* New York: Vintage, 1979. Print.

Saldaña-Portillo, María Josefina. "Reading a Silence: The 'Indian' in the Era of Zapatismo." *Nepantla: Views from South* 3.2 (2002): 287-314. Print.

——. *The Revolutionary Imagination in the Americas and the Age of Development.* Durham, NC: Duke UP, 2003. Print.

——. "Who's the Indian in Aztlán? Re-Writing Mestizaje, Indianism, and Chicanismo from the Lacandón." *The Latin American Subaltern Studies Reader*, ed. Ileana Rodriguez, Durham, NC: Duke UP, 2001. 402–23. Print.

Silko, Leslie Marmon. *Almanac of the Dead.* New York: Penguin, 1991. Print.

THE REPRESENTATION OF GLORIA ANZALDÚA'S BORDERLANDS THEORY IN WITI IHIMAERA'S *WHALE RIDER*: KAHU'S PROCESS OF AWAKENING TO BE THE MAORI'S VERSION OF *LA MESTIZA*

LAUREL BOSHOFF

Witi Ihimaera's *The Whale Rider,* published in English in 1987, illustrates how traditional culture must change and adapt in order to survive in the contemporary world. In an interview with the Pacific Islanders in Communications, Witi Ihimaera comments "([the]legend [Kahu transforms]) was a particular story for that particular era to affirm the nature of the Maori voyage, and that one needed to have courage to maintain one's identity. Today, it is so important to recognize that the world has indeed changed, but it takes time for tradition to be dismantled." Through Koro's rejection of Kahu, Ihimaera illustrates how abiding by stringent traditional patriarchal practices can silence, rather than foster, change. Koro's understanding of Maori traditions places Kahu in something similar to what Gloria Anzaldúa calls the "borderland," "a vague and undetermined place created by the emotional residue of an unnatural boundary. It is in a constant state of transition. The prohibited and forbidden are its inhabitants" (Anzaldúa 25). In order to become the first female whale rider, a Maori equivalent to the Anzaldúan *mestiza*, Kahu must break free from her borderland and no longer accept the silence forced upon her by being "prohibited and forbidden" in her culture. Kahu's search for autonomy symbolizes how "regardless of tradition and the way that society endeavors to make you conform or disempowers you—[you] must always strive to seek your dream and never let go of who you are, what you want to do, where you want to be, how you want to get there and what you want to find when you reach that destiny" (*piccom.org*). Once Kahu is able to embrace the Maori language and her ability to speak to the whales and dolphins, a step similar to the Anzaldúan embrace of the "wild tongue," she can break free from the borders to become her generation's whale rider, who will lead the new era of reawakening and preserving Maori traditions.

From the beginning of the novel, Kahu is confined within her society's borders, creating "the emotional residue of an unnatural boundary" that haunts her until Koro accepts and loves her (Anzaldúa 25). Koro, the "Super Maori," the emblem of tradition, and "The only 'legitimate' inhabitan[t]… in power" (Anzaldúa 25), immediately rejects Kahu, placing the blame for Kahu's birth on Nanny Flower's genes: "'I will have nothing to do with her. She has broken the male line of descent in our tribe…. It's your fault. Your female side was too strong'" (Ihimaera 13). Koro's immediate and steadfast rejection of Kahu based on her sex shows how Kahu is instantaneously and unquestionably placed in Maori borderlands, becoming, upon birth, part of the "prohibited and forbidden" participants in her culture (Anzaldúa 25). Until Kahu's awakening at the end of the novel, Koro consistently "identifies with the ancestors and embodies tradition; he has established the symbolic pact with authority" (Visser 67). But Irene Visser also observes that as a chief, "Koro is a hard ruler, and many of his acts are instances of 'tyranny and exclusion'" (67).[1] Raiwiri summarizes the tension between Kahu's birth and tradition:

> The trouble was that Koro Apierana could not reconcile his traditional beliefs about Maori leadership and rights with Kahu's birth. By Maori custom, leadership was hereditary, and normally the mantle of prestige fell from the eldest son to the eldest son. Except that in this case, there was an eldest daughter" (Ihimaera 15-16).

Through Koro's inability to "reconcile his traditional beliefs about Maori leadership," Kahu is "in a constant state of transition" because she is without a solidified and defined place in Maori culture (Anzaldúa 25). Koro's views on Maori tradition reflect how "Borders are set up to define the places that are safe and unsafe, to distinguish *us* from *them*. A border is a dividing line, a narrow strip along a steep edge" (Anzaldúa 25). In the instance of Koro and the Maori tradition, these borders literally "distinguish *us* from *them*;" they separate male and female. Kahu gradually exhibits how tradition must transform for the tribe to progress, meaning "Koro's fixation upon rigid tradition [echoes] his community's inability to draw upon its roots and find a path towards modernity" (De Souza 18). Koro constantly enforces the borders of his Maori culture in order to protect what he thinks is traditionally right, but in doing so, he silences Kahu, the person chosen by the Maori gods, the whales.

The preservation of Maori culture, according to Koro, relies on the separation between males and females: Kahu, Nanny Flowers, and all the other women have no role in his understanding of cultural borders. Kahu's name alone breaks the borders of the Maoris because it defies her sex and binds her to her ancestry, as Marnina Gonick notes, "she represents not only the future but the past" (313). Rawiri defends Koro's anger over Porourangi and Rehua's naming of Kahu, thus further breaking Maori traditional borders: "I could understand, however, why the old man was against the idea. Not only was Kahutia Te Rangi a man's name, but it was also the name of the ancestor of our village. Koro Apirana felt that naming a girl-child after the founder of our tribe was belittling Kahutia Te Rangi's prestige" (Ihimaera 19). Rawiri's understanding that "naming a girl-child after the founder of our tribe was belittling Kahutia Te Rangi's prestige" merely enforces Maori patriarchy: Rawiri is a male who has power and voice in his culture and is not kept within the horrible borderlands like Kahu. Rawiri and Koro's behavior and fear of "belittling" their ancestor's "prestige" reflects Anzaldúa's argument that "If a woman doesn't renounce herself in favor of the male she is selfish.... Woman is the stranger, the other. She is man's recognized nightmarish pieces, his Shadow-Beast. The sight of her sends him into a frenzy of anger and fear" (39). Koro is literally sent "into a frenzy of anger and fear" when Kahu is named after their ancestor: he leaves the house. Gonick views her inherited name as significant as it "juxtapos[es] [Kahu's] promise as a leader with the males of her community who live the consequences of colonialism in particularly damaging ways… the adult males of the community seem to have more strained relations to the land, the sea, and the cultural traditions" (312). Rawiri's reaction to Nanny Flowers' strong female presence and refusal to "renounce herself in favor of [Koro]" further enforces Koro's borders: "I guess the trouble was that Nanny Flowers was always 'stepping out of line.' Even though she had married into our tribe, she always made constant reference to her ancestor, Muriwai" (Ihimaera 19). Nanny Flowers' constant reference to her Muriwai ancestry and its matriarchal tradition causes "trouble" because it contradicts Koro and Rawiri's patriarchal views of tradition.

The tensions between Nanny Flowers' matriarchal views and Koro's patriarchal views on traditions and involvement in their culture clash when Nanny Flowers treats Kahu's afterbirth differently from Maori traditional demands. Riwiri tells us, "Rehua… had wanted to honor her husband by choosing a name from his people, not hers. That way, should she die, at least her firstborn child would be linked to her father's people and land… she wanted Kahu's afterbirth, including the birth cord, to be put in the earth on the marae in our village. Tradition called for its burial" (Ihimaera 20-1). Although tradition calls for the burial of Kahu's afterbirth and birth cord, Koro refuses to do it, handing over the power to Nanny Flowers. Unluckily for Koro, during the burial, Nanny Flowers predicts: "'Never mind, Kahu. You'll show him when you grow up. You'll fix the old paka'" (Ihimaera 23). Nanny Flowers' instructions for Kahu to "'show [Koro]… and fix the old paka'" exemplify the tension between matriarchy and patriarchy. Gonick argues that together Nanny Flowers and Kahu, "subvert mythic constructions of leadership as exclusively masculine. In doing so, a subversion of colonial discourses of Maori is also enacted: indigenous life is not dead; it is revitalized through 'the girl' subject" (315). With the words and actions of her grandmother, Kahu is forever bound to the land. Nanny Flowers, upon Porourangi's decision to send Kahu to Rehua's parents, states: "'Your birth cord is here. No matter where you may go, you will always return. You will never be lost to us'" (Ihimaera 29). Kahu must "leave the source, the mother, disengage from my family, *mi tierra, mi gente*, and all that picture stood for. [She] had to leave home so [she] could find [herself], find [her] own intrinsic nature buried under the personality that had been imposed on [her]" (Anzaldúa 38). Although Kahu returns to be "buried under the personality" of Koro, it is only through her having been away that her bond to Maori culture seems more special. Rawiri echoes Anzaldúa's sentiment about leaving home to find oneself: "When a child is growing up somewhere else, you can't see the small signs that mark her out as different, someone with a destiny. As I have said before, we were all looking somewhere else" (Ihimaera 32). Kahu's growth away from the Koro and Maori tradition makes her a stronger person because upon her return, her enthusiasm about Maori food, love for Koro, the symbol of tradition, and acceptance of the Maori's language and history indicates her special destiny.

When Kahu returns to the Maoris, she experiences and interacts with Koro's borders for the first time. Unfortunately, Koro's experience reflects how "The world is not a safe place to live in… Woman does not feel safe when her own culture, and white culture, are critical of her … Alienated from her [father²] culture, 'alien' in the dominant culture, the woman of color does not feel safe within the inner life of her self. Petrified, she can't respond, her face caught between *los intersticios*, the spaces between the different worlds she inhabits" (Anzaldúa 42). Since Kahu constantly searches for love from Koro, but is rejected because he wants a boy-child, "her own culture" is already setup to be "critical of her." Rawiri tells us "he had wanted an eldest boy-child, somebody more appropriate to teach the traditions of the village to… he had already begun to look in other families for such a boy-child" (Ihimaera 34). Since Kahu is of no use to Koro, she is "alienated from her [father] culture," so she "does not feel safe within the inner life of her self" because she cannot learn her Maori ancestry that would make her understand her destiny, her identity as the whale rider. Rawiri notifies us of Koro's official dismissal of Kahu and the other Maori women: "[Koro] said he wanted to begin a regular instruction period for the men so that we would be able to learn our history and our customs. Just the men, he added, because men were sacred… [the purpose was] to keep the Maori language going, and to increase the strength of the tribe. It was important, he said, for us to be so taught" (Ihimaera 35). Once the school is started, Rawiri describes the neglect of the females: "All of us felt the need to understand more about our roots.…

[Nanny Flowers] would sit with Kahu in her arms... watching the men walk past" (Ihimaera 48). The visualization of Kahu and Nanny Flowers sitting and "watching the men walk past" divides the sexes. Koro's early declaration that "men were sacred" and are the only ones who "would be able to learn our history and our customs" begs the question of what women's place in Maori society is, and as Nanny Flowers constantly reminds us: women are the givers of life, so should not the women be sacred too?

Upon the founding of Koro's school, Kahu asserts women's right to learn Maori traditions by biting Koro's toe. Koro tells the boys in his class: "But I do know the old man had the power to talk to the beasts and creatures of the sea. Alas, we have lost that power now.... [biting his toe] was part of the ritual to transfer his power to me" (Ihimaera 36). The biting of the toe transfers power to the next generation, so when Koro finds Kahu "biting on his big toe and making small snarling sounds as she played with it... [and then] she looked up at him and her eyes seemed to say, 'Don't think you're leaving *me* out of this,'" (Ihimaera 36). Kahu, by sucking Koro's toe, is attempting to suck the power out of the patriarch and put it in herself. Drawing upon her ancestral connections and the power inherent in this assertion, she starts "marking out a space that is both the future and the past" (313). Gonick even asserts that "[Kahu] may be said to represent a disruption of time—she is a new time, an interstitial time, both past and future. She is where the relations of time, memory, and hope for the future are reconfigured" (313). Koro, however, either does not comprehend or refuses to interact with Kahu because her attempt to transfer his power is unacceptable behavior that threatens his borders. This first rejection of Kahu's interaction with Koro's school shows how: "[She] [does] not make full use of [her] faculties... And there in front of [her] is the crossroads of choice: to feel a victim where someone else is in control and therefore responsible for the blame (being a victim and transferring the blame on culture, mother, father... absolves me of responsibility), or to feel strong, and, for the most part, in control" (Anzaldúa 43). Kahu can either surrender to Koro's rules about her presence or fight to retain her culture. Kahu apologizes but never stops trying to learn from Koro. Visser observes she does so without any attendant guilt: "she [does] not internaliz[e] any feelings of guilt; even though she is constantly made to feel her guilt by Koro, [Kahu] refuses to identify with it" (69). Kahu never submits to Koro's rules, which means she chooses the road that makes her "feel strong, and, for the most part, in control ... I suspect that Kahu overheard more than we thought. I am certain she must have been there when we learned that man was once able to talk, to communicate, with whales" (Ihimaera 39). Kahu's ability to persevere through Koro's banishment and anger over her persistence shows how she longs to embrace her destiny as the whale rider.

Kahu never surrenders to Koro's rejection because if she were to abide by his borders, she would never find her voice. Nanny Flowers describes "[Kahu is] hungry for *him*, the old paka. Hungry for his love," but, "the love Kahu received from Koro Apirana was the sort that dropped off the edge of the table.... But Kahu didn't seem to mind" (Ihimaera 34; 47). Kahu never fully submits to Koro's anger and rarely cries over his rejection because the love is not as important to her as the knowledge he has as the Maori leader. Kahu's behavior towards Koro relates with Anzaldúa's description of how: "Many times she wished to speak, to act, to protest, to challenge. The odds are heavy against her. She hid her feelings; she hid her truths; she concealed her fire; but she kept stroking the inner flame. She remained faceless and voiceless, but a light shone through her veil of silence" (Anzaldúa 45). Kahu's biting of Koro's toe and consistent appearance at the school are only two ways "a light shone through" Kahu's "veil of silence." While Kahu grows into her voice and powers, her actions begin a revolt against Koro's steadfast adherence to tradition. Visser notes the implications of Kahu's emerging challenge to Koro's rule: "Revolt, in its first meaning, denotes the transgression of a prohibition... but it also means repetition, working through, working-out (as in psychoanalysis). This 'coded' revolt[3] is not necessarily violent or destructive; the word is polyvalent; it has plasticity and can be used to denote reversal, transformation, abjuration, recovery, reconstruction of the past and of meaning" (68). Thus, rather than taking a path of violent resistance and resentment, Kahu follows her magical, inherited connection with the land and whales. When Rawiri and Kahu see the killer whales on the way back from the movie, "Kahu had begun to make eerie sounds in her throat.... It sounded as if she was warning them" (Ihimaera 45). These "eerie sounds" shine through "her veil of silence," and are only the beginning of Kahu's awakening to her language and identity.

Koro's obstinate refusal over Kahu's attempts at learning the Maori language causes Kahu to go into a state of self-disapproval. Kahu knows the cause of Koro's disapproval, and is constantly frustrated at being a girl. Kahu asks Rawiri: "Did you go to university, Uncle? Koro says it's a waste of time for a girl to go. Sometimes I wish I weren't a girl. Then Koro would love me more than he does. But I don't mind. What's it like being a boy Uncle?" (Ihimaera 83). Kahu no longer wants to be a girl because she is aware that "the issues [arise] from the fact that [she] is a girl... [she is] aware of [herself] as 'different,' when judged in terms of the prevailing expectations of traditional Maori culture, and [she] feel[s] dispossessed, alienated from [herself], and unloved as a result" (Fox 161). Kahu's heart-wrenching reaction, "it's not Paka's fault, Nanny... that I'm a girl," to Koro's absences at her recital further illustrates that she understands her place in the borderlands of Maori culture (Ihimaera 87). Kahu's emotional struggle resonates with what Anzaldúa identifies as *Coatlicue*, the goddess of life and death:

> We need *Coatlicue* to slow us up so that the psyche can assimilate previous experiences and process the changes. If we don't take time, she'll lay us low with an illness, forcing us to 'rest....' The soul uses everything to further its own making. These activities or *Coatlicue* states which disrupt the smooth flow (complacency) of life are exactly what propel the soul to do its work: make soul, increase consciousness of itself... Our greatest disappointments and painful experiences—if we can make meaning out of them—can lead us toward becoming more of who we are. (68)

Kahu must overcome her battle with forces similar to *Coatlicue*; Koro's horrific actions towards her are exactly what propel "[her] soul to do its work: make soul, increase consciousness of itself." As a young girl, Kahu "exist[s] on the brink of adolescence, where [she] grapple[s] with issues of identity as well as the impending feminization which [she does not] seem ready to accept as 'natural'. Occupying this boundary space between childhood and adulthood, [she is] presented as having access to a wiser form of knowledge" (Message 90). Since she is a young girl being blocked from understanding her identity, Kahu must rely on her inherent knowledge to find herself. Kahu's various proclamations that she wishes she was not a girl represent her Maori struggle with something like *Coatlicue* that attempts to "increase consciousness" of her whale rider soul.

Kahu and the overall Maori struggle with preserving their language resemble what Gloria Anzaldúa calls "wild tongues." Anzaldúa states; "Wild tongues can't be tamed, they can only be cut out…. We speak a patois, a forked tongue, a variation of two languages" (76-7). The Maori language that Koro works hard to bring back into his culture is "a forked tongue," because he, rather than the mainstream New Zealand society, must take the initiative to teach the Maori language. Anzaldúa emphasizes the importance of knowing your language, your wild tongue: "Ethnic identity is twin skin to linguistic identity—I am my language. Until I can take pride in my language, I cannot take pride in myself…. I will no longer be made to feel ashamed of existing… I will overcome the tradition of silence" (81). When Kahu performs at the school recital, Rawiri describes Kahu's pride in using the Maori "wild tongue:" "she smiled a brilliant smile at all of us. Her voice rang out with pride" (Ihimaera 85). Regrettably, Koro does not show up for Kahu's performance out of his strong opposition to her, so Kahu cannot "overcome the tradition of silence" because the silencer is not present. Kahu's love for the Maori language and self-identification with it is so strong that she won a contest in which she gave a speech only in Maori: "[Kahu's] tones rang with pride as she recited her genealogy, the family *whakapapa*… her aim in life was to fulfill the wishes of her grandfather and the tribe" (Ihimaera 86-7). It is not until Kahu can use the Maori language that she can take pride in her identity. Gonick sees this growth in language as crucial to Kahu's identity formation, observing that Kahu's reciting of her family's *whakapapa* "produce[s] the possibility of a political speech act for a Maori girl in the name of her desire that is radically delegitimated by the authoritative figure of the grandfather… She produces a radical crisis for established power. It's a critical subversion; a radical re-signification" (314). The *whakapapa*, like biting Koro's toe, signifies Kahu's longing for recognition. Kahu uses the Maori language to create her own identity, mixing tradition with her femininity, emphasizing how she not only wants "to fulfill the wishes of her grandfather and the tribe," but also bring them into the future with her tongue.

Ihimaera gradually builds Kahu's voice, a Maori version of Anzaldúan wild tongue. Kahu "waits till the waters are not so turbulent and the mountains not so slippery with sleet. Battered and bruised she waits, her bruises throwing her back upon her self and the rhythmic pulse of the feminine" (Anzaldúa 45). As Rawiri describes "[Kahu] was moving closer and closer to that point where she was in the right place at the right time, with the right understanding to accomplish the task that had been signed to her. In this respect there is no doubt in my mind that she had always been the right person" (Ihimaera 70). We get glimpses of Kahu growing into the language of the whales, the first instance during the movies, and the second, following Koro's story of killing the whales: "But she was so frightened. She was making a mewing sound in her throat. She seemed paralyzed with terror" (Ihimaera 52). Kahu's reaction to the slaughtering of whales not only solidifies a linguistic connection with the whales, but her emotional identification with them as their whale rider. The next morning, Rawiri finds Kahu on the beach talking to dolphins: "In the clear air I heard a chittering, chattering sound from the beach.… [Kahu] was standing facing the sea, listening to voices in the surf… I saw three silver shapes leaping into the dawn" (Ihimaera 54). The emotional horrors Kahu goes through the night before are soothed once she can use her language, her wild tongue. Visser again centers on the power of Kahu's wild tongue, which "seeks to purify; to remedy the ills of the present situation… confronting authority from a sense of belonging… Forgiveness, as demonstrated by [Kahu's] characteristic unconditional forgiveness of Koro, enables freedom from guilt and thus the breaking of the cycle of violence, sacrifice and exclusion" (70). The mixture of the Maori language and her ability to speak to whales and dolphins is a linguistic phenomenon that naturally transcends the tension between the traditional patriarchy and Kahu's healing femininity.

It is not until Kahu finds Koro's stone at the bottom of the ocean that Rawiri and Nanny Flowers fully understand the meaning of Kahu's Maori wild tongue, her whale language. Kahu's interactions with the dolphins at the bottom of the ocean expose her wild tongue ability to Rawiri and Nanny Flowers: "They circled around Kahu and seemed to be talking to her. She nodded and grabbed around its body… Kahu seemed to say 'Down there?' and the dolphins made a nodding notion" (Ihimaera 91). Kahu's communication with the dolphins displays "*la facultad*," "the capacity to see in surface phenomena the meaning of deeper realities, to see the deep structure below the surface. It is an instant 'sensing,' a quick perception arrived at without conscious reasoning" (Anzaldúa 60). Kahu's *la facultad* has multiple meanings through her ability to "see the deep structure below the surface" of Maori traditions, the physical ocean, and herself. Kahu instantly knows what she must do to find Koro's stone and, without hesitation, communicates and swims with the dolphins.

However, once Rawiri and Nanny Flowers discover Kahu's wild tongue, they silence Kahu by keeping her powers a secret. Their reaction exhibits how "The inability to respond is what is meant by responsibility, yet our cultures take away our ability to act—shackle us in the name of protection. Blocked, immobilized, we can't move forward, can't move backwards" (Anzaldúa 42-43). Nanny Flowers orders Rawiri: "'Not a word about this to Koro Apirana.... Not a word, Rawiri. Not a word about the stone or our Kahu... He's not ready yet'" (Ihimaera 92). Unintentionally, Nanny Flowers "shackle[s] [Kahu] in the name of protection" by not telling Koro, and thus enforces how "cultures take away [Kahu's] ability to act." Nanny Flowers temporarily silences Kahu's powers because she now knows Kahu is an important asset to the tribe; "Not only does she occupy or symbolize a boundary space, she also signifies the role of process and transition in the production of meaning" (Message 90). Although Kahu has already resisted being unable to move within Maori culture by Koro's traditional beliefs, she must also overcome Rawiri and Nanny Flowers' protection and recognition of her significance to the tribe.

The most dramatic and frustrating example of Kahu being forced into the borders is when Rawiri and Nanny Flowers keep the whale beaching from her. Rawiri tells Nanny Flowers: "'You better keep our Kahu at home today. Don't let her know what has happened'" (Ihimaera 101). Rawiri, who has been going to Koro's lessons, should know that the whale rider can hear the whales without being near them. Rawiri, rather than breaking from tradition, concerns himself with resolving the issue in a masculine way by getting all of his male friends together and handling everything through the strict patriarchal structure: no Maori women are invited to come help them. The scene is frustrating because once Rawiri returns, he finds

"Kahu way up on the bluff, calling out to sea. She was making that mewling sound and then cocking her head to listen for a reply. The sea was silent, eternal" (Ihimaera 107). Restraining Kahu simply causes a bigger problem in that the whales know the whale rider is present, but not saving the whales, which causes what Rawiri nicknames the "Second Coming" (Ihimaera 108).

The final restraint, and consequential silencing of Kahu, nearly causes the death of her people because Koro does not permit women, and especially Kahu around the sacred whale's beaching. Koro attempts to restrict Kahu so "[she] can't move forward, can't move backwards" due to his traditional belief that only the men should be involved in whale beachings (Anzaldúa 42-43). Nevertheless, Nanny Flowers opposes her husband's command: "I don't want you to interfere, Flowers. You know as well as I do that this is sacred work…You watch out. If I think you need the help, well, I shall change myself into a man. Just like Muriwai… I'll be like Muriwai if I have to. Kahu also, if she has to be" (Ihimaera 113).

This reference to Muriwai sends us back to when Kahu wished to be a boy to have Koro's love, but Nanny Flowers, rather than wanting love, wants action. Visser regards this scene as a significant point in Kahu's independence, noting that Nanny Flowers' assertion of Muriwai vocalizes Kahu's role as "the purifier [who] recognizes authority, the law, but [s]he claims that power must be broadened, to be shared by more people than just the leader, and so [s]he rebels against a restricted power in order to include a greater number of the 'brothers [/sisters]'" (69). Since Koro has consistently rejected her, Kahu patiently and respectfully waits for her chance to act rather than immediately speaking out to transform tradition. Koro permits Nanny Flowers to get the women together in the dinning hall, but orders that Nanny Flowers, "…keep Kahu away, e Kui… As for Kahu, she was staring at the floor, resigned, feeling sorry for herself" (Ihimaera 114). Rawiri thinks Kahu is "staring at the floor… feeling sorry for herself," but in reality, she is being placed in the borders during the time when she should be awakening as the whale rider.

Kahu, when she finally gets to the beach, embraces her role as whale rider, likening her role to Anzaldúa's "*la mestiza*," who is "a product of the transfer of the cultural and spiritual values of one group to another" (Anzaldúa 100). At the beach, the physical border between land and sea, "Ambivalence and unrest reside there and death is no stranger" (Anzaldúa 26). In order to accept her identity, Kahu must recognize the horrors of the border she must cross to become the whale rider, the Maori representation of *la mestiza*. Koro tells the men on the beach; "'If we are able to return it to the sea, then that will be proof that the oneness is still with us. If we are not able to return it, then this is because we have become weak. If it lives, we live. If it dies, we die'" (Ihimaera 117). Koro recognizes the sacred whale as the symbol of the Maori's survival but does not know how to resolve the problem. Kahu, during the chaos and fear, is able to gain knowledge from Koro for the first time:

> Why? Kahu asked Koro Apirana
>
> Our ancestor wants to die.
>
> But why?
>
> There is no place for it here in this world. The people who once commanded it are no longer here. He paused. When it dies, we die. I die
>
> *No*, Paka. And if it lives?
>
> Then we live also. (Ihimaera 123)

Koro's use of death to describe the importance of the sacred whale prompts Kahu to break free from Koro's strict borders and take on her role as whale rider.

Kahu's acceptance of her role as the whale rider demonstrates an awakening akin to the Anzaldúan "*Mestiza* consciousness." Kahu, by being the whale rider, is expected to save the sacred whale in order to protect her people. Kahu, realizing she must take action, goes and sings to the whale: "'*Karanga mai, karanga mai, karanga mai*' Call me. She raised her head and began to call to the whale… 'Oh sacred ancestor… I am coming to you. I am Kahu. Ko Kahutia Te Rangi, *ahau*….'" (Ihimaera 126). Kahu becomes the "product of the transfer of the cultural and spiritual values of one group," the Maori, "to another," the whales (Anzaldúa 100). Kahu, since she is so young and has not had training due to Koro's negligence, "began to weep. She wept because she was frightened. She wept because Paka would die if the whale died. She wept because she was lonely... She wept because Koro Apirana didn't love her. And she also wept because she didn't know what dying was like" (Ihimaera 129). By weeping, Kahu recognizes her place in Maori culture as the whale rider, and decides, "Let us go now... Let us return to the sea... Let the people live" (Ihimaera 129). Kahu's fear, but acceptance in the face of her culture's potential death, resembles how "Being... multilingual, speaking a patois, and in a state of perpetual transition the *mestiza* faces the dilemma of the mixed breed: which collectivity does the daughter of the darkskinned mother listen to?" (Anzaldúa 100). Kahu has no choice over which collective she belongs to because in order to save the Maori she must choose to go with the "collectivity" of the whales. Kahu must act to save her people. Gonick finds her means of doing so transformative: "Her ingenious solution to exclusion from inheriting the leadership position is that she refigures agentic leadership as based on performance rather than entitlement and in the process rewrites what entitlement means. [Kahu] does not simply act to become a leader or act like a leader; she acts leadership" (315). By using her wild tongue and embracing her role in the intertwined communities of the whales and the people of Whangara, Kahu becomes both communities' leader into the future. Without the proper knowledge of the whale rider, however, Kahu resigns herself to death when the bull dives: "I am not afraid to die, she whispered to herself.... She was Kahutia Te Rangi. She was Paikea. She was the whale rider. *Hui e, haumi e, taiki e.* Let it be done" (Ihimaera 133). Although, Kahu is no longer stuck in the borderlands of her culture, she is unnecessarily fearful due to her lack of knowledge about her position.

When the whales realize Kahu is the last spear Paikea threw into the future, Kahu gains more knowledge about her role as whale rider, resembling the "*Mestiza* consciousness." Interestingly, the mother whale, and not the bull, figures out Kahu's destiny: "*This is the last spear, the one which was to flower in the future... It is the seed of Paikea, she said, 'and we must return it to the land.'*" (Ihimaera 141). The bull whale agrees with his mate; "*Let this spear be planted in the years to come when the people are troubled and it is most needed.... We must return to the surface... We must return this new rider back to Whangara.*" (Ihimaera 142). In order for the Maori to culturally survive, Kahu must have a chance to physically lead her people, and illustrate how she "will break down the subject-object duality that

[kept] her prisoner and to show in the flesh through the images in her work how duality is transcended" (Anzaldúa 102). By being a female whale rider, Kahu physically transgresses the duality of her culture's traditions. She simultaneously breaks from and protects the human traditions that attempted to confine her by being the first female whale rider. The bull whale, once Kahu is returned to the land and he knows she is safe, decrees: *"Very well... Then let everyone live, and let the partnership between land and sea, whales and all humankind, also remain"* (Ihimaera 147). Gonick argues that Kahu's riding the sacred whale acknowledges her role as a link between the past and present, which "suggest[s] that memory is firmly situated in the present yet looks toward the future, the importance of learning to live with loss is articulated synonymously with a sense of possibility for the future" (313). Kahu's ability to actively break free from the borders placed on her and leave behind her life for the survival of her community foreshadows her powers as a future leader. Kahu tells Koro, when she wakes up:

> I fell off the whale. If I were a boy, I would have held on tight. I'm sorry, Paka, I'm not a boy...
>
> You're the best great-grandchild in the whole wide word, [Koro] said. Boy or girl, it doesn't matter.'
>
> Really Paka? Kahu gasped... Oh thank you, Paka. You're the best granddad in the whole wide world.
>
> I love you, Koro Apirana said. (Ihimaera 149)

Kahu still yearns for Koro's love and knowledge, and knows she cannot complete her destiny without him. Koro's newfound acceptance of Kahu further shows her *Mestiza* consciousness; "The answer to the problem... between males and females, lies in healing the split that originates in the very foundation of our lives, our culture, our languages, our thoughts" (Anzaldúa 102). Kahu, simply by being a female whale rider, is able to break the borders of her Maori culture to begin "[a] massive uprooting of dualistic thinking in the individual and collective consciousness [that] is the beginning of a long struggle" between the new world and old traditions (Anzaldúa 102). This powerful scene of the sacred whale's unquestioning acceptance of Kahu as his rider is a symbol of the tribe's new leadership; "[Kahu's] peaceful and compassionate 'coded revolt' against her grandfather's authority enable[s] a new structure of leadership for the community, which does not constitute a radical break with tradition and ritual, but rather re-connects the traditions and rituals of the past with a new structure of authority, characterized by inclusivity and shared leadership" (Visser 72). Thus, Kahu's gradual "uprooting" of Maori traditions allows the culture to survive and prosper in the modern world because the whales and the tribe's people are reconnected.

Although Kahu is a girl and was purposefully kept within the borders of Koro's perceptions of Maori tradition, and is thus not fully immersed in her culture's traditions, she continuously grows into a role that coincides with Anzaldúan *Mestiza* consciousness. Ihimaera describes: "*And the whale herd sang their gladness that the tribe would also live, because they knew that the girl would need to be carefully taught before she could claim the place for her people in the world*" (Ihimaera 147). The whales in the end force Kahu to return to the human collective so she can "claim the [future] place for her people in the world." Therefore, Kahu will fulfill her destiny as the whale rider when she is older, resembling Anzaldúa's expectations of *la mestiza*.

NOTES

1. The popularity of the motion picture of *The Whale Rider* initially eclipsed conversations and even scholarship about the novel. Commentators on the film, such as Visser, Gonick, Message, and De Souza, have catalyzed scholarly interest in where the novel and film intersect, evidencing how film can enrich interest in print.

2. Here I have changed "mother culture" to "father culture" because Kahu's link to Maori culture is through her father's blood, not her mother's.

3. Although this terminology is psychoanalytic in nature, it is Julia Kristeva's contention with Freud's myth of origin. See *Intimate Revolt* for more explanation.

WORKS CITED

Anzaldúa, Gloria. *Borderlands/La Frontera: The New Mestiza*. 3rd ed. San Francisco: Aunt Lute Books, 2007. Print.

De Souza, Pacale. "*Maoritanga* in *Whale Rider* and *Once Were Warriors*: A Problematic Rebirth Through Female Leaders." *Studies in Australian Cinema* 1.1 (2007): 15-27. *WilsonWeb*. Web. 1 September 2011.

Fox, Alistair. "Chapter 9: The Dilemma of the Maori New Man: Inter-generation Conflict in Witi Ihimaera's *The Matriarch, Bulibasha, The Whale Rider*, and *The Uncle's Story*." *The Ship of Dreams: Masculinity in Contemporary New Zealand Fiction*. Dunedin, New Zealand: Otago University Press, 2008. 153-169. Print.

Gonick, Marnina. "Indigenizing Girl Power: *The Whale Rider*, Decolonization, and the Project of Remembering." *Feminist Media Studies* 10.3 (2010): 305-19. Print.

Ihimaera, Witi. *The Whale Rider*. 1987. New York: Harcourt Inc., 2003. Print.

Message, Kyle. "*Whale Rider* and the Politics of Location." *Metro Magazine* 136 (2003): 86-90. *EBSCO*. Web. 1 September 2011.

Visser, Irene. "Exclusion and Revolt in Witi Ihimaera's *Whale Rider*." *Commonwealth* 30.2 (2008): 63-73. Print.

"Whale Rider: the Book. An Interview with *The Whale Rider* Author, Witi Ihimaera." *piccom. org*. Pacific Islanders in Communications, 2005. Web. 1 September 2011.

THE DOUBLE-FACED WOMAN AND THE TATTOOED MESTIZA: THE RHETORIC OF THE SIDESHOW AS SITE OF RESISTANCE IN THE WRITING OF GLORIA ANZALDÚA

CHELSEY PATTERSON

Throughout her writing, Gloria Anzaldúa continuously describes her discomfort with her identity and summons the rhetoric of the sideshow when she refers to herself as a tattooed woman and as an intersex individual. It is this rhetoric of the sideshow that I wish to critically examine in relation to Anzaldúa's theory of the new mestiza. I argue that the sideshow is an oppositional political space where Anzaldúa further contextualizes her own theories of identity, location, alterity, and hybridity. I further argue that Anzaldúa uses the rhetoric of the sideshow to accomplish four objectives: First, to help her readers confront their own fears, desires as well as racist and homophobic ideologies; second, to create a political space of possibility, transformation, reclamation and reinscription; third, to focus on the body as a site of resistance and fourth, to acknowledge and confront her own body as a historical narrative inscribed with racism and colonialism.

Since I will be using metaphor as a specific theoretical framework to guide this study, it is important to first consider the importance of metaphor in written texts and everyday existence. According to George Lakoff and Mark Johnson, metaphor is pervasive throughout Western thought and language. In fact, "our ordinary conceptual system, in terms of which we both think and act, is fundamentally metaphorical in nature" (Lakoff and Johnson 3). In a 2009 article in the *Boston Globe*, Drake Bennett describes how psycholinguists have recently discovered ways in which metaphors reveal how we think with our bodies, how experiments in temperature and weight, for example, have guided perceptions in how people interpret how "warm" or "cold" a stranger's personality is upon first meeting or how "weighty" a subject is based on the weight in a person's hand (1-2). Such experiments in metaphor support Lakoff and Johnson's argument of the importance of metaphor in everyday life, of metaphor existing at the root level of subconsciousness and language use, just as Rosemarie Garland Thomson, in "From Wonder to Error: A Genealogy of Freak Discourse in Modernity," argues that "the extraordinary body is fundamental to the narratives by which we make sense of ourselves and the world" (1). Thus, it is through the metaphor of the "extraordinary" or "freakish" body that we make sense of our surroundings; however, it is my intention throughout this essay to expand this argument so that it is through the extraordinary body that we interpret our subjectivity, intersectionality, and alterity.

In a previous study of the metaphors that are used throughout Anzaldúa's *Borderlands/La Frontera,* Erika Aigner-Varoz examines how Anzaldúa uses metaphors such as the serpent and the eagle as a "cultural and psychoanalytic criticism of self and society" as she "consciously attempts to change the popularized pejorative messages of such metaphors because they serve as destructive, limiting borders of culture and self" (48-49). Applying metaphor in this way, as a means of subverting pejoratives that damage or limit culture and self, can certainly be applied to Anzaldúa's choice of sideshow rhetoric, a rhetoric that has historically been associated with the outcasts of society, those who belonged on display for their "otherness" rather than be allowed admission to the rest of society. It is Anzaldúa herself who claims that metaphor can be used as a transformative power. In "Metaphors in the Tradition of the Shaman," Anzaldúa claims that by using metaphors, she is following in the tradition of the shaman, who creates images that provoke altered states of consciousness that are integral in the healing process.

Anzaldúa enlightens us: "We preserve ourselves through metaphor; through metaphor we protect ourselves. The resistance to change in a person is in direct proportion to the number of dead metaphors that person carries. But we can also change ourselves through metaphor" (122). It is Anzaldúa's hope, then, that metaphor both protect and change our perceptions of the self. By claiming the sideshow as a site of subversion, Anzaldúa thus serves to reclaim and reinscribe history, the history of the exiled, the exploited, and the outcast. By reclaiming such a history, Anzaldúa is able to reclaim her own identity and culture, to contextualize a third space within the rhetoric of the pejorative.

In order to fully comprehend the importance of Anzaldúa's sideshow metaphors, it is imperative to provide a historical background, albeit brief, of the American sideshow. The presence of human oddities has been displayed in traveling fairs and carnivals since at least 1102 in Europe. However, it was not until the late eighteenth and early nineteenth century that the American version of the "freak show" began to appear. It was the infamous P. T. Barnum that ultimately used his capitalistic skills to monopolize the market with his museum, originally known as Scudder's American Museum, located in lower Manhattan, which included a variety of live animals, fossils, taxidermy, and human oddities (Hartzman, 2-3). Eventually, the museum began touring as a legitimate circus and the sideshow, so named because of its location on the outskirts of town and its separation from the main circus tent and separate entrance fee, became a menagerie noted for its human oddities, most notably sword swallowers, tattooed women, conjoined and parasitic twins, and a variety of natural-born "freaks" and performers from across the world (Chemers 97). As a political site, the American sideshow is also well-known for its racism. Various Barnum sideshow acts displayed African Americans and Native Americans as exotic others, as literal freaks of nature who belonged alongside individuals born with missing limbs or otherwise deformed bodies. It is this exploitative side of the sideshow, which learned the methods of colonization and exploitation from its European counterpart that still haunts the collective imagination of the modern American carnival.

From the sideshow, the term *freak* emerged to describe this group of human oddities who were displayed behind giant colorful tapestries that often aggrandized or mislead the public about the degree of their astonishing abilities or disfigurements. The etymology of the term *freak* was initially associated with the sideshow acts themselves, as a pejorative term for individuals who were outcast, disowned, abnormal, unusual, deformed, mocked, hated, and feared based on their physical abnormalities. Not surprisingly, the term *freak* was associated not only with one's physical condition per se, but with "a way of thinking about and presenting people—a frame of mind and a set of practices" (Thomson 24). Thus, freakery as ideology is integral for presenting freakery as a site of political transformation. According to Lea Ramsdell in "Language and Identity Politics: The Linguistic Autobiographies of Latinos in the United States," "[l]anguage is identity and identity is political" (166). If individuals choose to call themselves *freaks*, as many modern sideshow performers and individuals within punk and tattooed subcultures often do, then the choice is a political one, a stand that marks a decision to rewrite history, not to erase, but to reclaim the moniker that was once used to label outcasts as subhuman. Ramsdell further notes the ways in which scholars investigate how "the self is invented by the language that is used to narrate its life story," referring to Paul DeMan's assertion that language precedes identity and allows individuals to develop their own subjectivity and connect with others (167). If language defines who we are and how we interact with others, then Ramsdell is correct in her declaration of language as a political act, as a means of creating identity and/or reacting against the identity that society has chosen for us. It is freakery as a political act that allowed the etymology of the term to evolve and become adopted by the '60s counterculture, who used the word like a mantra, as an active verb for uncommon practices or excesses. "At once an act and a condition, the designation *freak* proclaimed the counterculture's purposeful embrace of marginality" (Adams 141), as a category that reinscribed alterity as a badge of honor, of an overt rejection of conservative bourgeois values in lieu of something inherently more diverse, creative, open-minded, and abject. In fact, Rosemarie Garland Thomson, in her history and analysis of the freak show and the extraordinary body, defines the term *freak* as "something of a political gesture," as a term "whose use may function as an act of defiance, a political gesture of self-determination" (56). In other words, Thomson uses the term not to refer to individuals with physical abnormalities, as unusually gifted or challenged, but as a self-identified being who is "simultaneously and compulsively fascinating and repulsive, enticing and sickening" (Thomson 56). Thus, it is the freak who is able to traverse binaries, to defy conventional definitions and expectations, to question our notions of gender, sexuality, humanity, and sense of ourselves and our place in the world.

Gloria Anzaldúa, in *Borderlands/La Frontera,* argues that the work of mestiza consciousness "is to break down the subject-object duality that keeps her a prisoner and to show in the flesh and through the images in her work how duality is transcended" (102). She further contends that it is this emphasis on (Western) notions of dualities and contentions distinguishing between white/colored and male/female, for example, that must be eradicated and will result in "healing the split that originates in the very foundation of our lives, our culture, our languages, our thoughts" (102). It is this erasure of boundaries and binaries that characterizes Anzaldúa's new mestiza as a people "who inhabit multiple worlds because of their gender, sexuality, color, class, bodies, personality, spiritual beliefs, and/or other life experiences" (Anzaldúa 322). It is this being who possesses a "tolerance for contradiction and ambivalence" who finds a home within the rhetoric of the sideshow, particularly within the etymology of the term *freak,* a term that also resists Western binaries and contradictions, allowing the spectator to confront the possibilities of the "in-between" space that resides in the collective imagination.

Thomson contends that the freak "is an object of simultaneous horror and fascination because, in addition to whatever infirmities or abilities he or she exhibits, the freak is an *ambiguous* being whose existence imperils categories and oppositions dominant in social life" (57). Thomson claims that freaks resist categorical definition because they occupy "an impossible ground" that defies the binaries of human/animal, one being from another, nature/culture, man/woman, adults/children, humans/gods and living/dead, "our most fundamental categories of self-definition and boundaries dividing self from otherness" (57). This ambiguity, similar to Anzaldúa's ambiguity that is apparent within the new mestiza, creates a transformational space where a third sex, race, culture, class, spirituality, and physicality exist. Within the freak, new identities are declared, new ways of conceiving identity through the interstices of race, class, gender, sexuality, and nation. However, the breakdown of these binaries alone is not enough to claim that the freak further contextualizes and even problematizes Anzaldúa's new mestiza. To suggest so would trivialize Anzaldúa's theories and reduce them to a mere reflection of Bakhtinian conjecture. Philip McGowan's treatise on the American carnival entitled *American Carnival: Seeing and Reading American Culture,* argues that the American carnival is inherently anti-Bakhtinian in that it is dark, anti-subversive, and based on whiteness and capitalism. Essentially, McGowan contends that the American carnival is a space for the exhibition of otherness that allows the white viewer to continue such a reading of culture outside the carnival tent, is a site of capitalism, does not produce laughter, only fear of the racialized and exploited other, and disallows any space for subversiveness due to this capitalistic exploitation of the other (1-20). Although McGowan provides an excellent analysis of the essential differences between the European and the American carnival as well as provides a narrative of the commodification and racist intentions of the circus and sideshow circa the nineteenth century, McGowan also fails to consider the transgressive and resistant possibilities within the (post)modern sideshow and its ability to reinscribe history, which I believe that Anzaldúa attempts via her own use of the rhetoric of the sideshow, a rhetoric that encompasses the body as performance, a literal performance of subconscious fears, desires, and subjectivity.

The American sideshow as "contested site," (Chemers 3) as a space of hybridity, is similar to Derrida's "brisure," a "breaking and a joining at the same time, in the same place: difference and sameness in an apparently impossible simultaneity" (Young 26). This simultaneity of being one but not the other while being all and yet none, is at the heart of the new mestiza, who seeks to create a safe space, a third space where contradictions of race, class, identity and culture can polemically reside and distort meaning, all the while creating new definitions and sites of resistance. It is within the very semantics of the term *freak* itself that I argue a third space is found, a politically transformative space in which restrictive, categorical binaries are blurred and new possibilities of race, sexuality, class, and gender are reconfigured. Rachel Adams, in her analysis of the politicized nature of the sideshow, notes that her choice in using *freak* throughout her own text is not a disrespectful harkening back to the days when individuals were denied their right to humanity, who were objectified as entertainment and profit for others, but is instead "inspired, in part, by the critics and activists who have wrested the term *queer* from its original pejorative connotations, while insisting on the memory of violence and shame in its past. I am drawn to *freak* because, like *queer*, it is a concept that refuses the logic of identity politics, and the irreconcilable problems of inclusion and exclusion that necessarily accompany identitarian categories" (10). In this view, the freak exists as the new mestiza, who, although named, is absent of an identity that can be easily defined, who lives between and amongst nations, cultures, and categories, yet acknowledges a complicated and violent history within the very naming of herself and her multiple origins. While referring to *freak* within my argument and within Chicana theory, we must acknowledge this appellation as a legitimate term of resistance and give it its due agency as a political act, not as a pejorative that once more silences, shames, and commits acts of violence through its very language. I do not intend to apply the theory of the American sideshow lightly to Anzaldúa and her theories, nor is it my intention to de-politicize or trivialize Chicana theory; rather, I respectfully use the rhetoric of the sideshow as a signifier of transgressive possibilities for future polemics in regards to race, gender, class, sexuality, culture, and nationhood.

Anzaldúa's calculated use of the term *freak* throughout her work is used to specifically refer to the body. In "Spirituality, Sexuality, and the Body," a 1998 interview with Linda Smuckler, Anzaldúa describes her physical trauma with a hormone imbalance that caused her to menstruate at a very early age, arriving at pubescence while she was still a child. When describing this condition, Anzaldúa states that "I had this body that was a freak: I went into puberty and started bleeding when I was three months old; I had tremendous hot flashes; my breasts started growing when I was six. I was totally alien" (84). Anzaldúa uses the term *freak* here as a means of articulating her deep sense of alienation with the strangeness of her body, a sense that, according to Leslie Fiedler in *Freaks: Myths and Images of the Secret Self*, all pubescent adolescents feel upon the discovery of hair in strange places, growth spurts, and the emergence of breasts in females, which can cause young people to feel like the freaks in circus sideshows (31). Further in the Smuckler interview it is revealed that Anzaldúa has never entirely felt at ease with the trauma of her childhood illness, that in fact she still considers her early hormone imbalance as an aspect of her freakishness, as she confesses that within sexual and spiritual experiences, "all the Glorias are there," including "Gloria who's a freak" (Anzaldúa 85). This association between physical abnormality and the sideshow freak occurs again in "Creativity and Switching Modes of Consciousness," when she again refers to her childhood hormone imbalance, which "made me a freak" (103) and then further within the same text she switches gears and escapes the pain of the body to focus on psychic pain as a result of her artistic inclinations:

> All my escape modes had problems: I couldn't be in the outer world all the time because that was painful. I couldn't be in the inner world all the time because that was painful, too. I couldn't be in the artistic world— off creating through paint, or through words- because that meant confronting all my fears and all the problems in my life that I was trying to resolve and bring to order through the writing. So I became very adept at switching from one mode of consciousness to another. (104)

This switching of consciousness, of being neither inside nor outside, of "feeling like a freak, like I had no skin," is similar to the hybrid consciousness felt by sideshow freaks, who blur traditional binaries in favor of more enlightened modes of being, who force us to feel uncomfortable in our displeasure of such blurring. Anzaldúa struggles with both her outer self-designation as freak and her inner self-designation of freak. Anzaldúa's self-identification with the freak as physical and psychic otherness, as a secret self that allows for the transgression of binaries, boundaries, of opposition to fixed identity, is apparent within the other sideshow characters and tropes that she alludes to throughout her writing, such as the tattooed woman, the conjoined and parasitic twin, and the hermaphrodite.

The tattooed woman appears in Anzaldua's writing in "Haciendo caras, una entrada," when Anzaldúa discusses the relevance of "face": "'Face' is the surface of the body that is the most noticeably inscribed by social structures, marked with instructions on how to be *mujer, macho,* working-class, Chicana. As mestizas— biologically and/or culturally mixed—we have different surfaces for each aspect of identity, each inscribed by a particular subculture. We are 'written' all over, or should I say, carved and tattooed with the sharp needles of experience" (Anzaldúa 124). In this excerpt, Anzaldúa uses the rhetoric of the sideshow—in this case, the tattooed woman, to help contextualize the new mestiza, an individual that is *permanently* marked with experience, culture, and her identity as a Chicana, but who is simultaneously tattooed with the impermanence of sexuality, gender, class, nationality, and spirituality—aspects of her identity that might appear one day, but disappear the next, or might appear simultaneously as the mere outline of a trace, an absence in the presence. This ambivalence is likewise depicted through the imagery of the tattooed woman, who is at once a liberated, speaking body while also serving as a palimpsest of the history of colonized inscription.

According to Christine Braunberger in "Revolting Bodies: The Monster Beauty of Tattooed Women," the tattooed female body serves as a speaking body, one that transgresses and writes against the text of women's silence that culture has written for them:

> In a culture built on women's silence and bent on maintaining silence as a primary part of the relationship between women's bodies and cultural writing, the rules have been simple. The written body may only speak from a patriarchal script that tries to limit women's voices and bodies to supporting roles and scenery. So on a woman's body any tattoo becomes the symbol of bodily excess. (1)

Thus, the female tattooed body serves as liberation from the silent, objectified body, inscribed with androcentric constraints of piety, decency, virginity, silence, and beauty. As such, these "speaking bodies," as defined by Braunberger, write back to the larger male society, largely in an attempt to redefine standards of beauty, as Margot Mifflin argues in *Bodies of Subversion*, when she contends that women's tattoos serve as "passkeys to the psyches of women who are rewriting accepted notions of feminine beauty and self-expression" (vi). This contention that tattoos are a form of rebellion against traditional standards of beauty appears often in such discussions by white theorists or when applied blindly to encompass all women (read as "all women are white"). Although Mifflin's book does attempt to include a multicultural aspect, her discussion of tattooed Latinas is reduced to a mere three paragraphs and is overshadowed by the offensive presumption that Latinas who are interested in tattoos must therefore be gang members, whose tattoos are affiliated with gang membership, boyfriends, children, or Catholicism (134). However, Mifflin (albeit briefly) does discuss the subversive potential in the rise of the tattooed image of La Malinche amongst young Latina college students and her increase in popularity "because of the ambiguities and complexities of her historical role, and the belief that historians have been unfair to her and misrepresented her because she's a woman" (135). It is this ambiguity and misrepresentation that Anzaldúa discusses within the heart of the new mestiza that is represented within the face of the tattooed woman, who wears her markings "as a self-inflicted wound—at once a mark that abjects the bearer, and an assertion of control over abjection" (Fleming 25). In other words, the new mestiza, the tattooed woman, is able to "speak back" with her body, yet is also stigmatized, or abjected, by her community for such transgressions. According to Juliet Fleming in "The Renaissance Tattoo," this simultaneous control over abjection and victimization because of abjection results in the tattoo as occupation of "the no-place of abjection," the third space of the border between subjectivities of colonization (McCarron 88). Such abjection, rather than mere rebellion of traditional standards of beauty, is more relevant when considering the "Chicana canvas," the permanent site of transformation of the tattooed Chicana body (Santos 93). According to Xuan Santos in "The Chicana Canvas: Doing Class, Gender, Race, and Sexuality through Tattooing in East Los Angeles," tattooed Chicanas are particularly transgressive since their machismo culture does not accept female bodies that "speak back" through body modification. Once this Chicana canvas has been reclaimed, it "becomes an active means of self-affirmation that can express oppositions to barriers imposed by class, gender, race, and sexuality" (93). This Chicana canvas is a much more powerful form of reclamation, one that seeks resistance beyond white women's aesthetic concerns. This reclamation harkens back to tattooed women in the sideshow, whose tattoos were usually associated with domination, sexuality, and colonization. These "white" (it can be argued that these women were not actually Anglicized, for the ink under their skin placed them in a category beyond racial categorization) tattooed women of the Victorian era were given false captivity narratives and thus read through the eyes of their male overseers, who told the audience that such women were captured by natives and tattooed against their will. In such narratives, then, the tattoo needle's insertion into these women amounted to the rape of femininity, the violation of the sacred in exchange for the profane (Osterud). The tattooed woman of the sideshow, then, like the new mestiza, is located within the racialized shadow of colonization, exploitation, and commodification, yet is simultaneously liberated by the flesh's ability to speak against the constraints of a singular identity, a singular race, origin, or location.

The hermaphrodite, like the tattooed woman, also plays a key figure in the work of Anzaldúa. In the poem, "The Occupant," Anzaldúa describes awakening one morning to discover a male occupying her body, so that "A cock's growing out of my cunt/I'm getting hair on my chest" (22). At first, this crowding of the body is almost comical, as is evident by Anzaldúa's satirical line, "I'm for sharing/ but this is absurd;" (10-11) however, the final six lines are devastating in their implications of colonization:

> One of us has got to go
>
> One of us is going to
> occupy the other to death
> One of us is going to emerge sobbing
> with sorrow from the bloody
> remnant of the other. (Anzaldúa 12-17)

It is interesting that the title of this poem is "The Occupant," and refers to the unwanted occupation of another, an entity that is determined to emerge victorious with the wounded pieces of the other instead of meld into a being of multiple interpretations, of fractured identities and possibilities. This idea of the colonized Other plays a prominent role in the figure of the hermaphrodite, the half man half woman, the bearded lady, the conjoined or parasitic twin, and even the epignathic parasite, an integral spectacle of the sideshow, a doubleness that problematicizes the body politic. In particular, the congenital hermaphrodite sought to obliterate the demarcated boundaries of sex and gender, allowing for a third space of identity construction in which the colonized and the colonizer were one and the same, thus making room for new spaces of knowledge construction: "The hermaphrodite cannot be slotted into a binary logic. Neither is it simply a 'third sex' that exposes the fatal frailty of that logic. The difficulties that hermaphroditism presented to early modern systems of classification suggest that those systems were often themselves unstable" (Gilbert 31). Thus, the hermaphrodite challenged the sideshow audience's heteronormative and colonial ideology, challenging them to reconsider the definition of male and female and of self and other.

The conjoined twin was likewise an important aspect of the American sideshow, fascinating scientists, physicians, philosophers and the working class, whose curiosity was piqued because of the belief that "conjoined twins pose[d] a most literal challenge to the borders of personal identity by placing a multiplied self where there is usually only one, and by questioning where individual agency begins and ends" (Pingree 174). This obsession with borders, with the "multiplied self," aroused not only a fascination in the American public, but instigated an integral fear in the loss of individual subjectivity and led to the popularity of such sideshow conjoined twins such as Millie-Christine, the "Two-Headed Nightingale" (1851-1912), and The Hilton Sisters, Daisy and Violet, "San Antonio's Siamese Twins" (1908-1969). This fear of the Other was so intense amongst sideshow customers that "the myth of the double merged with that of the multiple monster to create a myth of the Monstrous Self and an identically Monstrous Other *joined together till death do them part*" (Fiedler 205). This simultaneous fear and fascination with the Monstrous Self was evident in the public's insistence on viewing the physical point of contact where the double bodies connected to one another, where the illusion of separation could be made, since separation "and thus the triumph of individuality, was always a preferable condition" (Durbach 65). Anzaldúa presents the metaphor of the conjoined twin in "Dream of the Double-Faced Woman," a short piece from the sixth chapter of her unpublished autohistoria, *La Serpiente Que Se Come Su Cola: The Death and Rebirth Rites-of-Passage of a Chicana Lesbian*. The piece outlines how important it is not to separate the spirit from the flesh or even the political from the spiritual, a separation that she refers to as the "body-split" (Anzaldúa 71). Anzaldúa further contextualizes this theory in "now let us shift... the path of conocimiento...inner work, public acts," in which she discusses the image of the double-faced woman that she has drawn in a journal, an image of double-headed, double-faced woman in which one woman is looking ahead and the other is looking to the side. According to Anzaldúa, such a doubling is similar to the effect of residing on a physical border between nations, that "living between cultures results in 'seeing' double, first from the perspective of one culture, then from the perspective of another. Seeing from two or more perspectives simultaneously renders those cultures transparent" (*Home* 549). Thus, the double-headedness allows for a greater vision of possibilities, is perhaps the very image of the new mestiza, the inhabitant of multiple selves and worlds, who resides in-between and amongst various sexualities, spiritualities, nationalities, languages, cultures, genders, classes, races, and lives. Furthermore, Anzaldúa contends that such a double vision results in a spiritual transformation that allows one access to nepantla, where "you sense more keenly the overlap between the material and spiritual worlds; you're in both places simultaneously— you glimpse el espíritu—see the body as inspirited. Nepantla is the point of contact where the "mundane" and the "numinous" converge, where you're in full awareness of the present moment" (*Home* 549). This double-faced woman, then, most certainly evokes the spirit of the conjoined twin of the sideshow, a double being whose perceived lack of individuality evoked fear and revulsion in spectators, for their overt abhorrence of the monstrous Other, a being who lacked distinct borders between self and other, yet found happiness and self-content within that doubleness, who appropriated their own double flesh as site of resistance, who often refused the idea of becoming separated, of losing their double vision, as it were.

In addition to the conjoined twin, the parasitic twin, the twin that existed as a few extra appendages attached to the arms or legs, or existed as an amalgamation of tiny, not fully formed body parts attached to the side or stomach, is also a key metaphor used within the work of Anzaldúa. For example, in "La Prieta," Anzaldúa alludes to Shiva, the Hindu deity with several appendages: "You say my name is ambivalence? Think of me as Shiva, a many-armed and legged body with one foot on brown soil, one on white, one in straight society, one in the gay world, the man's world, the women's, one limb in the literary world, another in the working class, the socialist, and the occult worlds. A sort of spider woman hanging by one thin strand of web" (*Reader* 45-46). Anzaldúa is thus a being with parasitic limbs, no longer an easily identifiable individual with a fixed gender, sexuality, or personality. It was the parasitic twins of the sideshows that often promoted such sexual ambiguity, as was the case with "Lalloo the Double-Bodied Hindoo Boy," whose parasitic twin consisted of a toddler-sized pair of arms and trunk that were attached to his stomach. Lalloo's twin possessed "a version of a penis," but Lalloo dressed the parasite in girl's clothing, naming her Lala and "it was thus precisely the sexual ambiguity of the parasite, which could not be comfortably contained under the sign of either male or female, that made this act so intriguing" (Durbach 68). It was this intrigue that complicated the spectator's fear, a sexual intrigue that allowed for the focus of the parasitic and the conjoined twins' sexual anatomy that allowed for graphic "scientific" discussions of the formation of the parasite's genitalia and whether or not female conjoined twins shared the same vagina and anus. The metaphor of Shiva, of the parasitic twin, then, encapsulates the body as site of resistance, as denial of a single gender or sexuality, as the encapsulation of the ambiguity of fear and desire, as the metaphor for the public's open confrontation with the monstrous, a challenge to sexual mores and sexist ideologies.

In conclusion, I believe that Anzaldúa perhaps unconsciously applies the metaphor of the sideshow within her work as a way to problematize and enhance the concept of the new mestiza, evoking the imagery of the tattooed woman, the mirror maze, the hermaphrodite, and the twin. By evoking such symbolism, Anzaldúa also helps readers confront their own ideologies and helps to create a space of transformation through the obliteration of dichotomies, and acknowledges the body as site of colonization and resistance.

WORKS CITED

Adams, Rachel. *Sideshow U.S.A.* Chicago: University of Chicago Press, 2001. Print.

Aigner-Varoz, Erika. "Metaphors of a Mestiza Consciousness: Anzaldua's *Borderlands/La Frontera.*" *MELUS* 25.2 (2000): 47-62. Print.

Anzaldúa, Gloria E. *Borderlands/La Frontera: The New Mestiza.* 2nd ed. San Francisco: Aunt Lute, 1999. Print.

---. "Creativity and Switching Modes of Consciousness." *The Gloria Anzaldúa Reader.* Ed.AnaLouise Keating. Durham: Duke UP, 2009. Print.

---. "Dream of the Double-Faced Woman." *The Gloria Anzaldúa Reader.* Ed. AnaLouise Keating. Durham: Duke UP, 2009. Print.

---. "Haciendo caras, una entrada." *The Gloria Anzaldúa Reader.* Ed. AnaLouise Keating. Durham: Duke UP, 2009. Print.

---. "La Prieta." *The Gloria Anzaldúa Reader.* Ed. AnaLouise Keating. Durham: Duke UP, 2009. Print.

---. "now let us shift...the path of conocimiento...inner work, public acts." In *This Bridge We Call Home: Radical Visions for Transformation.* Ed. Gloria E. Anzaldúa and AnaLouise Keating. New York: Routledge, 2002. Print.

---. "The Occupant." *The Gloria Anzaldúa Reader.* Ed. AnaLouise Keating. Durham: Duke UP, 2009. Print.

---. "Spirituality, Sexuality, and the Body: An Interview with Linda Smuckler." *The Gloria Anzaldúa Reader.* Ed. AnaLouise Keating. Durham: Duke UP, 2009. Print.

---. "Turning Points: An Interview with Linda Smuckler (1982)." In *Gloria E. Anzaldúa: Interviews/Entrevistas.* Ed. AnaLouise Keating. New York: Routledge, 2000. Print.

Bennett, Drake. "Thinking Literally: The Surprising Ways that Metaphors Shape Your World." *Boston Globe* 27 September 2009. Print.

Braunberger, Christine. "Revolting Bodies: The Monster Beauty of Tattooed Women." *NWSA* 12.2 (2000). Print.

Chemers, Michael M. *Staging Stigma: A Critical Examination of the American Freak Show.* New York: Palgrave Macmillan, 2008. Print.

Durbach, Nadja. *Spectacle of Deformity: Freak Shows and Modern British Culture.* Berkeley: University of California Press, 2009. Print.

Fiedler, Leslie. *Freaks: Myths and Images of the Secret Self.* New York: Doubleday, 1993. Print.

Gilbert, Ruth. *Early Modern Hermaphrodites: Sex and Other Stories.* New York: Palgrave, 2002. Print.

Hartzman, Marc. *American Sideshow: An Encyclopedia of History's Most Wondrous and Curiously Strange Performers.* New York: Penguin, 2005. Print.

Lakoff, George and Mark Johnson. *Metaphors We Live By.* Chicago: University of Chicago Press, 1980. Print.

McCarron, Kevin. "Skin and Self-Indictment: Prison Tattoos, Race, and Heroin Addiction." *ESC* 34.1 (2008): 85-102. Print.

McGowan, Philip. *American Carnival: Seeing and Reading American Culture.* Westport: Greenwood Press, 2001. Print.

Mifflin, Margot. *Bodies of Subversion: A Secret History of Women and Tattoo.* New York: Juno, 2001. Print.

Osterud, Amelia Klem. *The Tattooed Lady: A History.* Golden: Speak Press, 2009. Print.

Pingree, Allison. "The 'Exceptions That Prove the Rule': Daisy and Violet Hilton, the 'New Woman,' and the Bonds of Marriage." In *Freakery: Cultural Spectacles of the Extraordinary Body.* Ed. Rosemarie Garland Thomson. New York: New York UP, 1996. Print.

Ramsdell, Lea. "Language and Identity Politics: The Linguistic Autobiographies of Latinos in the United States," *Journal of Modern Literature* 28.1 (2004): 166-176. Print.

Santos, Xuan. "The Chicana Canvas: Doing Class, Gender, Race, and Sexuality through Tattooing in East Los Angeles." *NWSA* 21.3 (2009): 91-120. Print.

Thomson, Rosemarie Garland, ed. *Freakery: Cultural Spectacles of the Extraordinary Body.* New York: New York University Press, 1996. Print.

Young, Robert J. C. *Colonial Desire: Hybridity in Theory, Culture and Race.* New York: Routledge, 1995. Print.

"NEW MESTIZA CONSCIOUSNESS" AS TRAVELING THEORY? APPLYING ANZALDÚAN THOUGHT TO CARIBBEAN AMERICAN FICTION

MARION ROHRLEITNER

In "Notes on Travel and Theory" James Clifford argues that theory is inherently "a product of displacement, comparison, a certain distance. To theorize," he says, "one leaves home."[1] Clifford locates the main difference between the etymological origin of the Greek theorin and the current usage of theory in the contemporary absence of a stable, unified point of departure and return. Cultural, economic, and social multiplicity and contradictions dominate the lives of migrant majorities in the late twentieth- and early twenty-first centuries. Home, if it ever was, no longer is one safe space, one place of origin, one locale, but consists of a mind-boggling complexity of often uneasy, but also potentially productive, simultaneities.

It is here, in the pluralizing understanding of identity and home, where I propose to make a connection between traveling theory and two of Gloria Anzaldúa's key terms—"new mestiza consciousness" as the consciousness of lived ambiguity, and "Nepantla" as the state of being "in-between." The concepts embodied in these terms offer important insights into the workings of liminal identities in contemporary postcolonial fiction. Even though Anzaldúa's contributions to identity formation in conflicted "contact zones" are at least as complex and relevant as Edward Said's discussions of exile, James Clifford's traveling theories, Homi Bhabha's musings on hybridity, and Michael Warner's exploration of gendered liminal spaces, her theories still have not sufficiently traveled to literatures and contact zones beyond the U.S.-Mexico borderlands.[2] This relative scarcity of a scholarly engagement with Anzaldúa's work outside of Chicana/o and border studies is a loss, because, as María Socorro Tabuenca-Córdoba has pointed out, Anzaldúa "…invites the reader to cross into other realms and really look into those realms. It allows us to investigate our own identities by questioning them, and it invites us to question our national identities too" (29). From this perspective, Anzaldúa's theories inherently lend themselves to traveling, given the self-reflexive demands she places on her readers. This does not mean that Anzaldúa's body of work needs to be accepted as hagiography or turned into universal truth. On the contrary, one of the benefits of reading Anzaldúa's work critically allows us to be ever more attentive to the absences, silences, distortions, and blindspots in our own thinking.

This essay thus has two main goals: first, to model how two of Anzaldúa's critical terms, "new mestiza conciousness" and "Nepantla," can be understood as examples of traveling theory in their own right; second, to show what happens when Anzaldúa's theory travels from the U.S.-Mexico borderlands to the island of Hispaniola, specifically how "mestiza consciousness" and "Nepantla" can facilitate a more complex reading of liminal identities in Loída Maritza Pérez's *Geographies of Home* (1999) and Edwidge Danticat's *The Farming of Bones* (1998). The main female protagonist of each novel develops a "new mestiza consciousness" by carving out a space for her ambiguous gender and/or racial identity amidst hostile environments that demand uniform alliances with one nation, one ethnicity, and one gender only.

ANZALDÚA AND TRAVELING THEORIES

In his 1982 essay "Traveling Theory," Edward Said ponders what happens to theoretical concepts when they travel to geographical spaces, cultures, languages, and times other than those in which they were first formulated. In his initial assessment, Said asserts that travel often results in a dilution of the theory's original force and urgency as a result of it being removed from its immediate source—its specific cultural, political, and geographical context. This dilution, according to Said, is particularly pronounced once a particular theory is discovered and adopted by established scholars in often elitist academic settings.[3]

When Said returns to his thoughts on traveling theory twelve years later in "Traveling Theory Revisited," he offers a different option: the possibility that theory can actually be reinvigorated in productive ways when it is applied to cultural contexts outside of the theory's original conception.[4] Said invites readers to reconsider the intellectual and political possibilities inherent in transporting and adapting a geographically and culturally specific theory to a radically different set of circumstances. At the same time he cautions against the temptations of uninformed appropriation. In traveling theory, Said finds"…the possibility of actively different locales, sites, situations for theory, without facile universalism or overgeneral totalizing":

> To speak here only of borrowing and adaptation is not adequate. There is a particular and intellectual, and perhaps moral community of a remarkable kind…the exercise involved in figuring out where the theory went and how in getting there its fiery core was reignited is invigorating…it is another voyage central to intellectual life in the late twentieth century. (2002, 452)

Rather than universally dismissing the validity of traveling theories, Said promotes the notion that engagement with geographically and culturally specific theories by "outsiders" actually constitutes one of the central intellectual endeavors of the contemporary critic. The dispersal of theories via migration, Said realizes, is the very force that potentially rejuvenates the revolutionary potential of the theoretical formulation. The prerequisite for such engagement must, of course, be a sensitive, respectful, and informed treatment of and familiarity with content and context of the original theory.[5] In a 1997 interview, Ann Reuman directly asked Gloria Anzaldúa, "Do you feel that your borderlands metaphor has been appropriated or misunderstood?" Anzaldúa graciously responded, "What I'm thrilled about is that people have seen themselves reflected in my work enough so that they can get in dialogue with themselves" (6). Her theory, Anzaldúa suggests, is intended to enable everyone who is willing to seriously engage with it to discover previously unknown or inaccessible aspects of their psyche. She elaborates:

> I think what's probably one of the riskier things that I did in *Borderlands/ La Frontera* was to open up the concept of mestizaje, of the new mestiza and hybridity, to be non-exclusive, to be inclusive of white people and people from other communities. And the risk was in having again Euro-Americans take over the space. (6)

Anzaldúa's concern is legitimate, and it is very true that her work has often been used as and reduced to a token example of Chicana writing and borderlands theory.

Yet Anzaldúa courageously takes these risks, for example when she identifies shared themes and issues in her and Adrienne Rich's work, building bridges between white middle-class and Chicana working-class feminisms. She states, "All of what Adrienne Rich has written and what I have written is about getting out of this cage of limitations imposed by our respective cultures, and the loss of language, the loss of gender…" (43). The building and maintenance of such cross-cultural bridges has been an important feature of much of Anzaldúa's work from *This Bridge Called My Back* to *This Bridge We Call Home*. In her preface to *This Bridge We Call Home*, Anzaldúa for example beautifully illustrates the multiple meanings of bridges, which deserves to be quoted at length. She describes bridges as

> …. passageways, conduits, and connectors that connote transitioning, crossing borders, and changing perspectives. Bridges span liminal (threshold) spaces between worlds, spaces I call *Nepantla*, a Nahuatl word meaning tierra entre medio. Transformations occur in this in-between space, an unstable, precarious always-in-transition space lacking clear boundaries. Nepantla es tierra desconocida, and living in this liminal zone means being in a constant state of displacement – an

uncomfortable, even alarming feeling. Most of us dwell in nepantla so much of the time it's become a sort of home. (1)

Anzaldúa foregrounds alienation and deterritorialization as painful but necessary prerequisites for transformation. If we dwell in a too comfortable place for too long, she suggests, we tend to stagnate and fear change, and yet change is as unavoidable as it is necessary for growth. Living in Nepantla is not always a conscious choice; many who are socially marginalized are relegated to this uncomfortable space in between, and the liminal space of dislocation, originally considered the opposite of home, changes the very notion of what home signifies by allowing the nepantleras to discover previously unknown aspects of themselves in this liminal space.

Liminality is by definition located in the outskirts of society, in a space where otherwise dominant or generally accepted norms are not enforced and thus eventually called into question. It is an anarchic space, which allows for a radical remaking of the self without fear of state-sponsored control or coercive discipline. Feared and vilified as dangerous, Nepantla also becomes a space of unprecedented freedom. By allowing Anzaldúa's "new mestiza consciousness" and "Nepantla" to travel to the domains of a Dominican American and a Haitian American novel, I am trying to construct a bridge between Chicana and Caribbean diasporic writers based on their shared experiences as members of marginalized communities. As Anzaldúa asserts in *Borderlands/La Frontera*,

> The psychological borderlands, the sexual borderlands and the spiritual borderlands are not particular to the Southwest. In fact, the Borderlands are physically present wherever two or more cultures edge each other, where people of different races occupy the same territory, where under, lower, middle and upper classes touch, where the space between two individuals shrinks with intimacy. (2007, 19)

The experiences of those who are marginalized because of their national origin, skin color, religious beliefs, or sexual orientation call for a new consciousness that is able to negotiate "habitually incompatible frames of references...and cultural collision" (2007, 100) and to form non-sanctioned, but safe intimate spaces.

Anzaldúa famously calls this "a new mestiza consciousness, una consciencia de mujer" (2007, 99) and links her identity as a Chicana lesbian writer to that of a Nahuatl, a shape-shifting shaman, whose "ability to travel through worlds, to jump from one locale to the other, or one particular identity to the other" (2007, 13) also exemplifies the need to constantly adapt to and negotiate new and often hostile environments. The inhabitants of Nepantla, and those who develop and master a mestiza consciousness, are often immigrants, migrants, documented as well as undocumented, and the outcasts, "queers" of the nation, who cannot or do not want to be assimilated and absorbed into limiting binaries.

ANZALDÚA AND CARIBBEAN AMERICAN FICTION

Following a philosophical approach based in the concept of Nepantla, home becomes an ever-shifting idea that is created while moving. As Haitian American writer Edwidge Danticat said about the majority of the world's population at the turn of the millenium, "Migration *is* home." Fellow author and scholar Myriam J. A. Chancy directly connects her sense of self as a Haitian-born immigrant to Canada to Anzaldúa's notion of mestiza identity. She remembers, "as a graduate student, I really connected to Gloria Anzaldúa's work, in terms of borderlands and border countries and the whole idea of mestiza consciousness. And part of it was being mixed race" (79-80). When Anzaldúa's new consciousness of the border-crossing multiracial, multilingual, multicultural migrant mestiza travels to the island of Hispaniola, a concept that was born in the U.S.-Mexico borderlands is transposed into the equally contested, violent, and racialized Dominican-Haitian borderlands.

Similar to the South Texas border of Anzaldúa's childhood and youth, the Dominican-Haitian border does not simply denote a clean separation along a national border. The forced binary physicality of borders also extends to the proliferation of mutually exclusive binary gender roles and identities, which make individuals choose one over another identity, when in reality most are made of multiplicities. Myriam J. A. Chancy effectively connects these two aspects of borders and asserts with regard to Hispaniola, "the majority of Haitian women and Dominican women are trying to transcend the limitations of our gender, and that is a form of border crossing" (81). Chancy's awareness of the multiple locations and manifestations of borders, beyond national and physical ones, reflects a discourse that has traveled successfully from Anzaldúa's South Texas to the Caribbean, and also puts Anzaldúa's work in conversation with queer theorists such as Michael Warner, Judith Halberstam, and Joseph Allen Boone. Boone explicitly connects queer and borderlands theory in the introduction to *Queer Frontiers,* suggesting, "Queer theory, too, may be conceived as a borderland and a frontier, a space of transition and a still largely unexplored geography" (9). This sense of exploration conceives of liminal spaces as locales for opportunity rather than confinement, and allows Dominican American writers like Loída Maritza Pérez, Ana Lara, and Nelly Rosario as well as Haitian American writers such as Edwidge Danticat and Myriam J. A. Chancy to reformulate their experiences of migration within a larger history of gendered and racialized binaries.

My selection of Loída Maritza Pérez's *Geographies of Home* and Edwidge Danticat's *The Farming of Bones* as examples of the possibilities inherent in Anzaldúa's traveling theory is not a random choice among relevant Caribbean American texts. Pérez is a Dominican-born author who now lives in New Mexico, and Danticat is a 2009 MacArthur fellow who immigrated to the United States from Haiti at age twelve. These immigrant authors were born on two opposing sides of a much contested, racialized border along the Massacre River which divides the island of Hispaniola in a predominantly Kreyol speaking Haiti in the West and a predominantly Spanish-speaking Dominican Republic in the East. The populations of both countries, whose multiracial heritage includes Taíno, Carib, West African, Spanish, and French influences, have been ideologically pitted against each other since the Treaty of Ryswick (1697) divided the former Spanish colony of Hispaniola into the French owned Saint-Domingue in the West, and the Spanish-owned Santo Domingo in the East. This colonial division gained new urgency after the Haitian Revolution produced the first independent Black nation in the New World in 1804, and when the newly declared Republic of Ayiti occupied the Spanish colony twice before the final independence of Santo Domingo from Spain in 1865. These historical rivalries were, however, not seen as based in an essential racial difference between Haitians and Dominicans until the dictatorship of Rafael Leonidas Trujillo y Molina (1930-1961), who invented a national Dominican identity grounded in Spanish "pureza de sangre" rather than the cultural, linguistic, and ethnic mestizaje celebrated by Anzaldúa.

The Farming of Bones is a historical novel set during and in the aftermath of the 1937 massacre, and explicitly addresses the violence that ensues when a nation becomes obsessed with notions of imagined racial purity. *Geographies of Home* on the other hand, is set alternately in New York City and upstate New York in the 1990s, and seems to be far removed from such racialized concerns. Even a cursory reading of the novel, however, soon reveals the persistence of such racialized notions in Dominican immigrant communities, especially when paired with already existing racism in the United States. Both novels feature female protagonists who, I argue, embody a new mestiza in search of their own Nepantla.

THE EVOLUTION OF "NEW MESTIZA CONSCIOUSNESS" IN *GEOGRAPHIES OF HOME*

In Loída Maritza Pérez's debut novel *Geographies of Home*, the main protagonist Ileana decides to leave the posh New England campus where she is a student on a much-desired full stipend, and to return to her parents' dilapidated home in Brooklyn, once she hears news of her older sister Marina's mental breakdown. Ileana is the youngest daughter of fourteen siblings born to Dominican immigrant parents. Her family considers her an aberration on all accounts— Ileana "should have been a boy since her sex had been predicted from the shape of Aurelia's pointy stomach and [because] all her siblings had been born to form alternate pairs of the same sex, a sequence only Ileana had disrupted" (4). Her precarious status in the family order is exacerbated by her being the first daughter to attend college, and in addition, a college five hours away from her parents' home in Brooklyn. Her sister Marina is a rape survivor who rejects her Afro-Dominican heritage and embraces an imaginary "pure" Spanish descent, echoing the national fantasy of dictators Trujillo and Balaguer. Her fanatical religiosity and internalized racism bring her ever closer to the brink of madness.

Marina's exploration of the dark depths of her psyche can be understood in the context of what Anzaldúa calls "La herencia de Coatlicue/ The Coatlicue State" in the fourth chapter of *Borderlands/La Frontera*. Anzaldúa testifies, "There are many defense strategies that the self uses to escape the agony of inadequacy…I have split from and disowned parts of myself that others rejected. I have used rage to drive others away and to insulate myself against exposure" (2007, 67). Marina's mental breakdown is a result of her denying a large part of who she is—historically, physically, and culturally—and the "Shadow Beast" comes back to haunt her at night. Coatlicue, in her manifestation of the "Shadow Beast" of addiction, depression, and self-hatred is, for Marina, "the dark night of the soul, hiding oneself in the dark cave, reaching the bottom" (13). Marina becomes a prisoner of her own worst fears. In an ugly, jealous exchange with her younger sister shortly after Ileana's return from college, Marina hisses, "I am Hispanic, not black" (38). Silvio Torres-Saillant locates this denial of Blackness in the Dominican Republic not so much in self-hatred, but in a different conceptualization of race. He argues, "Black Dominicans do not see blackness as the central component of their identity, but privilege their nationality instead, which implies participation in a culture, a language community, and the sharing of a lived experience" (1090). If we are to believe this assessment, then Marina's internalized racism is not so much a result of her identity as the daughter of Dominican immigrants but rather the outcome of a collusion between Dominican nationality-based in Hispanidad and a U.S. based racial notion of the "one-drop rule"—another intriguing case of traveling theory. In either case, Marina is unable to see the world beyond limiting gender and race binaries and lashes out against anyone who threatens her worldview.

Anzaldúa reminds us that a crucial part of new mestiza consciousness consists in the ability to develop a "tolerance for contradictions, a tolerance for ambiguity" (101)—ambiguities in terms of language, cultural values, racial and gender identities, and sexual orientation. According to Anzaldúa the "queer," the outcasts of each nation, are often also those whose necessarily heightened sensibilities are able to detect the lower frequencies of cultural anxieties and change. Ileana is one such outcast: to her family she is a traitor who left home and refuses to play the subservient role of a respectable woman in Dominican Seventh Day Adventist families. On the campus of her alma mater, she is an exotic beauty whose conservative dress code is considered off-putting and ridiculous. To her sister Marina, her androgynous appearance and detached demeanor threaten the strict binaries of male and female, blackness and whiteness, on which Marina's sense of self depends and which is, simultaneously, the source of her self-hatred.

Both Marina and Ileana inhabit and embody different aspects of Nepantla - Marina in the dark depths of her psyche, in which the Shadow Beast taunts and humiliates her; and Ileana in the androgynous body and rebellious mind of a first generation Seventh Day Adventist Dominican American, who is a foreigner both in her family's home and on the university campus where she tries to reinvent herself. Here Nepantla is not the romanticized space of uncritical fantasies of a colorblind, hybrid society; on the contrary, Nepantla is a refuge and a curse to those who are to open themselves to the possibility of plurality. Similar to Mary Louise Pratt's definition of the contact zone as a space where "cultures meet and, at times violently, grapple with each other" (605), Anzaldúa's notion of the border as a place "where the Third World grates against the first and bleeds" (2007, 25), Nepantla is not a peaceful place, but one that challenges pre-existing assumptions and is therefore filled with opportunity for change.

"Queers" are frequent inhabitants of this difficult yet exciting space. Anzaldúa's assertion, "As a mestiza I have no country, my homeland cast me out; ...(As a lesbian I have no race, my own people disclaim me; but I am all races because there is the queer of me in all races)" (2007, 102) corresponds directly to Ileana's lived experience. The only true family Ileana finds consists precisely in a community of "queers" represented by her openly gay friend Ed, who becomes a part of her "makeshift" familia from scratch.

Ileana finds the strength to reject her family's violence and embrace the many contradictions she inhabits only at the very end of the narrative, after Marina, in a raging attempt to firmly establish Ileana's gender identity, rapes her in her parents' home. Only after having survived both the rape and her father's violent, accusatory response to it, Ileana embraces her identity as a nepantlera, and discovers the freedom a mestiza consciousness brings. The concluding sentences of *Geographies of Home* are an echo of mestiza consciousness as formulated in *Borderlands/La Frontera*: "...her soul had transformed into a complex and resilient thing able to accommodate the best and the worst. Everything she had experienced…She would leave no memories behind. All of them were her self. All of them were home" (321). In true mestiza fashion Ileana learns to "juggle cultures" and embraces the conflicted entirety of her heritage, in which "Nothing is thrust out, the good and the bad and the ugly, nothing rejected, nothing abandoned" (101).

FINDING NEPANTLA IN *THE FARMING OF BONES*

Edwidge Danticat's second novel, *The Farming of Bones*, was published to much critical acclaim in 1998. It retells the notorious 1937 massacre of tens of thousands Haitian migrants in the Haitian-Dominican border region near Dajabón from the intimate perspective of Amabelle Desir, a young orphaned Haitian migrant who, mutilated for life, survives the massacre, and loses her lover Sebastien and her closest friends in the horrific event. Amabelle does not only inhabit a physical Nepantla as multilingual, multicultural border region in the Northwest of the Dominican Republic; as a survivor of the massacre, she also inhabits the dangerous psychic space between survivor's guilt and the living dead.

In an interview with Karin Ikas, appended to the 2007 of *Borderlands/La Frontera*, Anzaldúa defines the concept of Nepantla in more detail. She describes the term as "a Nahuatl word for the space between two bodies of water, the space between two worlds. It is a limited space, a space where you are not this or that, but where you are changing" (237). This space of uncomfortable transition does, however, always also hold the potential for productive transformation.

A focus on Anzaldúa's reference to bodies of water proves particularly fruitful when analyzing key passages in Danticat's novel. Water, especially rivers, are powerful symbols of transition in many cultures, from the river Lethe that both connects and separates the realm of the living from the realm of the dead in Greek mythology to the Ohio river, which separated slave-holding states from free states, to the Río Grande/Río Bravo, which demarcates the border between the United States and Mexico since the Treaty of Guadalupe Hidalgo. Throughout *The Farming of Bones*, the aptly named Massacre River has great significance for Amabelle Desir's sense of self.[6] It is the location where her parents drowned during a vicious flood when she was still a young child; it is also the site of the most traumatic event of her life, the night of early October 1937, when Dominican paramilitary troops, disguised as local farmers, took machetes to their Haitian Dominican neighbors. Last but not least, the river is also the setting of the richly ambiguous final scene in the novel. Many years after the massacre, Amabelle returns to the Dominican Republic to confront her former employer, Señora Valencia, whose husband Pico was a high official in Trujillo's army, with her role in the massacre and inquire about the possible survival of her loved ones. Faced with the Dominican woman's utter refusal to acknowledge her complacent complicity with the gruesome events of October 1937, Amabelle decides to return to the actual site of her trauma and immerses herself in the shallow waters of the Massacre River. The ending of the novel is intentionally ambiguous: Does Amabelle drown herself in the river to join her parents and her loved ones in the afterlife? Or does she perform a cleansing ritual and emerge from the waters reinvigorated? Or does she, like the mythological soucouyant figure in Danticat's short story "Nineteen Thirty-Seven," dive through the waters to emerge on the other side, unscathed?

What matters perhaps most is that Amabelle, who is a figure paralyzed in mourning and who has dedicated her life to remembering every detail of her relationship with Sebastien Onius, finally dares to take action and strives to relinquish the tight grasp of a "past [that] is more like flesh than air" (281). The water, which literally and metaphorically represents death to Amabelle, becomes a location of potential liberation and self-affirmation—a site of Nepantla. Throughout the novel Amabelle has tried to find such a space, as when she testifies earlier: "All I want to do is find a place to lay it down now and again, a safe nest where it will neither be scattered by the winds, nor remain forever buried beneath the sod" (266). The soothing, warm quality of the water allows her to "lie down," and the quality of water, forever in motion, prevents her from being interred. Entering the river thus insinuates a positive change in Amabelle's life. She is, after all, "looking for the dawn" (310), a new sunrise in the final scene of the novel. According to Lynn Chun Ink, *The Farming of Bones* calls for "a new method of reading communal identity that in fact re-imagines geographic and psychic boundaries in a way that has yet to be explored" (805). This new way of reading postcolonial fiction by Caribbean American writers such as Pérez and

Danticat may well be facilitated by using theoretical concepts developed not by Eurocentric critics, but by philosophers such as Anzaldúa, whose work is grounded in a world view of the Americas that privileges mestizaje over purity and requires a "tolerance for ambiguity" rather than the blind reiteration of limiting binaries.

While Anzaldúa's theories are firmly grounded in the cultural and geo-political context of the U.S.-Mexico borderlands, postcolonial literary and cultural studies, especially those dedicated to exploring the mutually constitutive character of heterosexism and racism in colonized spaces, will gain significant momentum when incorporating concepts such as "new mestiza consciousness" and "Nepantla" into their active vocabulary.

NOTES

1 http://www2.ucsc.edu/culturalstudies/PUBS/Inscriptions/vol_5/clifford.html

2 With this comment I do not wish to promote a utilitarian approach towards Anzaldúa's work; instead, I propose the great significance and import of Anzaldúa's work beyond Chicana feminism and the universal appeal of her theory which is grounded in the historical and socio-political specificity of the U.S.-Mexico borderlands.

3 Edward Said's exemplary study focuses on Georg Lukács's theory of reification and its application and adaptation by Lucien Goldmann at Harvard and Raymond Williams at Cambridge.

4 Said's persuasive examples include Adorno's study of Arnold Schönberg's dissonant music as a critique of Lukács's optimistic resolution to reification and Frantz Fanon's radical application of Lukács's subject-object dialectic to the struggle for Algerian independence.

5 Said specifies the need to pay attention to specificity as follows: "One would not, could not want to assimilate Viennese twelve-tone music to the Algerian resistance to French colonialism: the disparities are too grotesque to even articulate."

6 In an eerie foreshadowing of history, the Massacre River was, however, not named after the notorious 1937 massacre. The Dajabón river was renamed after a particularly bloody battle between eighteenth-century Spanish colonial forces and French buccaneers.

WORKS CITED

"A Meridians Roundtable with Edwidge Danticat, Loída Maritza Pérez, Myriam J. A. Chancy, and Nelly Rosario." *Meridians* 5.1 (2004): 69-91. Print.

Anzaldúa, Gloria. *Borderlands/La Frontera: The New Mestiza.* 3rd ed. San Francisco: Aunt Lute Books, 2007 (1986). Print.

----- and Cherríe Moraga, eds. *This Bride Called My Back: Writings by Radical Women of Color.* San Francisco: Kitchen Table Press, 1981. Print.

----- and AnaLouise Keating, eds. *This Bridge We Call Home: Radical Visions for Transformation.* New York: Routledge, 2002. Print.

Boone, Joseph Allen, ed. *Queer Frontiers: Millennial Geographies, Genders, and Generations.* Madison: The U of Wisconsin P, 2000. Print.

Caliz-Montoro, Carmen. *Writing from the Borderlands: A Study of Chicano, Afro-Caribbean, and Native Literatures in North America.* Toronto: TSAR Publications, 2000. Print.

Clifford, James. "Notes on Travel and Theory." http://www2.ucsc.edu/culturalstudies/PUBS/Inscriptions/vol_5/Clifford.html. Online.

Costa, Maria Dolores, ed. *Latina Lesbian Writers and Artists.* Binghamton: Harrington Park Press, 2003. Print.

Danticat, Edwidge. *The Farming of Bones.* New York: Penguin, 1998. Print.

-----. "Nineteen Thirty-Seven." *Krik? Krak!* New York: Vintage, 1995. Print.

Ink, Lynn Chun. "Remaking Identity, Unmaking Nation: Historical Recovery and the Reconstruction of Community in *In the Time of the Butterflies* and *The Farming of Bones*". *Callaloo* 27 (2004): 788-807.

Lugones, María. "On Borderlands/La Frontera: An Interpretive Essay." *Hypatia* 7. 4 *Lesbian Philosophy* (Autumn, 1992): 31-37. Print.

Pérez, Loída Maritza. *Geographies of Home.* New York: Penguin, 1999. Print.

Pratt, Mary Louise. "Arts of the Contact Zone." *Ways of Reading: An Anthology for Writers.* Eds. David Bartholomae and Anthony Petrosky. Boston: Bedford P, 2002. 497-518. Print.

Reumann, Ann E. and Gloria Anzaldúa. "Coming Into Play: An Interview with Gloria Anzaldúa." *MELUS* 25.2 (Summer 2000): 3-45. Print.

Said, Edward W. "Traveling Theory." *The World, the Text, and the Critic.* Cambridge: Harvard UP, 1983. 226-247. Print.

----- "Traveling Theory Revisited." *Reflections on Exile and Other Essays.* Cambridge: Harvard UP, 2002. Print.

Tabuenca-Córdoba, María Socorro. "Twenty Years of Borderlands: A Reading from the Border." *El Mundo Zurdo: Selected Works from the Meetings of the Society for the Study of Gloria Anzaldúa 2007 & 2009.* Eds. Norma E Cantú, Christina L. Gutiérrez, Norma Alarcón and Rita E. Urquijo-Ruiz. San Francisco: Aunt Lute Books, 2010. 25-31. Print.

Torres-Saillant, Silvio. "The Tribulations of Blackness: Stages in Dominican Racial Identity." *Callaloo* 23.3 (Summer 2000): 1086-1111. Print.

CONTRIBUTORS

Norma Alarcón is a noted Chicana theorist and scholar. She is Professor Emerita of Ethnic Studies, University of California, Berkeley. She received her doctorate in Latin American Literature and Culture from Indiana University. Her path breaking essays shaped Chicana Studies and paved the way for contemporary theories of Chicana subjectivity. For over 25 years she owned and ran Third Woman Press, publishing key writers and texts in Chicana and Latina Studies. Writers such as Sandra Cisneros and Ana Castillo were first published in Third Woman Press. She resides in San Antonio and is currently working on a collection of her essays.

Sunshine Maria Anderson's journey towards entering higher education has been a long one. She transferred from East Los Angeles College in 2009 to UCLA, and is now finishing a degree with two Majors: one in Chicana and Chicano Studies and the second in Art History. She has participated in research through the Undergraduate Research Center (URC) as an Undergraduate Research Fellow and the Undergraduate Research Scholars Program (URSP), and she presented at the "International Conference on the Life and Work of Gloria Anzaldúa" in 2010 (her first conference). She considers herself a non-traditional student who balances being a mother and full time student. Her interests are primarily in the arts, specifically as a tool for transformation, healing, and empowerment within underserved communities. She hopes to open up a museum titled "Mexican American Museum of Art" (MAMA) in Los Angeles.

Laurel Boshoff graduated from Skidmore College in Saratoga Springs, New York in 2009 with a BA in English and Government. She received my M.A. in English from The University of Texas at San Antonio in May 2011. She will pursue doctoral studies and hopes to focus on Transatlantic Nineteenth-Century Literature. Her ultimate goal is to become an English professor, which will allow her to share her love for literature with students and colleagues.

Marcos del Hierro is a third-year PhD student in the English Department at Texas A&M University at College Station. He received his MA in English and American Literature at the University of Texas at El Paso. His academic interests include hip-hop studies, Chican@ studies, and cultural rhetorics. He recently was awarded the 2011 Charles Gordone Prize in creative nonfiction.

Theresa Delgadillo is an Assistant Professor of Comparative Ethnic and American Studies at Ohio State University. Her research and teaching focus on gender, race and religion; Afro-Latinidad and Latino/as in the Midwest. She has published articles and chapters in collected volumes. Her book *Spiritual Mestizaje: Religion, Gender, Race and Nation in Contemporary Chicana Narrative* was published by Duke University Press in 2011.

Aurora Levins Morales is, in her words, "a writer, an artist, a historian... also an activist, a healer, a revolutionary who tell[s] stories with medicinal powers." She is the author of *Medicine Stories, Remedios: Stories of Earth and Iron from the History of Puertorriqueñas*, and the co-author of *Getting Home Alive* and *Cosecha & Other Stories* with her mother, Rosario Morales.

Qwo-Li Driskill is a mixedblood Cherokee Two-Spirit writer, activist, performer and scholar. S/he is the author of *Walking with Ghosts: Poems* and the co-editor of *Queer Indigenous Studies: Critical Interventions in Theory, Politics, and Literature* and *Sovereign Erotics: A Collection of Two-Spirit Literature*. Qwo-Li is an assistant professor in the Department of English at Texas A&M University.

Leah Lakshmi Piepzna-Samarasinha is a queer disabled Sri Lankan writer, teacher and cultural worker. The author of *Consensual Genocide* and co-editor of *The Revolution Starts At Home: Confronting Intimate Violence in Activist Communities* (South End, 2011), her work has appeared in several anthologies, including *Persistence: Still Butch and Femme*, *We Don't Need Another Wave*, and *A Girl's Guide to Taking Over The World*. Her second book of poetry, *Love Cake*, and first memoir, *Dirty River*, are forthcoming.

Josh T. Franco grew up in Odessa, Texas. Currently, he is in the PhD program in Art History at Binghamton University in Binghamton, New York. He splits his time between New York (Binghamton, New York City) and Texas (Marfa, Austin, San Antonio).

María del Socorro (Coco) Gutiérrez-Magallanes is an *Irvine Scholar* with a Bachelor of Arts in Sociology and Latin American and Iberian Literary and Cultural Studies from Occidental College in Los Angeles, California. She holds an M.A. in Latin American Studies from Universidad Nacional Autónoma de México, UNAM. She is currently a Ph.D. Candidate from UNAM in the Facultad de Ciencias Políticas y Sociales and the Programa Universitario de Estudios de Género with a dissertation project on autobiographical writings a *contrapunto* of Gloria Anzaldúa and Roque Dalton. Coco is a *border crosser* since childhood, a *Mexican born Chicana* from Guadalajara, South Central Los Angeles and México City, by choice, and a *Nepantlera* de corazón y por convicción.

George Hartley, Associate Professor of English at Ohio University, is the author of many essays on Gloria Anzaldúa and on Chicana/o literature and culture more generally. He is currently writing a book on Anzaldúa—or to be more accurate, that book is currently writing him. His other books are *Textual Politics and the Language Poets* (Indiana UP 1989) and *The Abyss of Representation: Marxism and the Postmodern Sublime* (Duke UP 2003).

Tiffany Ana López is Associate Professor in the Theatre Department at the University of California, Riverside. Her research focuses on issues of trauma and violence and the ways that theater, literature, and art provide avenues for personal healing, community building, and social change. She has published numerous essays, articles, chapters, and reviews in books and journals, including *Theatre Journal* and *Performing the US Latina and Latino Borderlands*. She is the editor of the short story anthology, *Growing Up Chicana/o* (1993) and co-editor of *Chicana/Latina Studies: The Journal of Mujeres Activas en Letras y Cambio Social* (since 2006).

Melina M. Martínez has received a bachelor's degree from the University of Texas at Brownsville and Texas Southmost College in Arts Education. She is a Certified Texas Educator pursuing a Master's degree in Curriculum and Instruction with an Emphasis in Art Education. She is scheduled to graduate in the summer of 2011.

Chelsey Patterson is currently a graduate student working towards her PhD in the English department at the University of Texas at San Antonio. Her research interests currently include sideshow studies, critical race theory, and postmortem racism within the field of medicine. She was born and raised in Corpus Christi, Texas.

Laura E. Pérez is an associate professor and graduate advisor of the doctoral program in the Department of Ethnic Studies, at the University of California, Berkeley. She is also a core faculty member of the graduate program in Performance Studies and an affiliated faculty member of the Department of Women's Studies and the Center for Latin American Studies. Her research, teaching, and writing focus on post-sixties U.S. Latina/o literary, visual, and performance arts; "U.S. women of color" (a.k.a "third world") feminist and queer thought; art and spirituality; racialization and the cultural politics and economics of the artworld(s); and theories of oppositionality and decolonization. She is the author of *Chicana Art: The Politics of Spiritual and Aesthetic Altarities* (Duke UP 2007). In spring of 2009, she co-curated, with Delilah Montoya, the art exhibition "Chicana Badgirls: Las Hociconas," at the 516 Gallery, in Albuquerque. In spring of 2011, she curated "Labor+a(r)t+orio: Latin@ Bay Area Arts Now," at the Richmond Arts Center, California.

Kamala Platt, Ph.D., M.F.A. is a writer, artist, profesora, activist & independent scholar living in South Texas and at The Meadowlark Center in Kansas. Her work focuses on women's cultural poetics of environmental justice in fronteras of resistance to walls, militarization/war, environmental racism and ecological destruction. Her first collection of poetry, *On the Line,* is now available from its publisher, Wings Press.

Marion Rohrleitner is assistant professor of English and affiliated faculty in the Women's Studies and African American Studies Programs at the University of Texas at El Paso, where she teaches 20th and 21st century American, Latina/o, and Caribbean literatures as well as literatures of the African Diaspora. Her articles and book reviews have appeared in *Antípodas*, *American Quarterly*, and *Latino*

Studies. Her first book, *Diasporic Bodies: Contemporary Historical Fictions and the Intimate Public Sphere,* is currently under review.

Sonia Saldívar-Hull is a Professor of English and the founding Director of the Women's Studies Institute at University of Texas, San Antonio, where she also directs the Women's Studies Program. *Feminism on the Border: Chicana Politics and Literature,* her book on Chicana feminist theory, was published by the University of California Press (2000). Her publications include numerous book chapters, articles and introductory essays on Chicana literature, feminism, and the cultural intersections of borderland studies. She has been co-editor of *Latin America Otherwise: Languages, Empires, Nations,* a book series with Duke University Press, since 1997.

Rita E. Urquijo-Ruiz is a Mexicana/Chicana who claims Sonora and California as her homes. She is an Associate Professor of Spanish in Modern Languages & Literatures at Trinity University. Her areas of interest are Mexican and Chicana/o literatures and cultures, gender/sexuality, and theater/performance studies. She is also a poet and a performance artist. *She is the co-editor of Global Mexican Cultural Productions (Palgrave Macmillan 2011) and El Mundo Zurdo (Aunt Lute 2010).* Her book: *Wild Tongues: Transnational Mexican Popular Culture* is forthcoming in the Chicana Matters Series at the University of Texas Press.

Deborah Kuetzpalin Vasquez, a home girl from San Anto, is a multi-media Chicana artist. Observing the Chican@ Movement through the lens of a child has shaped her life, work, and the creation of Citlali, la Chicana Superhero. She obtained her Bachelors of Arts from Texas Woman's University and her Masters of Fine Arts from the University of Wisconsin Madison. She also studied traditional culture at Universidad Nahuatl in Ocotepec, Mexico. Currently works in clay, collage, installation, and film shorts.

Linda Winterbottom teaches at the University of the Incarnate Word. She earned her Ph.D. in English and American Literature at the University of Texas at San Antonio. She specializes in Caribbean American and U.S. Multiethnic literature as well as Creative Writing.